—A—
DICTIONARY
of
Irish Place-Names

—A—
DICTIONARY
of
Irish Place-Names

Adrian Room

Appletree Press

First published and printed by
The Appletree Press Ltd
7 James Street South
Belfast BT2 8DL
1986

9 8 7 6 5 4 3 2 1

British Library Cataloguing in Publication Data
Room, Adrian
A dictionary of Irish place-names.
1. Ireland—Gazetteers
I. Title
914.15'003'21   DA979

ISBN O-86281-132-5

Contents

Acknowledgements

I should like to acknowledge the professional assistance of a number of people in preparing material for the entries in the Dictionary.

In Northern Ireland I owe much to Mr Jack McCoy, Senior Assistant Librarian (Local History) at Ballynahinch Public Library, Co. Down. He and his team have tirelessly tracked down and passed on to me much useful information concerning individual place-names, whether in Northern Ireland or in the Republic. I am also grateful to Mrs R. M. Andrews, Treasurer of the Ulster Place-name Society, for providing me with copies of the Society's *Bulletin*. Most sadly, the leading authority on Northern Irish place-names, Mrs Deirdre Flanagan, died suddenly just as I was on the point of consulting her on certain names.

In the Republic, I owe much to the help and advice of Mr Art Ó Maolfabhail, Chief Placenames Officer at the Ordnance Survey Office, Dublin. He made me fully aware of the complexities lurking behind many Irish place-names, and of the pitfalls to be avoided. Also in Dublin, I am most grateful to Aideen Ryan for translating passages of relevant material on place-names from Irish publications. I hasten to add here that any inconsistencies or errors in the rendering of Irish words and phrases is entirely my own responsibility. I hope there will be few.

Last but most certainly not least I would like to say how grateful I am to Paul Woodman and Erica Shipley of the Permanent Committee on Geographical Names for British Official Use at the Royal Geographical Society in London . They made much helpful and valuable material available to me from their unique library of gazetteers, maps, and works on place-names.

Any positive value the present Dictionary may have is largely due to the help of these people. Any defects must be laid at my own door.

Adrian Room
January 1986

Introduction

(Names printed in italics have their own entries in the Dictionary)

The history and topography of a country are usually reflected in its place-names, as recorded in the languages of the people who have settled there, and this is certainly true of Ireland, both in the Republic and in Northern Ireland. Ireland's history begins with a rather misty, semi-legendary period dominated by the names of pagan and Christian chiefs, rulers and saints, and many of these appear in place-names throughout the land. It is frequently difficult or even impossible to trace the individual concerned, and little or nothing, for example, is known about the man called Aisil who gave his name to *Athassel,* or the Ing whose name is preserved in *Dromin,* Co. Louth. It can usually be assumed that places containing the name of Patrick and Brigid, such as *Downpatrick* and *Kilbreedy,* refer to *the* St Patrick and St Brigid who are two of Ireland's greatest saints and certainly historical figures. But often there are many saints of the same name – even over thirty called Columb (Colm), apart from the famous St Columba (Columcille) – so that the identification of a particular saint in a place-name is just as difficult as that of any other individual, whether Christian or pagan.

The country's later history involves first, the Anglo-Norman invasion begun by Richard de Clare ('Strongbow') in 1170 and second, the English and Scottish settlements ('Plantations') of the sixteenth and seventeenth centuries. Here, the personal names are generally better documented, although local knowledge and research is often needed to determine, for example, who the Font of *Fontstown* was, or the Bennett of *Bennettsbridge.*

To judge by its place-names alone, whether they contain a personal name or not, Ireland is revealed as a land that contains (or contained, since many are now non-existent or in ruins) a wealth of churches, monasteries, abbeys and religious establishments on the one hand, and a formidable array of forts, castles, strongholds and defensive posts on the other. Place-names abound with words such as *cill, mainistir, dún, caiseal, ráth,* and *lios,* denoting different types of religious and military settlements, and most such names have, in their other half, if not a personal name then a descriptive word or a topographical feature as a

7

defining element. A glance at the many 'Kil-' or 'Kill-' names in the dictionary, for example, will show not only the personal names of founders, landowners and saints (*Kilbarrack, Kilcash, Killeany, Killorglin*), but also simple adjectives (*Kilbeg, Kilglass, Killard, Killeen, Kilmore, Kilrea*) and natural features of the landscape such as woods or trees (*Kilbaha, Kildare, Killeter, Killinure, Kilross*) or other objects (*Kilclief, Kilclooney, Kilcooney, Kilcurry, Killashee, Killavallen, Killough, Killycluggin*).

Enough examples have been given here to show that, hardly surprisingly, the majority of Ireland's place-names are in Irish, existing today in an English spelling that is usually an approximation, and often a distortion, of the original. For many such names, a translation into English should suffice to make them meaningful. *Donaghmore*, for example, represents *Domhnach Mór*, and so is 'big church'. *Moneyglass* is *An Muine Glas*, 'the green grove', and *Raheen* is *An Ráithín*, 'the little ring-fort'. As mentioned, many names consist of two halves, with the second often a personal name or noun in the genitive case, with or without the Irish definite article (*an* or *na*). Thus *Annamoe* is *Áth na mBó*, 'ford of the cows', indicating a regular crossing place for cattle over the river, and *Carrigadrohid* is *Carraig an Droichid*, 'rock of the bridge', denoting a rock at or near the point where a bridge crosses the river. Where the second half of such names is an inanimate object, such as a wood, marsh, bridge or church, the sense in English is really more 'at' or 'by' rather than 'of', so that *Carrigatogher* should be understood as 'bridge by a causeway', and *Killashee*, already quoted, as 'church at the fairy hill'. Where the first part of the name indicates a large place, such as a plain or valley, this may actually contain the second, so that *Glenfarne* is 'valley with elder trees', and *Inishcealtra is* 'island with churches'.

Mention of 'fairy hill' here is a further reminder that many Irish place-names arise from legend, and that *Inishbofin* has more to it than a simply descriptive 'island of the white cow', as it literally translates. A white cow is not just a white cow here, but a symbol of purity, fertility and nutrition. Not for nothing is the Irish name for the Milky Way *Bealach na Bó Finne*, 'way of the white cow'.

After the names of Irish origin come the English names, although some apparently English names are actually corruptions of the Irish. *Crowhill*, therefore, is not a hill where crows nest, *Cranfield* is not a field where cranes live, *Ferns* is not a place of ferns and *Longford* is not a place by a long ford.

Most English names can be easily recognised by their obviously non-Irish personal name (*Barrington's Bridge, Edgeworthstown*), or by their clearly English components (*Fivemiletown, Greyabbey*). It should be said, however, that in some such cases it is likely that the English is a translation of the original Irish, although in certain instances it is difficult to determine whether the English name was translated from the Irish or the Irish from the English.

Today, however, there are fewer English names than there were, and many quite well-known English place-names, established at the time of the Plantations, have now reverted to the original Irish. The once familiar King's County, Queen's County, Kingstown and Queenstown are today *Offaly, Laois, Dun Laoghaire* and *Cóbh*, among others.

Some of the most modern names are English, too, including *Arthurstown, Eglinton, Helen's Bay* and *Riverstown* (Co. Cork), all nineteenth-century names, and a small but interesting group of English names are those that derive from inns, such as Buckandhounds, Fox and Geese, Pass-if-you-can and Redcow, all near Dublin.

English names often begin with 'Castle-' or 'Newtown-', or have an initial letter found only rarely or not at all in the Irish alphabet, such as H-, J-, K-, O-, V- and W-.

Longford was mentioned as being a misleading name, since there is no long ford there. (The name is a corruption of Irish *longphort*, 'fortress'.) But how about *Waterford?* This, too, is a corruption, and does not mean 'ford over the water'. The origin of the name, however, is not Irish but Norse, and an important reminder that the Vikings were in Ireland for some two hundred years from the ninth century. The impression they made was not as great as in England or Scotland, but the fact that they were in Ireland at all is recorded in some quite well-known place-names (almost all sea-inlets or ports) on the east and south-east coast. Among the most familiar Scandinavian names in Ireland are those of *Strangford, Carlingford, Wicklow, Howth, Ireland's Eye* and *Waterford*. One of the furthest inland is *Leixlip*.

The three languages that are found in Ireland's place-names are thus Irish (often originally Old Irish, spoken in the seventh to tenth centuries), English (usually so-called 'Modern' i.e. post-1500 English) and Old Norse, with Anglo-Norman influence seen in several personal names. The Romans never came to Ireland, so there is no direct Latin influence, as there is elsewhere in the British Isles.

Where place-names are not historical in some way, referring to a particular event such as a battle or the building of a church, they are almost entirely topographical, relating to Ireland's dominant natural features – rivers, lakes, mountains, hills, bogs, woods, valleys, streams, islands, rocks and plains among them. Sometimes a feature is referred to by different words, and English 'hill' can translate Irish *ard, brí, cabhán, céide, cnap, cnoc, corr, drom, leitir, maol, mullach, siodh* and *tulach,* among others. Each of these words singles out a certain aspect of the hill, such as its size, shape or use, or points to a predominant part of it, such as its summit or side. *Céide,* for example, is a flat-topped hill, and *cnap* a little round one. *Drom* is a long, low hill, and *leitir* a hillside that is constantly wet with running streams. *Maol* is a bald or bare hill, and *siodh* one where fairies were believed to live. *Tulach* is a small hill that was often used for assemblies. In a land that is full of hills ('the fair hills of Éire'), such distinguishing words arise naturally, and survive in today's place-names.

In general, it is still possible to visit a place with a 'natural feature' name, and find the feature existing even today. This is particularly so of the larger, more 'immovable' features such as islands, valleys, promontories and hills. But in many locations the original feature that gave its name to the place will have been obliterated or lost, especially if the site has developed into a town or city. Who can now locate the original 'ferny nook' of *Coleraine,* for example, or even point to the particular stretch of the river Liffey that was the 'black pool' of *Dublin?* Furthermore, lakes can dry up or be drained, woods are thinned and cut down, fords are replaced by bridges, and rocky landscapes are levelled. When this happens, a place-name that was originally simply descriptive becomes historic, reminding us today that once, long ago, this is how the place was seen by the people who named it.

The correct interpretation of Ireland's place-names, whether Irish or English in origin, is not always easy. Not only has the spelling and pronunciation of many names changed over the years, but some places have acquired more than one name. The best-known example of this is *Dublin* itself, since its official name is *Baile Átha Cliath,* as the postmark on any letter will show. Which here is the 'correct' name? The answer is that they both are, except that the more widely known and used name of *Dublin* has been distorted from the original Irish (today, *dubh-linn*), while the official name is orthographically and lexically correct.

Some idea of the situation can be seen by comparing the official spellings of the names of postal towns in *Ainmneacha Gaeilge na mBailte Poist* (see the Bibliography) with earlier place-name listings, such as the *Dictionary of Irish Placenames* by Risteárd Ó Foghluda. The modern Post Office name of Jennymount, Belfast, for example, is *Tulach Shíne* in Irish, 'stormy hillock' (the English is a corruption of this, and there was never any Jenny here). The earlier work, however, gives the Irish name of this same place as *Bothar na Trágha,* 'road of the strand'. Similarly *Milford,* in Co. Donegal, is now *Baile na nGallóglach,* 'townland of the gallowglasses', whereas earlier, and not all that long ago, it was *Béal na nGallóglach*, 'river-mouth of the gallowglasses'. As it happens, either name could apply, since the village is actually at the mouth of a river at the head of Mulroy Bay.

The similarity of *béal* to *baile*, especially when either can be rendered in English as 'Bally-', points to another hazard, and detailed local research is often necessary to establish which is correct. The same situation arises with the very many 'Kill-' names, where this element can represent either Irish *cill*, 'church' or *coill*, 'wood'. In more than a few cases the long favoured derivation may in fact be incorrect, that is, wrongly preserved in the Irish name, so that what seems to translate as 'grey church', for example, could actually turn out to be 'grey wood'. When neither church nor wood no longer exists, the only recourse is to written records – if *they* exist and if they themselves are reliable! Further complications have been caused by recent spelling reforms in the Irish language itself, and by the passing of the Placenames Act of 1975 in the Republic, when many postal towns acquired further respellings. (In Northern Ireland, most place-names except the most modern have their Irish equivalents, but these are not normally displayed publicly on signposts or used officially by the Post Office, as they are south of the border.)

This degree of instability has led to some difficulty in compiling the present Dictionary, especially since I have attempted to give the Irish equivalent of every English name, where it exists, even in Northern Ireland. Wherever possible, the Irish spelling has been taken from the 1969 *Ainmneacha Gaeilge na mBailte Poist*. This does not, of course, list minor names or natural features, so these I have taken either from the earlier gazetteer (by Risteárd Ó Foghludha) or from the 1970 map *Éire* listed in the Bibliography. Even the spelling of the English names (whether genuinely English or, as most often, versions of the Irish) varies from one source to another, and here, too, I have tried to be consistent. Where interpretations of a name are dubious, I have given the one that seems the most probable, taking into account historical and local topographical factors wherever possible.

All entries give four basic pieces of information, in this order: 1) English spelling of name; 2) county where place is located (with 'Belfast' instead of 'Antrim' when the place is a district in this city); 3) Irish spelling or version; 4) interpretation. Where a name is particularly well known or complex or 'obscure', I have added a brief commentary. Where several places of the same name are found in different counties, I have stated simply 'several' in place of the county name. In such cases the Irish name may not be exactly the same for all the places, and may even be quite different. See *Milford*, for example.

Two Appendices give the basic meanings of common Irish root words found in place-names, and some indication is given there of the different shades of meaning for words that translate into English simply as 'hill', 'church', etc.

Finally, a select Bibliography is given for the reader who wishes to pursue further some particular or more detailed aspect of the place-names of one of Europe's loveliest lands.

A

Abbey (Galway), An Mhainistir, 'the monastery'.
The Kinalehin Friary near here was originally founded *c.* 1340 for the Carthusians by John de Cogan, but was abandoned by them *c.* 1370 and taken over by the Franciscans.

Abbeydorney (Kerry), Mainistir Ó dTorna, 'monastery of the Uí Torna'.
The Cistercian abbey whose remains lie to the north of the village was founded in the mid-12th century.

Abbeyfeale (Limerick), Mainistir na Féile, 'abbey of the (river) Feale'.
The Cistercian abbey by the river Feale here was founded in 1188 by Brian Ó Brien.

Abbeygormacan (Galway), Mainistir Uí Ghormacáin, 'abbey of the O Gormagans.'
The Augustinian abbey here was founded by a chief of the O Gormagans.

Abbeyknockmoy (Galway), Mainistir Chnoc Muaidhe, 'abbey of the hill of Muaidh'.
The nearby Cistercian abbey of Collis Victoriae was founded in the 12th century by Cathal O Conor, king of Connacht, in memory of victory over the Anglo-Norman forces. Muaidh in the Irish name is a woman's name.

Abbeylara (Longford), Mainistir Leathrátha, 'monastery of the half ring-fort'.
Remains of the original Cistercian abbey can still be seen here.

Abbeyleix (Laois), Mainistir Laoise, 'monastery of Laois'.
The original Cistercian abbey De Lege Dei, founded in 1184 by Conor O More, has now disappeared.

Abbeyshrule (Longford), Mainistir Shruthla, 'monastery of the stream'.
Remains of the Cistercian abbey, colonised by monks from Mellifont in the mid-12th century, can still be seen here by the river Inny.

Abbestrowry (Cork), Mainistir an tSruthair, 'monastery of the stream'.
Ruins of the Cistercian abbey can still be seen here nearby on the bank of the river Ilen.

Achonry (Sligo), Achadh Conair, 'Conaire's field'.

Acoose Lough (Kerry), Loch Dhá Chuas, 'lake of the two caves'.

Acton (Armagh).
The village was founded by Sir Toby Poyntz in the 16th century and named after his family's native village in England, Iron Acton, Gloucestershire.

Adamstown (Wexford).
Adam may have been a member of the Devereux family who built the castle here in 1556.

Adare (Limerick), Áth Dara, 'ford of (the) oak grove'.
There are still oak trees here by the river Maigue.

Addergoole (Mayo, Galway), Eadarghóbail, '(place) between two (river) forks'.
The Mayo place is by the river Addergoole in a long glen leading to Lough Conn. The land is low-lying and marshy here and there are several streams. Compare **Adrigole**.

Adrigole (Cork), Eadargóil, '(place) between two (river) forks'.
The former village on Bantry Bay is on Adrigole Harbour where the Adrigole River flows down into it from Lough Glen. There are other streams here.

Affane (Waterford), Áth Mheadhoin, 'middle ford'.
The ford is over the river Blackwater, about two miles below Cappoquin.

Agha (several), Achadh, 'field'.

Aghaboe (Laois), Achadh Bhó, 'field of (the) cow'.

Aghabog (Monaghan), Achadh Bog, 'soft field'.

Aghaboy (Longford), Achadh Buidhe, 'yellow field'.

Aghada (Cork), Áth Fhada, 'long ford'.
Aghada is south of Cóbh, facing it over Cork Harbour. There is no river here and the name may really be *Achadh Fhada*, 'long field'.

Aghadoe (Kerry), Achadh Dá Eó, 'field of the two yews'.

Adhadowey (Derry), Achadh Dubhthaigh, 'Dubhthai's field'.

Aghadown (Cork), Achadh Dúin, 'field of the fort'.

Aghagallon (Antrim), Achadh Gallan, 'field of the standing stone'.

Aghagower (Mayo), Achadh Fhobhair, 'field of the well'.
The well came to be called St Patrick's well, named after the monastery dedicated to him here.

Aghalane (Cavan), Achadh Leathan, 'wide field'.

Aghalee (Antrim), Achadh Lí, 'Lí's field'.

Aghamarta (Cork), Achadh Mhártain, 'Martin's field'.

Aghamore (several), Achadh Mór, 'big field'.

Aghanloo (Derry), Áth Lú, 'Lú's little ford'.
Aghanloo is on the river Roe and Lough Foyle.

Aghavannagh (Wicklow), Achadh an Mhéanaigh, 'field of the middle (mountain)'.
Old forms of the name suggest that the true origin is *Achadh mBeannach*, 'hilly field'.

Aghavea (Fermanagh), Achadh Bheithe, 'field of the birch trees'

Aghaville (Cork), Achadh an Bhile, 'field of the ancient tree'.

Aghaviller (Kilkenny), Achadh an Bhiolair, 'field of the watercress'.

Agherton (Derry), Achadh ar Toín, 'field on the low ground'.
Agherton is near the Atlantic coast, on the river Bann.

Aghinver (Fermanagh), Achadh Inbhir, 'field of the estuary'.
Aghinver is on Lough Erne.

Aghmacart (Laois), Achadh Mhic Airt, 'field of the son of Art'.

Aghowle (Wicklow), Achadh Abhall, 'field of (the) orchard'.

Aglish (Kilkenny), An Eaglais, 'the church'.
This is a common name, and at many of the places so called the ruins of an old church still exist, as they do in Waterford and Kerry, for example.

Aglishcloghane (Tipperary), Eaglais Clo-cháin, 'church of the stepping stones'.

Ahakista (Cork), Áthan Chiste, 'ford of the treasure'.
If this is the true origin, some battle treasure may be referred to.

Ahaphuca (Cork), Áth an Phúca, 'ford of the hobgoblin'.
The ford here was where the bridge now crosses the Ounageeragh, on the boundary between Limerick and Cork.

Ahascragh (Galway), Áth Eascrach, 'ford of the sandhill'.
The place is named after the river here, which flows into the Suck.

Aherlow (Tipperary), Eatharlach, 'valley'.
This is a small river flowing in a still attractive valley in the Galtee Mountains.

Ahoghill (Antrim), Áth Eóchaille, 'ford of (the) yew trees'.
Ahoghill is on the rivers Bann and Maine, and the ford could have been over either or both.

Aille (Galway, Mayo), An Aill, 'the cliff'.

Aldergrove (Antrim), An Garrán Fearnóige, 'the alder grove'.

Allenwood (Antrim), Fiodh Alúine, 'wood of Allen'.

Andersonstown (Belfast), Baile Andarsan, 'Anderson's town'.

Annaclone (Down), Eanach Cluana, 'marsh of the meadow'.
The river Bann here flows through low, boggy land.

Annacloy (Down), Áth na Coithe, 'ford of the stone'.
Annacloy is on the river of the same name.

Annacotty (Limerick), Áth na Coite, 'ford of the little boat'.
The village is on the Mulkear river, about a mile from the Shannon, and it is possible that small boats could have come up as far as this at some time.

Annaduff (Leitrim), Eanach Dubh, 'black marsh'.

Annagassan (Louth), Áth na gCasán, 'ford of the paths'.
The 'paths' were probably the two rivers Glyde and Dee, which join near this village.

Annagh (several), Eanach, 'marsh'.

Annaghaskin (Dublin), Eanach Sheascán, 'marsh of (the) eels'.

Annaghdown (Galway), Eanach Dhúin, 'marsh of (the) fort'.
There is still a ruined castle here on (the) shore of Lough Corrib, and although this may not be the original fort, it was probably built on its site.

Annaghmore (Sligo), Eanach Mór, 'big marsh'.

Annahilt (Down), Eanach Eilte, 'marsh of (the) doe'.

Annahone (Tyrone), Eanach Eoghain, 'Eoghan's march'.

Annalong (Down), Áth na Long, 'ford of the ships'.
Annalong is on the Irish Sea coast with a deep-water harbour, and for long has been the only place of shelter for fishing boats here. The ford would have been over the river Annalong here, near where the ships were anchored.

Annamoe (Wicklow), Áth na mBó, 'ford of the cows'.
The ford was almost certainly where the bridge is now, and this would have been the regular crossing-place for cattle.

Annayalla (Monaghan), Eanaigh Gheala, 'bright marshes'.
The 'brightness' or whiteness (Irish geal, 'white') may have been from whitish grass or conspicuous white flowers here.

Annestown (Waterford), Bun Abha, 'river mouth'.
This name appears to be a faulty English rendering of the original Irish, although it is not recorded in its present form before the nineteenth century.

Anny (Monaghan), Eanaighe, 'marsh'.

Antrim (Antrim), Aontroim, 'one house'.
The meaning is uncertain, but 'solitary farm' is one possibility, from Irish aon, 'one', 'single' and treabh, 'house', 'family'. Some have derived it from trom, genitive truim, 'elder tree', although this seems less likely.

An Uaimh (Meath), An Uaimh, 'the cave'.
See **Navan**.

Aran Island (Donegal), Árainn Mhór, 'big Aran'.
The literal derivation of Aran is Irish ára, dative árainn, 'loin', 'kidney'. Here this means 'arched back', 'ridge'. The Aran

Islands, Galway, have the same origin. The biggest island there is called Inishmore ('great island'). Then come Inishman ('middle island') and Inisheer ('eastern island'). The relevant Irish words for these names are inis, mór, meadhón, ear; 'island', 'great', 'middle', 'east'.

Arboe (Tyrone), Árd Bó, 'cow height'.
There is no obvious 'height' here, but the land does slope up gradually from the western shore of Lough Neagh.

Ardagh (several), Ardach, 'high field'.
In Limerick, Ardagh is at the foot of Slieve Luachra.

Ardamine (Wexford), Árd Ladhrann, 'height of the (river) fork'.

Ardara (Donegal), Árd an Ratha, 'height of the ring-fort'.
The name comes from the ring-fort nearly on the top of the cliffs here, although the village of Ardara itself is in a deep valley.

Ardaragh (Down), Árd Darach, 'height of oaks'.

Ardbraccan (Meath), Árd Breacan, 'St Brecan's height'.
St Brecan built a 6th-century church here before he went to Aran, where his main establishment was.

Ardcarn (Roscommon), Árd Carna, 'height of the carn'.
The reference is to a monumental heap of stones here on Lough Key and by the Shannon.

Ardcath (Meath), Árd Cath, 'height of (the) battle'.
This must be a historic reference of some kind.

Ardee (Louth), Baile Átha Fhirdia, 'town of Ferdia's ford'.
Ferdia (or Fear-Diadh) was a Connacht warrior said to have been killed here in the first century by his former companion Cú Chullain when he was attempting to prevent Queen Maeve's forces from entering Ulster. A plaque on the bridge over the Dee here refers to this event.

Ardeevin (Roscommon), Árd Aoibhinn, 'beautiful height'.

Arderin (Laois), Árd Éireann, 'height of Erin (i.e. Ireland)'.
This is the highest mountain in the Slieve

15

Bloom range, but not the highest in Ireland (which is Carrantuohill, in Mac Gilly-cuddy's Reeks, Kerry).

Ardfert (Kerry), Árd Fhearta, 'height of the grave'.

Ardfinnan (Tipperary), Árd Fhíonáin, 'St Fíonán's height'.

The monastery here was founded in the 7th century by St Fíonán the Leper. There are no traces of it now, but the Protestant church stands on its site.

Ardglass (Down), Árd Ghlais, 'green height'.

Ardglass is on a gentle slope that runs down to the bay here.

Ardgroom (Cork), Dhá Dhrom, 'two ridges'.

Ardkeen (Down), Árd Caoin, 'pleasant height'.

Ardkeen is on a peninsula between Lough Strangford and the Irish Channel.

Ardlougher (Cavan), Árd Luachra, 'height of the rushes'.

Ardmillan (Down), Árd an Mhuilinn, 'height of the mill'.

The ruins of the mill can still be seen here.

Ardmore (several), An Áird Mhór, 'the great height'.

Most places of this name are headlands. The Waterford Ardmore is a famous ancient monastic site.

Ardmulchen (Meath), Árd Maolchon, 'Maelchon's height'.

Ardnacrusha (several), Árd na Croise, 'height of the cross'.

Ardnaree (Mayo), Árd na Ria, 'height of the executions'.

This is the popular translation of the name, referring to the four foster brothers who murdered their master, Ceallach, bishop of Kilmoremoy, and were hanged here by his brother.

Ard Oilean (Kerry), Árdoileán, 'high island'.

This now uninhabited island is also known by the English name of High Island.

Ardpatrick (Limerick), Árd Pádraig, 'St Patrick's height'.

The name comes from the hill here, where monastic remains can still be seen on the site where St Patrick is said to have founded the original establishment.

Ardrahan (Galway), Raithin, 'height of the ferns'.

The area round here is noticeably hilly.

Ardress (Armagh, Galway), Árd Dreasa, 'height of the brambles'.

Ardskeagh (Cork), Árd Scia, 'height of bushes'.

Ards (Peninsula) (Down), An Áird, 'the point'.

The 's' is an English plural addition to the Irish word.

Ardstraw (Tyrone), Árd Sratha, 'height of the riverside land'.

Ardtole (Down), Árd Tuathail, 'Tuathal's height'.

Arigna (Roscommon), An Airgnigh, 'the destroyer'.

The name refers to the river here as one that erodes its banks.

Arklow (Wicklow), An tInbhear Mór, 'the big estuary'.

The English name is an adaptation of the original Old Norse, meaning 'Arnkel's meadow' (Old Norse *ló*, 'meadow'). The Irish name refers to the estuary of the Avoca.

Arless (Laois), An Árdlios, 'the high ring-fort'.

Armagh (Armagh), Árd Mhacha, 'Macha's height'.

The name traditionally refers to Queen Macha ('of the golden hair') who founded Emain Macha (known formerly as Emania and now called Navan Fort) on the hill here some time in the third century B.C. The county name comes from that of the town.

Armoy (Antrim), Oirthear Maí, 'eastern end of the plain'.

Artane (Dublin), Árd Aidhin, 'Aidhean's height'.

Arthurstown (Wexford).

Named after Arthur, Lord Templemore, who founded it in the early 19th century.

Articlave (Derry), Árd an Chléibh, 'height of the basket'.

This name probably refers to a natural, basket-shaped feature here.

Artigarvan (Tyrone), Árd Tí Garbháin, 'height of the house of Garbhán'.

Ashbourne (Meath), Cill Dhéagláin, 'St Declan's church'.

The Irish name often appears in its anglicised form of Killeglan (which see).

Ashford (Limerick), Ceapach na Corcóige, 'field of the hive'.
Compare the next entry, where the English and Irish names agree.

Ashford (Wicklow), Áth na Fuinseoige, 'ford of the ash'.

Ashtown (Dublin), Baile Ás, 'Ashe's town'.

Askeaton (Limerick), Eas Géitine, 'Géitine's waterfall'.
The waterfall or cataract (Irish *eas*) is on the Deel River near here.

Athassel (Tipperary), Áth Aisil, 'Aisil's ford'.
The ford was over the Suir River here.

Athboy (Meath), Baile Átha Buí, 'town of the yellow ford'.
The river here has the same name.

Athenry (Galway), Baile Átha an Rí, 'town of the king's ford'.
The place is said to have been founded by an early English colony and named for an English king, perhaps originally as 'Kingstown' or something similar, with the present Irish name (and its anglicised version) being a translation of this.

Athgoe (Dublin), Áth Góain, 'ford of the smith'.

Athlacca (Limerick), An tÁth Leacach, 'the stony ford'.
The ford was over the Morning Star River here, above its junction with the Maigue.

Athleague (Roscommon), Áth Liag, 'ford of the stone'.
The name is traditionally said to refer to a stone or boulder in the river Suck here which is never covered even when the river floods. If the stone ever is covered, Athleague will be flooded, says a local tale.

Athlone (Westmeath), Baile Átha Luain, 'town of the ford of Luan'.
There is an important crossing of the Shannon here. Luan is a man's name.

Athy (Kildare), Baile Átha Í, 'town of the ford of Ae'.
The name is that of a Munster chief killed in an 11th-century battle here.

Auburn (Westmeath), Achadh na Gréine, 'field of the sunny place'.
The original Irish name of the village was Lissoy, i.e. *Lios Uaimhe*, 'fort of the cave'.

The present English name is due to Oliver Goldsmith, whose poem 'The Deserted Village', (published 1770) was based on Lissoy, and has as its opening line: 'Sweet Auburn! loveliest village of the plain.' There are over ten places called Auburn in the United States, and they all took their name from this village, which itself adopted the new name soon after Goldsmith's poem appeared. (Some American place name dictionaries claim that the name was based on the little Yorkshire village of Auburn, now in Humberside near Bridlington, but this is not the case.)

Augher (Tyrone), Eochair, 'border'.
Augher is three miles from the border with Monaghan.

Aughinish (Donegal, Clare), Each Inis, 'horse island'.
These places were probably named after favourite horse pastures. The Clare village is also known as Newquay.

Aughnacloy (Tyrone), Achadh na Cloiche, 'field of the stones'.
The name perhaps refers to one or more prominent stones here, or ones that were connected with some ritual or even a historic event.

Aughnamullen (Monaghan), Achadh na Muileann, 'field of the mills.
There were still several flaxmills and bleaching mills here in the late 19th century.

Aughrim (Galway, Wicklow), Eachroim, 'horse ridge'.
The Galway Aughrim was the scene of the battle of 12 July 1691, which decided the Jacobite war and was a turning point in Irish history.

Aughris (Sligo), Eachros, 'horse peninsula'.
This name is more likely to refer to a battle site than a grazing ground for horses.

Avalbane (Monaghan), Abhall Bán, 'white orchard'.
The name probably refers to the abundant blossom here.

Avoca (Wicklow), Abhóca.
This name is a modern adaptation of Ptolemy's ancient name *Oboka*, used to refer to this stretch of the Avonmore River. The former Irish name was *An Droichead*

Nua, 'the new bridge'.

Avonbeg (Wicklow), An Abhainn Bheag, 'the little river'.

This is the middle of three head streams of the Avoca, and is 'little' by contrast with the Avonmore, into which it flows at the 'Meeting of the Waters'.

Avonmore (Wicklow), Abhainn Mhór, 'great river'.

This river is said to have been called *Dea*, 'goddess', originally, and so to have had a name identical to the English river Dee. The source of the river is the point where several small streams join near Glendalough.

B

Bagenalstown, see **Muine Bheag**.

Baile Átha Cliath, see **Dublin**.

Bailey (Lighthouse) (Dublin).
The lighthouse is at Howth, to the east of Dublin, where it was built in 1814 on the site of an ancient fortress (Irish *baile*).

Bailieborough (Cavan), Coill an Chollaigh, 'wood of the boar'.
The English name does not derive from Irish *baile*, 'farm', 'town' but from a surname.

Balbriggan (Dublin), Baile Brigín, 'Brigín's homestead'.

Baldongan (Castle) (Dublin), Baile Dhonnagáin, 'Donnagán's homestead'.
The former castle here was dismantled by the royalists in the 17th century.

Baldonnell (Aerodrome) (Dublin), Baile Dhónaill, 'Dónal's homestead'.

Baldoyle (Dublin), Baile Dúill, 'Dubhghall's homestead'.
The personal name can be literally understood as 'black foreigner', 'dark stranger'.

Balla (Mayo), Balla, 'wall'.
The name refers to the *Tobar Mhuire*, known in English as the Blessed Well (i.e. of the Blessed Virgin Mary), to the west of Balla. This was enclosed by a wall, traditionally by St Mochua (Mo-Chua) in the 7th century, when he founded a monastery here.

Ballacolla (Laois), Baile Cholla, 'town of the hard land'.

Ballagh (Limerick), An Bealach, 'the road', 'the way'.
This name occurs elsewhere, as in Roscommon and Tipperary.

Ballaghaderreen (Mayo), Bealach an Doirín, 'road of the little oak grove'.

Ballaghkeen (Wexford), Béal Átha Caoin, '(place at the) mouth of the beautiful ford'.

Ballaghlea (Galway), Bealach Liath, 'grey road'.

Ballickmoyler (Laois), Baile Mhic Mhaoilir, 'townland of the son of the servant of Mary', 'Mac Moyland's homestead'.

Ballina (several), Béal an Átha, '(place at the) mouth of the ford'.
In the case of Ballina, Mayo, the name may mean 'ford mouth of the wood', from Irish *bel-átha-an-fheada*.

Ballinaboy (several), Béal an Áth Buidhe, '(place at the) mouth of the yellow ford'.
In the case of Ballinaboy, Galway, the name may mean '(place at the) mouth of the ford of the bay', from the Irish *Béal Átha na Bá*.

Ballinaclash (Wicklow), Baile na Claise, 'townland of the trench'.
The 'trench' is the hollow through which the river runs.

Ballinaclogher (Kerry), Baile na gClochar, 'townland of the stone buildings'.

Ballinaclough (Tipperary), Baile na Cloiche, 'townland of the stones'.

Ballinacor (Wicklow), Baile na Corra, 'townland of the weir'.
Ballinacor is on the Avonbeg River.

Ballinadee (Cork), Baile na Daibhche, 'townland of the cauldron'.
The name refers to a whirlpool somewhere here in the river Bandon.

Ballinafad (Sligo), Béal an Átha Fada, '(place at the) mouth of the long ford'.
Ballinafad is at the south-west corner of Lough Arrow.

Ballinagar (Offaly), Béal Átha na gCarr, '(place at the) mouth of the ford of the waggon'.
The name refers to a regular crossing place here for drays or waggons.

Ballinahinch (Tipperary), Baile na hInse, 'townland of the river meadow'.

Ballinakill (Kerry), Baile na Coille, 'homestead of the wood'.

Ballinalack (Westmeath), Béal Átha na Leac, 'ford-mouth of the flagstones'.
There is a bridge here now, but the original ford across the river Inny was actually covered in flagstones.

Ballinalee (Longford), Béal Átha na Lao, 'ford-mouth of the calves'.
This would have been a regular crossing point for calves. Compare **Annamoe**.

Ballinamona (Cork), Baile na Móna, 'townland of the bog'.

Ballinamore (several), Béal an Átha Móir, 'mouth of the big ford'.

Ballinamuck (Longford), Béal Átha na Muc, 'ford-mouth of the pigs'.

As with Ballinalee, this would have been a regular crossing point for the animals.

Ballinard (Limerick), Baile an Áird, 'townland of the height'.

The land here slopes noticeably to the west.

Ballinascarthy (Cork), Béal na Scairte, 'ford-mouth of the thicket'.

Ballinasloe (Galway), Béal Átha na Sluaighe, 'ford-mouth of the gathering'.

Whatever the original 'gathering' was, it was almost certainly the forerunner of the present livestock market, which is the largest in Ireland and developed out of the famous horse fairs held here.

Ballinchalla (Mayo), Baile an Chaladh, 'townland of the landing place'.

Ballinchalla is on Lough Mask.

Ballinclare (Sligo), Caisleán Bhéil an Chláir, 'castle of the town of the plain'.

Ballincollig (Cork), Baile an Chollaigh, 'homestead of the boar'.

Ballincurry (Tipperary), Baile an Churraigh, 'townland of the marsh'.

Ballindarragh (Fermanagh), Baile na Dara, 'townland of the oak'.

Ballinderreen (Galway), Baile an Doirín, 'townland of the small oak grove'.

Ballinderry (several), Baile an Doire, 'homestead of the oak grove'.

Ballindroit (Donegal), Baile an Droichid, 'town of the bridge'.

The river here is the Dale (or Deele).

Ballineanig (Kerry), Baile an Aonaigh, 'townland of the fair'.

Ballineen (Cork), Béal Átha Fhínín, 'Fínín's ford-mouth'.

Ballingarry (Limerick, Tipperary), Baile an Gharraí, 'homestead of the garden'.

Ballingeary (Cork), Béal Átha an Ghaorthaidh, 'ford-mouth of the wooded valley'.

The river here is the Lee.

Ballingurteen (Cork), Baile an Ghoirtín, 'townland of the small field'.

Ballinlough (several), Baile an Locha, 'townland of the lake'.

In some cases the original lake will have been drained or may have dried up.

Ballin Prior (Kerry), Baile an Phrióra, 'the prior's townland'.

Ballinrobe (Mayo), Baile an Róba, 'homestead of the (river) Robe'.

Ballinskelligs (Kerry), Baile an Sceilg, 'homestead of Skellig Island'.

Irish *sceillig* means 'splinter', 'rocky pinnacle', 'crag'; *see* **Skelligs**.

Ballinspittle (Cork), Béal Átha an Spidéil, 'ford-mouth of the hospital'.

Ballintaggart (Kerry), Baile an tSagairt, 'homestead of the priest'.

Ballintemple (several), Baile an Teampaill, 'townland of the church'.

Ballintober (Mayo, Roscommon), Baile an Tobair, 'homestead of the well'.

The Roscommon Ballintober is also known as Toberbride, and the name refers to a holy well here dedicated to St Brigid. The Mayo well is north-west of the town, just south-east of the remains of the church, where it is known as Tober Patrick.

Ballintogher (Sligo), Baile an Tóchair, 'townland of the causeway'.

Ballintoy (Antrim), Baile an Tuaighe, 'townland of the north'.

The village is in the extreme north of the country, by the coast.

Ballintra (Donegal), Baile an tSratha, 'homestead of the river meadow'.

Ballintra is on the river of the same name.

Ballintubbert (Laois), Baile an Tiobrad, 'townland of the well'.

Ballinure (several), Baile an Iúir, 'townland of the yew tree'.

Ballinvoher (several), Baile an Bhóthair, 'townland of the road'.

Ballivor (Meath), Baile Íomhair, 'Íomhar's townland'.

Ballough (several), An Bealach, 'the road', 'the way'.

Ballsbridge (Dublin), Droichead na Dothra, 'dodder bridge'.

The bridge, named after someone called Ball, was built in 1751.

Ballyanne (Wexford), Baile Anna, 'Anne's town'.

Ballybane (Cork), Baile Bán, 'white townland'.

Ballybarrack (Louth), Baile Balraic, 'Balrac's townland'.

Ballybay (Monahan), Béal Átha Beithe, 'ford-mouth of the birch tree'.

Ballybeg (several), An Baile Beag, 'the small homestead'.

Ballybetagh (Dublin), Baile Biataigh, 'townland of the hospitaller'.

The reference is to a measure of land, originally one thirtieth of a barony, or 480 Irish acres. Such a measure was usually known as a 'ballybetagh'.

Ballyboe (Donegal), Baile Bó, 'cow homestead'.

As with Ballybetagh, this name was used to denote a measure of land.

Ballybofey (Donegal), Bealach Féich, 'Fiach's road'.

The 'Bally' here is thus Irish *bealach*, not the expected *baile*, 'homestead'.

Ballyboggan (Meath), Baile Uí Bhogáin, 'townland of the descendants of Bhogán'.

Ballybogey (Antrim), Baile an Bhogaigh, 'townland of the bog'.

Ballybough (Dublin), Baile Bocht, 'poor townland'.

Ballyboy (Offaly), Baile Átha Buidhe, 'town of the yellow ford'.

The name is found elsewhere, and in most cases derives from Baile Buidhe, 'yellow townland'. The Offaly Ballyboy is on the river Silver.

Ballybrack (Dublin), An Baile Breac, 'the speckled townland'.

Ballybrien (Longford), Baile Bhriain, 'Brian's townland'.

Ballybritt (Offaly), Baile an Bhriotaigh, 'Briotach's townland'.

Ballybrittas (Laois), Baile Briotáis, 'homestead of (the) brattice'.

This is the literal meaning of the Irish, with 'brattice' being a medieval wooden fort used in sieges. But the name is probably distorted, and perhaps should really be 'speckled townland' (as for Ballybrack), indicated a settlement with dwellings dotted about.

Ballybrophy (Laois), Baile Uí Bhróithe, 'townland of Brophy's descendants'.

Ballybunion (Kerry), Baile an Bhuinneanaigh, 'Bunion's homestead'.

Ballycahill (Tipperary), Bealach Achaille, 'road of Achaille'.

Ballycanew (Wexford), Baile Uí Chonnmhaí, 'townland of the descendants of Conway'.

Ballycarney (Wexford), Baile Uí Chearnaigh, 'townland of the descendants of Carney'.

Ballycarry (Antrim), Baile Cora, 'homestead of the weir'.

Ballycastle (Antrim), Baile an Chaistil, 'farmstead of the castle'.

The castle is no longer here. Its site was The Diamond, in Ballycastle Old Town.

Ballycastle (Mayo), Baile an Chaisil, 'homestead of the stone fort'.

In this name the Irish word *caiseal* has become the English 'castle'. A more accurate English spelling of the name would therefore be 'Ballycashel'. See **Cashel,** and compare with Antrim Ballycastle.

Ballyclare (Antrim), Bealach Cláir, 'road of the plain'.

Compare the next name.

Ballyclare (Roscommon), Baile an Chláir, 'townland of the plain'.

Compare the previous name.

Ballyclerihan (Tipperary), Baile Uí Chleireacháin, 'townland of the descendants of Clerahan'.

Ballyclough (Cork), Baile Cloch, 'townland of stones'.

This name is also found elsewhere.

Ballyconnell (Cavan), Béal Átha Conaill, 'ford-mouth of Conall'.

According to tradition, Conall Carnagh (or Cearnach), one of the most famous of the Red Branch knights of Ulster, was killed here in the 1st century.

Ballyconry (Kerry), Baile Conraoi, 'Conraoi's townland'.

Ballycotton (Cork), Baile Choitín, 'Cottin's townland'.

Ballycowan (Offaly), Baile Cobhainn, 'Cobhann's homestead.'

Ballycrovane (Cork), Béal an Churraigh Bháin, '(place at the) mouth of the white marsh'.

Ballycroy (Mayo), Baile Chruaigh, 'townland of the summit'.

Ballydaheen (Cork), Baile Dáithín, 'little Dáith's townland'.

21

Ballydangan (Roscommon), Baile Daingean, 'townland of the fort'.

Ballydavid (Kerry), Baile na nGall, 'townland of the foreigners'.

The English name appears to be a distortion of the Irish, in place of the expected 'Ballynagall'.

Ballydehob (Cork), Béal an Dá Chab, 'entrance of the two mouths'.

This name must refer to some local feature here. Ballydehob is at the base of Mount Gabriel on the shores of Roaringwater Bay.

Ballydesmond (Cork), Baile Deasumhan, 'Desmond's townland'.

For over a hundred years from the 1830s, Ballydesmond was known as Kingwilliamstown, after the English king William IV (reigned 1830-7).

Ballydooley (Roscommon), Baile Uí Dhúbhlaoich, 'townland of the descendants of Dooley'.

Ballyduff (several), An Baile Dubh, 'the black homestead'.

Ballyduggan (Down), Baile Uí Dhúgáin, 'townland of the descendants of Duggan'.

Ballyeaston (Antrim), Baile Uistín, 'Austin's townland'.

Ballyeighter (Clare), Baile Íochtair, 'lower town'.

Ballyfeard (Cork), Baile Feá Aird, 'townland of the high wood'.

Ballyferriter (Kerry), Baile an Fheirtéaraigh, 'Ferriter's townland'.

Ballyforan (Roscommon), Béal Átha Feorainne, 'ford-mouth of the river meadow'.

Ballyfoyle (several), Baile an Phoill, 'townland of the hole'.

Ballygally (Antrim), Baile Geithligh, 'Geithleach's homestead'.

Ballygar (Galway), Béal Átha Ghártha, 'ford-mouth of the enclosed garden'.

Ballygarrett (Wexford), Baile Ghearóid, 'Gearóid's townland'.

Ballygawley (Tyrone, Sligo), Baile Uí Dhálaigh, 'townland of the descendants of Daly'.

Ballyglass (Mayo), An Baile Glas, 'the green homestead'.

Ballyglunin (Galway), Béal Átha Glúinín, 'Glúinín's ford-mouth'.

Ballygowan (Down), Baile Mhic Gabhann, 'townland of Mac Gowan'.

Ballygrogan (Cork), Baile Uí Ghrógáin, 'townland of the descendants of Grogan'.

Ballyhaise (Cavan), Béal Átha hÉis', 'Éis' ford-mouth'.

Ballyhalbert (Down), Baile Thalbóid, 'Talbot's homestead'.

Ballyhale (Kilkenny), Baile Héil, 'Howel's homestead'.

Ballyhaunis (Mayo), Béal Átha hAmhnais, 'ford-mouth of the battle'.

Ballyhean (Mayo), Béal Átha hÉin, 'ford-mouth of the bird'.

Ballyheigue (Kerry), Baile Uí Thaidhg, 'townland of the descendants of Taidhg'.

Ballyholme (Down), Baile Hóm, 'creek town'.

Ballyhooly (Cork), Baile Átha hÚlla, 'town of the ford of the apples'.

Ballyhornan (Down), Baile Uí Chornáin, 'townland of the descendants of Fearnan'.

Ballyhusty (Tipperary), Baile Hoiste, 'Hoiste's townland'.

Ballyiriston (Donegal), Baile Ireastain, 'townland of Irestan'.

Ballyjamesduff (Cavan), Baile Shéamais Dhuibh, 'James Duff's town'.

The name is that of the English officer who fought in Ireland during the 1798 rising.

Ballykeel (Antrim), An Baile Caol, 'the narrow townland'.

Ballykeeran (Westmeath), Bealach Caorthainn, 'road of the rowan trees'.

As with Ballybofey, the 'Bally' here is not the usual Irish *baile*.

Ballykelly (Derry), Baile Uí Cheallaigh, 'homestead of the descendants of Kelly'.

Ballykilleen (Offaly), Baile an Chillín, 'townland of the (monk's) cell'.

Ballykinler (Down), Baile Coinnleora, 'townland of the candlestick'.

The site here is said to have been granted by John de Courcy to Christchurch, Dublin, for the upkeep of a perpetual light burning before the cross in this church.

Ballylanders (Limerick), Baile an Londraigh, 'Landers' homestead'.

The name appears to be that of an English family called Landers.

Ballylarkin (Kilkenny), Baile Uí Lorcain,

'homestead of the descendants of Larkin'.

Ballylesson (Down), Baile na Leasán, 'townland of the small forts'.

Ballylickey (Cork), Béal Átha Leice, 'fordmouth of the flagstones'.

Ballylickey is at the point where the river Ouvane enters a creek of Bantry Bay. The flagstones were still here quite recently.

Ballyliffen (Donegal), Baile Lifín, 'Liffin's homestead'.

Ballylinan (Laois), Baile Uí Laigheanáin, 'townland of the descendants of Linan'.

Ballyline (Kilkenny), Baile Uí Fhlainn, 'townland of the descendants of Flynn'.

Ballylongford (Kerry), Béal Átha Longfoirt, 'ford-mouth of the fortress.'

The fortress concerned is the one at Carrigafoyle castle, two miles away.

Ballylough (Antrim), Baile an Locha, 'townland of the lake'.

Ballymacallion (Derry), Baile Mhac Ailín, 'townland of the son of Allion'.

Ballymacarberry (Waterford), Baile Mhac Cairbre, 'townland of the son of Cairbre'.

Ballymacarret (Belfast), Baile Mhic Gearóid, 'townland of the son of Carret'.

Ballymachugh (Cavan), Baile Mhic Aodha, 'townland of the son of Hugh'.

Ballymack (Kilkenny), Baile Mac Cua, 'townland of the sons of Cua'.

Ballymackesy (Wexford), Baile Uí Mhacasa, 'townland of Mackessy'.

Ballymacoda (Cork), Baile Mhac Óda, 'townland of the son of Óda'.

Ballymagorry (Tyrone), Baile Mhic Gofraidh, 'townland of the son of Gorry'.

Ballymahon (Longford), Baile Uí Mhatháin, 'homestead of the descendants of Mahon'.

Ballymakeera (Cork), Baile Mhic Íre, 'townland of the son of Íre'.

Ballymalis (Kerry), Béal Átha Málais, 'Málas' ford-mouth'.

Ballymartin (Down), Baile Mhic Giolla Mhártain, 'townland of Mac Gilmartin'.

The modern Irish surname Mac Gilmartin means 'devotees of St Martin', with 'Gil-' from Irish *giolla*, 'lad', 'servant', 'devotee'.

Ballymascanlan (Lough), Baile Mhic Scanláin, 'homestead of the son of Scanlán'.

Ballymena (Antrim), An Baile Meánach, 'the middle town'.

Ballymena is near the middle of Co. Antrim at a point where many roads converge. However, its name dates back to a time before the county was established, and there are other places of the name that are not in the middle of a county. The name thus means more 'central township', 'place where roads meet'.

Ballymoe (Galway), Béal Átha Mó, 'fordmouth of Mó'.

Ballymoney (Antrim), Baile Muine, 'homestead of the thicket'.

There are other places of the name, e.g. in Wexford, and for some of these the origin may be *Baile Monaidh*, 'homestead of the moor'.

Ballymoon (Carlow), Bealach Múna, 'Múna's road'.

Compare **Ballybofey** and **Ballykeeran**, where the 'Bally-' is not the usual Irish *baile*.

Ballymore (several), An Baile Mór, 'the big town'.

If a place with this name is on a river, the *baile* might be *béal* and so refer to the mouth of the ford.

Ballymore Eustace (Kildare), An Baile Mór, 'the big homestead'.

The second half of the name refers to the members of the Anglo-Norman Fitz Eustace family, who were the hereditary constables of the Archbishop of Dublin's manor here from 1373 to about 1524.

Ballymote (Sligo), Baile an Mhóta, 'homestead of the mound'.

The mound referred to was almost certainly the motte of the 13th-century Anglo-Norman castle of Rathdrony, just over a mile west of Ballymote.

Ballymullen (Kerry), Bale an Mhuilinn, 'townland of the mill'.

There are other places of the name, and in some case the *baile* could be *béal* and so refer to a ford-mouth, as mentioned for Ballymore.

Ballymurphy (Carlow), Baile Uí Mhurchú, 'townland of the descendants of Murphy'.

Ballymurray (Roscommon), Baile Uí Mhuirígh, 'townland of the descendants of Murray'.

Ballynabola (Wexford), Baile na Buaile,

'townland of the summer pasture'.

Ballynacally (Clare), Baile na Caillí, 'townland of the hag'.

Ballynacarriga (Cork), Baule na Carraige, 'townland of the rock'.

Ballynacarrow (Sligo), Baile na Ceathrú, 'townland of the quarter'.

A quarter was a land measure, the fourth part of a 'ballybetagh' (see **Ballybetagh**).

Ballynacurry (Armagh), Baile na Cairthe, 'townland of the standing stone'.

Ballynaclogh (Tipperary), Baile na Cloiche, 'townland of the stone'.

The district here is well known for its limestone and marble.

Ballynacorra (Cork), Baile na Cora, 'townland of the weir'.

Ballynacourty (several), Baile na Cúirte, 'townland of the mansion'.

Ballynadrummy (Kildare), Baile na Druiminne, 'homestead of the white-backed cow'.

Ballynafeigh (Belfast), Baile na Faiche, 'townland of the playing field'.

A *faithche* was a level green area in front of a fort or residence that was used for games, sports, public receptions, and so on, something like a modern public park.

Ballynafid (Westmeath), Baile na Feide, 'townland of the little stream'.

Ballynagall (Kerry), Baile na nGall, 'townland of the foreigners'.

The 'foreigners' would have been the English.

Ballynaglogh (Cork), Baile na gCloch, 'townland of the stones'.

Ballynagore (Westmeath), Béal Átha na nGabhar, 'ford-mouth of the goats'.

This would have been a regular crossing point for the animals over the Brosna River.

Ballynahaglish (Mayo, Kerry), Baile na hEaglaise, 'townland of the church'.

Ballynahinch (Down, Tipperary), Baile na hInse, 'homestead of the island'.

In the case of the Ballynahinch in Co. Down, the site was probably an 'island' between the river, the lake (now drained and laid out as playing fields), and a stream which ran from the lake into the river. More generally, the location here was a pocket of dry land surrounded by hills, the river, and bogland.

Ballynahinch Lake (Galway), Loch Bhaile na hInse, 'lake of the homestead of the island'.

One island in the lake has an ancient castle that belonged to the Martin family here.

Ballynahown (Westmeath), Baile na hAbhann, 'townland of the river'.

Ballynakill (several), Baile na Cille, 'townland of the church'.

In some places so named, the origin may well be *Baile na Coille*, 'townland of the wood'.

Ballynalackan (Clare), Baile na Leacan, 'townland of the hillside'.

Ballynapark (Wicklow), Baile na Páirce, 'townland of the field'.

Ballynaskeagh (Down), Baile na Sceach, 'townland of the whitethorn bushes'.

Ballynastuckaun (Galway), Baile na Stocán, 'townland of the tree stumps'.

Irish *stocán* has several meanings, including 'tree stump', 'rock', and 'hill', and any of these could apply here.

Ballyneety (Limerick), Baile an Fhaoitigh, 'White's townland'.

The name is the English surname White.

Ballyness (Derry, Tyrone), Baile an Easa, 'townland of the waterfall'.

Ballynoe (Down), An Baile Nua, 'the new homestead'.

Ballynure (Antrim), Baile an Iúir, 'homestead of the yew'.

Ballyorgan (Limerick), Baile Uí Argáin, 'Organ's township'.

Ballyporeen (Tipperary), Béal Átha Póirín, 'Poreen's ford-mouth'.

Ballyragget (Kilkenny), Béal Átha Ragad, 'ford mouth of Ragget'.

The name is that of the Anglo-Norman family Le Ragged, who had lands here in the 13th century.

Ballyraheen (Wicklow), Baile an Ráithín, 'townland of the small ring-fort'.

Ballyrashane (Antrim), Baile Rath Seáin, 'townland of John's fort'.

Ballyroe (Kerry), Baile Rua, 'red-coloured townland'.

Ballyronan (Derry), Baile Uí Rónáin, 'townland of the descendants of Rónán'.

Ballyroney (Down), Baile Uí Ruanaí, 'town-land of the descendants of Ruanaí'.

Ballysadare (Sligo), Baile Easa Dara, 'homestead of the waterfall of the oak'.
The waterfall is that of the Owenmore River, which flows down a series of shelving rocks to Ballysadare Bay.

Ballyskeery (Mayo), Baile Ease Caoire, 'townland of the narrow waterfall'.
The letter *l* of Irish *caoile*, 'narrow' has changed to *r*, by association with *caor*, genitive *caoire*, 'ball', 'berry', which would be meaningless here.

Ballysallough (Down), Baile Salach, 'dirty townland'.

Ballyshannon (Donegal), Béal Átha Seanaidh, 'ford-mouth of the hillside'.
The town is on a steep bank overlooking the river Erne.

Ballyshrule (Galway), Baile Sruthail, 'townland of the stream'.

Ballysillan (Belfast), Baile na Saileán, 'townland of the willow groves'.

Ballysimon (Limerick), Béal Átha Síomoin, 'Simon's ford-mouth'.

Ballysteen (Limerick), Baile Stiabhna, 'townland of Istiadhan'.

Ballytarsna (Tipperary), Baile Trasna, 'cross-town'.
The name denotes the transverse location of the place, where it 'runs across' an otherwise straight road or route.

Ballytore (Kildare), Béal Átha an Tuair, 'ford-mouth of the bleaching green'.
A 'bleaching green' is a place suitable for drying clothes or other objects, in particular one by a stream, where the things can be washed.

Ballyvaughan (Clare), Baile Uí Bheacháin, 'townland of the descendants of Behan'.

Ballyvourney (Cork), Baile Bhuirne, 'homestead of the stony place'.

Ballyvoyle (Waterford), Baile Uí Bhaoghill, 'townland of the descendants of Boyle'.

Ballywalter (Down), Baile Bháltair, 'Walter's homestead'.

Ballywilliam (Wexford), Baile Liam, 'William's homestead'.

Ballywillin (Longdord), Baile an Mhuilinn, 'townland of the mill'.

Balmoral (Belfast, Down), Baile Mór Aille,

'townland of the big cliff'.
The Scottish Balmoral has a different meaning — 'village in the big clearing'.

Balrath (Meath), Baile na Rátha, 'homestead of the ring-fort'.

Balrothery (Dublin), Baile an Ridire, 'townland of the knight'.

Baltimore (Cork), Dún na Séad, 'fort of the jewels'.
The present Irish name is different from the English, which represents *Baile na Tighe Mór*, 'townland of the big house'. Irish *sead* is a general word denoting anything of value, although in historic times meaning some precious posession, which could be anything from a jewel to a young cow. In the English name, the 'big house' (Irish *teach mór*) would have been a country gentleman's residence. The American Baltimore derives its name from this Irish place, through the hereditary title of the Calvert family whose seat (*teach mór*) was the barony here.

Baltinglass (Wicklow), Bealach Conglais, 'road of Cúglas'.
The personal name Cuglas is said to derive from *Cú Ghlas*, 'greyhound'.

Baltray (Louth), Baile Trá, 'homestead of (the) strand'.
Baltray is at the mouth of the river Boyne.

Banagher (Derry, Offaly), Beanacher, 'place of pointed hills'.
The Banagher in Offaly is said to be named from the sharp rocks in the river Shannon here, with Irish *beann* meaning any pointed object from a peak to a pinnacle.

Banbridge (Down), Droichead na Banna, 'bridge on the (river) Bann'.

Bandon (Cork), Droichead na Bandan, 'bridge on the (river) Bandon'.
It is possible that the name of this river and of the Bann (*see* **Banbridge**) may mean 'goddess', and be related to Irish *bean*, 'woman'.

Bangor (Down), Beannchar, 'pointed arrangement'.
As a monastic establishment, Bangor was a daughter foundation of Bangor in North Wales. The common Celtic name is believed to refer to the pointed sticks or rods in the wattled fence that surrounded

the settlement. The Irish Bangor was originally known as Bangor Mór to distinguish it from the Welsh one, and as if to imply that it had developed independently.

Bangorerris (Mayo), Baingear Iorrais, 'pointed hill of Erris'.

Bann, *see* **Bandon**.

Bannow (Wexford), Cuan an Bhainbh, 'harbour of the young pig'.
The place here is now just the site of a former town.

Bansha (Tipperary), An Bháinseach, 'the grassy spot'.
The village is on an attractive site below the east end of a wooded ridge (the Slievenamuck Hills), at the mouth of the Glen of Aherlow.

Banteer (Cork), Bántír, 'fair country'.

Bantry (Cork), Beanntraí, '(place of) Beann's people'.
In traditional early legend, Beann was one of the sons of Conor Mac Nessa, the 1st-century king of Ulster. Some see the name as actually meaning 'hilly strand', as if deriving from *Beanntraighe* (*beann*, 'headland', 'hill' and *traigh*, 'strand', 'shore').

Barfordstown (Meath), Baile Bharfoird, 'Barford's town'.

Barna (several), Bearna, 'gap'.
This name usually indicates a gap through hills or mountains, such as a pass.

Barnaderg (Galway), Bearna Dhearg, 'red gap'.

Barnageera (Dublin), Barr na gCaorach, 'summit of the sheep'.

Barnagh (Limerick), Bearnach, 'gapped'.

Barnatra (Mayo), Barr na Trá, 'top of the strand'.

Barnesmore (Donegal), An Bearnas Mór, 'the great gap'.
The glen here is known as the Gap of Barnesmore.

Baronscourt (Tyrone), Cúirt an Bharúin, 'the baron's court'.
The original name of the location here, preserved in the remains of Derrywoone Castle, was *Doire Eoghain,* 'Eoghan's oak grove'. The present name is from the Georgian mansion built here in 1741 as the seat of the Duke of Abercorn. The estate has three semi-artificial lakes, called

Loughs Catherine, Fanny and Mary, and nearby hills are called Bessie Bell and Mary Gray. The lakes are named after members of the family (the Scottish Hamiltons, Dukes of Abercorn), and the two hills were named by the family after the heroines of a Scottish ballad.

Barraduff (Kerry), Barra Dubh, 'black top'.

Barrington's Bridge (Limerick).
The bridge was built in 1818 by Sir Jonah Barrington, judge in the admiralty court.

Barryscourt (Cork), Cúirt an Bharraigh, 'Barry's court'.

Baslick (Roscommon), Baislic Mhór, 'big church'.
The ruins of the old abbey can still be seen here.

Batterjohn (Meath), Bóthar Sheáin, 'John's road'.

Batterstown (Meath), Baile an Bhóthair, 'townland of the road'.

Bawnboy (Cavan), An Bábhún Buí, 'the yellow enclosure'.
A 'bawn' was an enclosure for cattle.

Baytown Park (Meath), Páirc Bhaile Beithe, 'park of the townland of the birch'.
The English name is a corruption of the Irish, half translated.

Bealaha (Clare), Béal Átha, 'ford-mouth'.

Bear Haven (Cork), Béarra.
According to legend, Owenmore, the 2nd-century king of Munster, spent nine years in Spain and there married Beara, daughter of the Spanish king. On his return to Ireland he landed on the north side of Bantry Bay and called the place *Beara* after his wife.

Bective (Meath), Beicteach.
Bective is a 12th-century daughter foundation of Mellifont, and its present name is said to be a corruption of its original Latin one, *De Beatitudine*, through such spellings as *Bekty, Bekedy*, and so on.

Bedlam (Donegal), An Bhealtaine, 'Beltane'.
The name is that of the Irish May Festival, held both here and elsewhere.

Beclare (Galway), Béal Chláir, 'mouth of (the) plain'.

Belcoo (Fermanagh), Béal Cú, 'mouth of the narrow neck of land'.
The original Irish *caol*, 'narrow part' has

become *cú*, 'dog', probably by association with *éal*, 'mouth'. Belcoo is in fact on an isthmus between the Upper and Lower Loughs Macnean.

Belderrig (Mayo), Béal Deirg, 'Dearg's estuary'.

Belfast (Antrim), Béal Feirste, '(ford-) mouth of the sandbank'.

The sandbank of the name is the one that formed at the point where the little river Farset (which took its own name from the sandbank, Irish *fearsad*) joined the Lagan, a short distance below Queen's Bridge. Another small river, the Owenvarna or Blackstaff, joined the Lagan further upstream, and the tongue of dry land stretched out between the two towards the opposite shore on the Co. Down side. At low tide the river could be forded here, probably at a point now marked by a continuation of Ann Street. The crossing was an important one, and only fell out of use when Long Bridge was built.

Belgooly (Cork), Béal Guala, 'entrance of the hill-shoulder'.

Bellacorick (Mayo), Béal Átha Chomhraic, 'ford-mouth of the confluence'.

Bellaghy (Derry), Baile Eachaidh, 'townland of the horseman'.

This is almost certainly a distortion of the original Irish, which may have meant 'mouth of the muddy place', from *beal*, 'mouth' and *laitheach*, 'mud', 'mire'. The Irish for 'horseman' is *eachaidhe*.

Bellanagare (Roscommon), Béal Átha na gCarr, 'ford-mouth of the waggons'.

Bellanaleck (Fermanagh), Bealach na Leice, 'road of the flagstone'.

Bellanamullia (Roscommon), Béal Átha na mBuillí, 'ford-mouth of the blows'.

The name appears to refer to some battle here. It may, however, be a corruption of some other word, such as *muileann*, 'mill'.

Bellananagh (Cavan), Béal Átha na nEach, 'ford-mouth of the horses'.

Bellarena (Derry), Baile an Mhargaidh, 'townland of the market'.

Bellavally (Cavan), Béal an Bhealaigh, 'mouth of the pass'.

Belleek (several), Béal Leice, 'ford-mouth of the flagstone'.

At Belleek in Fermanagh, a flat rock in the river-bed appeared as a smooth, level floor when the water grew shallow in summer.

Belleeks (Armagh), Béal Leice, 'ford-mouth of the flagstone'.

This is the same as the previous name.

Bellewstown Meath, Baile an Bheileogaigh, 'Bellew's town'.

Bellurgan (Louth), Baile Lorgan, 'town of the strip of land'.

Belmullet (Mayo), Béal an Mhuirthead, 'entrance of the Mullet Peninsula'.

Beltany (Donegal), An Bhealtaine, 'Beltane'.

For the sense of this name, see **Bedlan**. There are two places called Beltany in Donegal, and other variations of the name elsewhere.

Beltra (Mayo, Sligo), Béal Trá, 'entrance to For the sense of this name, see **Bedlam**.

Belvelly (Cork), Béal an Bhealaigh, 'entrance to the road'.

Benbo (Leitrim), Beanna Bó, 'peaks of the cow'.

This mountain derives its name from the appearance of its double peak, resembling the horns of a cow.

Benbrack (Cavan), Beann Bhreac, 'speckled hill'.

Ben Bulben (Sligo), Beann Ghulbain, 'beak pinnacle'.

This mountain is well known for its unusual 'profiles'.

Benburb (Tyrone), An Bhinn Bhorb, 'the rough peak'.

Irish *borb* means 'sharp', 'rough', 'projecting', and this last sense is appropriate for the settlement here, which developed near a cliff overhanging the river Blackwater.

Benmore (Antrim), Beann Mhór, 'great peak'.

This headland has a number of high rocks and a precipice.

Bennettsbridge (Kilkenny), Droichead Binéid, 'Bennett's Bridge'.

Bessbrook (Aramagh), An Sruthán, 'the brook'.

The first part of the name derives from that of Elizabeth Carlile, of Newry, who married John Pollock, founder of a linen manufacturing business here. His house, Bess Brook, was near the Camlough River, and was named partly after his wife, partly after the little river.

Bettystown (Meath), Baile an Bhaitaigh, 'Betagh's homestead'.

Billis (Cavan), Na Bilí, 'the ancient trees'.
The Irish name has acquired an English plural 's'.

Binnion (Donegal), Beinnín, 'small peak'.

Birdhill (Tipperary), Cnocán an Éin Fhinn, 'hill of the white bird'.

Birr (Offaly), Biorra, 'watery place'.
The former name of Birr was Parsonstown, after Sir Lawrence Parsons of Leicestershire, to whom the settlement was assigned by James I in 1620. Birr is on the river Camcor.

Blackrock (Dublin), An Charraig Dhubh, 'the black rock'.
The name is found elsewhere, with slightly differing Irish versions; see the next two entries.

Blackrock (Louth), Na Creagacha Dubha, 'the black rocks'.

Blackrock Castle (Cork), Caisleán na Ducharraige, 'castle of the black rock'.

Blackstaff (Belfast), Abhainn Bheara, 'river of (the) staff'.
The little Belfast river, known also as the Owenvarna (from the Irish), has a name that denotes the staves or stakes formerly used to provide a crossing over it. See also **Belfast**.

Blackwatertown (Armagh), An Port Mór, 'the big fort'.
The English name refers to the river Blackwater here. The fort was built in 1584.

Blackwood (Kildare), Coill Dubh, 'black wood'.

Blanchardstown (Dublin), Baile Bhlainsear, 'Blanchard's town'.
Blanchard is an Anglo-Norman family name. The place-name here was recorded in 1249 as *Villa Blanchard*.

Blaney (Fermanagh), Bléinigh, 'narrow strip of land'.

Blaris (Down), Bláras, 'exposed place'.
The Irish root word for this name is *blár*, used of a field or other site that is bare and exposed, unlike a sheltered place.

Blarney (Cork), An Bhlarna, 'the small field'.

Blennerville (Kerry), Cathair Uí Mhóráin, 'stone fort of the descendants of Moran'.
The English name here is based on a family name.

Blessington (Wicklow), Baile Coimín, 'Comyn's townland'.
The earlier English name here, based on the present Irish one, was 'Ballycomin'. This was understood as deriving from *baile comaoine*, 'townland of favour' (from *comaoin*, 'favour', 'recompense', 'Holy Communion'), and this was mistakenly rendered into English as Blessington, i.e. 'town of blessing'.

Bloody Bridge (Down), Droichead na Fola, 'bridge of blood'.
The name arose here after 1641, when there was a massacre of Planters at the old road bridge, to the west of the present bridge and car park.

Bloody Foreland (Donegal), Cnoc Fola, 'hill of blood'.
This name is said to describe the red sunsets seen from the hill here.

Blue Ball (Offaly), An Phailís, 'the palisade'.
The English name appears to derive from an inn here.

Bodenstown (Kildare), Baile Bodún, 'Boden's town'.

Bofin, Lough (Galway), Loch Bó Finne, 'lake of (the) white cow'.

Boghadoon (Mayo), Both an Dúin, 'hut of the fort'.

Boher (Offaly), An Bóthar, 'the road'.

Boheraphuca (Offaly), Bóthar an Phúca, 'road of the hobgoblin'.

Boheravaghera (Waterford), Bóthar an Mhachaire, 'road of the plain'.

Boherboy (Cork), An Bóthar Buidhe, 'the yellow road'.
The road referred to is the one between Milltown and Banteer.

Boherlahan (Tipperary), An Bóthar Leathan, 'the wide road'.

Bohermeen (Meath), An Bóthar Mín, 'the smooth road'.

Boherroe (Roscommon), An Bóthar Ruadh, 'the red road'.

Boho (Fermanagh), Botha, 'huts'.
The name indicates a tribal settlement of some kind.

Bohola (Mayo), Both Chomhla, 'Comhla's cell'.
The church here is now in ruins.
Boley (Kildare), Buaile, 'summer pasture'.
Bonamargy (Antrim), Bun na Mairge, 'mouth of the (river) Margy'.
The friary so named here was founded in 1500.
Boolavonteen (Waterford), Buaile an Mhóintin, 'summer pasture of the little bog'.
Boolteens (Kerry), Na Buailtíní, 'the little summer pastures'.
Boolyglass (Kilkenny), Buaile Ghlas, 'green summer pasture'.
Booterstown (Dublin), Baile an Bhóthair, 'townland of the road'.
The road was, and still is, one of the main ones leading south from Dublin.
Borris (Carlow), An Bhuiríos, 'the borough'.
This is an Anglo-Norman name given to a borough town established by them.
Borris-in-Ossory (Laois), Buiríos Mór Osraí, 'the big borough of Ossory'.
Ossory is the name of an ancient territory here.
Borrisokane (Tipperary), Buiríos Uí Chéin, 'borough of the descendants of Cein'.
This name may in fact have a different origin, and derive from achadh caoin, 'smooth field', rather than a personal name.
Borrisoleigh (Tipperary), Buiríos Ó Luigheach, 'borough of the descendants of Luigheach'.
Bouladuff (Tipperary), An Bhuaile Dhubh, 'the black summer pasture'.
Bourney (Tipperary), Boirne, 'rocky lands'.
Boveva (Derry), Boith Mhéabha, 'Maeve's hut'.
Maeve is a woman's name, famous as that of the legendary queen of Connacht who led an invasion of Ulster.
Boylagh (Donegal), Baoigheallach, 'territory of the descendants of Boyle'.
Boyle (Roscommon), Mainistir na Búille, 'monastery of the (river) Boyle'.
The 12th-century Cistercian monastery, on the north side of the town, is now in ruins.
Boyne (Kildare/Offaly/Meath), An Bhóinn, '(river of) the white cow'.
The river name traditionally comes from

Boand, a goddess who inhabited it, with her own name based on bo bhán, 'white cow'.
Boyounagh (Galway), Buíbheanach, 'yellow marsh'.
The marsh would be 'yellow' either from the colour of its grass or from its flowers.
Bracklagh (Galway), Breaclach, 'speckled place'.
Bracklyn (Westmeath), Breaclainn, 'speckled meadow'.
Braid (Antrim), Brághaid, 'gorge'.
The name refers to the deep glen through which the river flows.
Brandon Mountain (Kerry), Cnoc Bréanain, 'St Brendan's hill'.
St Brendan had his retreat here in the 6th century, and remains of his cell, oratory and well can still be seen on the summit of the hill.
Bray (Wicklow), Bré, 'hill'.
The hill of the name is nearby Bray Head, which rises to nearly 800 ft (240m).
Bready (Tyrone), An Bhréadaigh, 'the broken land'.
Breenagh (Donegal), Na Bruíneacha, 'evil-smelling stream'.
Brickens (Mayo), Na Broicíní, 'the badger warrens'.
Bride Bridge (Waterford), Droichead na Bríde, 'bridge of the (river) Bride'.
Brideswell (Roscommon), Tobar Bríde, 'St Brigid's well'.
The well here was formerly famous for its cures.
Bridgend (Donegal), Ceann an Droichid, 'end of the bridge'.
Bridgetown (several), Baile an Droichid, 'town of the bridge'.
Brigown (Cork), Brí Gobhan, 'hill of the smith'.
Brittas (Dublin, Limerick), An Briotás, 'the brattice'.
A brattice was either a wooden tower used in medieval siege operations, or a covered gallery on a castle wall. The first of these is the likely sense here.
Broadford (several), Áth Leathan, 'broad ford'.
Brookeborough (Fermanagh), Achadh Lon, 'field of blackbirds'.

29

The English name derives from that of the Brooke family whose seat was here at Colebrooke. Descendants of the original family included Alan Francis Brooke, the 1st Viscount Alanbrooke, and Sir Basil Brooke, the 1st Viscount Brookeborough, former prime minister of Northern Ireland.

Broomfield (Monaghan), Achadh an Bhrúim, 'field of the broom'.

Broughshane (Antrim), Bruach Sheáin, 'John's house'.

The Irish word that gives the first half of the name is probably brugh, 'house', 'palace', 'fort', not bruach, 'brink', 'bank', 'border'.

Brownstown (Meath), Baile an Bhrúnaigh, 'Brown's town'.

Bruff (Limerick), An Brú, 'the fort'.

Bruree (Limerick), Brú Rí, 'king's fort'.

This was the chief seat of Oillill Ólum, the 2nd-century king of Munster, and later, in the 7th century, of the petty kings of the Dal gCais.

Bullaun (Galway), Bollán, 'well in a rock'.

Bunacurry (Mayo), Bun an Churraigh, 'end of the marsh'.

Bunalty (Mayo), Bun Aillte, 'bottom of the cliff'.

Bunbeg (Donegal), An Bun Beag, 'the small river-mouth'.

Bunclody (Wexford), Bun Clóidí, 'mouth of the (river) Clody'.

The former name of Bunclody was Newtownbarry, after James Barry, sovereign of Naas.

Buncrana (Donegal), Bun Cranncha, 'mouth of the (river) Crana'.

Bunduff (Leitrim), Bun Duibhe, 'mouth of the (river) Duff'.

Bunlahy (Longford), Bun Lathaighe, 'end of the marsh'.

Bunmahon (Waterford), Bun Machan, 'mouth of the (river) Mahon'.

Bunnahowen (Mayo), Bun na hAbhna, 'mouth of the river'.

Bunratty (Clare), Bun Raite, 'mouth of the (river) Ratty'.

The river is also called the Owenogarney, after the O Carneys' territory here.

Burncourt (Tipperary), An Chúirt Dóite, 'the burnt court'.

The former name of the house here was Clogheen ('small stones'), built by Sir Richard Everard of Ballyboy in 1641. Nine years later it was burnt down by Cromwell, as the present name of the location shows.

Burnfoot (Donegal), Bun na hAbhann, 'mouth of the river'.

The English name renders the Irish, i.e. 'foot of the burn'. Burnfoot is on Lough Swilly.

Burren, The (Clare, Down), Boirinn, 'stony place'.

Burrishoole (Mayo), Buiríos Umhaill, 'borough of Umhall'.

Burtonport (Donegal), Ailt an Chorráin, 'ravine of the curve'.

The English name comes from William Burton, 4th Marquis Conyngham, who established a port here in the late 18th century in order to compete with the port opened on nearby Rutland Island by the Duke of Rutland.

Bushfield (Tipperary), Cnoc na Sceach, 'hill of the whitethorn bushes'.

Bushmills (Antrim), Muileann na Buaise, 'mill of the (river) Bush'.

Buttevant (Cork), Cill na Mallach, 'church of the summits'.

The English name is popularly supposed to derive from the French warcry of the de Barrys, Boutez an avant, but is much more likely to represent Norman French botavant, a term for a defensive outwork.

Byrnes Grove (Kilkenny), Choill Uí Bhriain, 'grove of the descendants of Byrne'.

C

Cabra (Down, Dublin), An Chabrach, 'the poor land'.

Cadamstown (Kildare, Offaly), Baile Mhic Ádaim, 'townland of the son of Adam'.

Caha Mountains (Cork/Kerry), Cnoic na Ceachan, 'hills of showers'.

Caher (several), An Chathair, 'the stone fort'.

Caherbarnagh (several), An Chathair Bhearnach, 'the gapped fort'.
The name refers to a dilapidated fort, with gaps where clay or stones have been removed.

Caherconlish (Limerick), Cathair Chinn Lis, 'fort at the head of the ring-fort'.
The name implies a stone fort (*cathair*) built near an earthern one (*lios*).

Caherconree (Kerry), Cathair Conraoi, 'Cúraoi's fort'.
This is a mountain 2,713 ft (814m) high, with the fort on a promontory at 2,050 ft (615m).

Caherdaniel (Kerry), Cathair Dónall, 'Dónall's fort'.
The fort of the name is by the road about half a mile west of the village.

Caherlistrane (Galway), Cathair Loistreáin, 'fort of the place where corn is burnt off the ear'.
The second part of the name is Irish *loiscreán*, referring to corn that has not been threshed in the normal way but burnt off the ear.

Cahermore (Cork), Cathair Mhór, 'great fort'.

Cahir (several), An Chathair, 'the stone fort'.
This is an alternative spelling to Caher. Cahir in Tipperary was known in full as *Cathair-duna-iascaigh*, 'fort of the fortification abounding in fish'. The name relates to a rocky island in the river Suir. There is now a 15th-century castle on the site of the original fort.

Cahirciveen (Kerry), Cathair Saidhbhín, 'little Sadhbh's fort'.
Sadhbh is a woman's name, sometimes anglicised as Sabina.

Caledon (Tyrone), Cionn Aird, 'high head'.

The former English name, corresponding to the Irish, was Kenard. The present name derives from the Earls of Caledon, whose seat was here.

Callow (Mayo), An Caladh, 'the riverside meadow'.
Irish *caladh* has the basic meaning 'shore', 'port', usually implying a place where boats can land. Callow is by the lough of the same name.

Caltra (Galway), An Chealtrach, 'the burial ground'.

Camaross (Wexford), Camros, 'crooked wood'.

Camlough (Armagh), Camloch, 'crooked lake'.

Camolin (Wexford), Cam Eolaing, 'Eolang's bend'.

Camp (Kerry), An Com, 'the hollow'.
Camp is at the seaward end of Glen Fas.

Campile (Wexford), Ceann Poill, 'head of (the) creek'.

Cappagh (several), An Cheapach, 'the plot of land'.
The name implies land that is suitable for agricultural use.

Capparoe (Tipperary), An Cheapach Rua, 'the red-coloured plot of land'.

Cappawhite (Tipperary), An Cheapach, 'the plot of land'.
The second half of the name is the family surname White.

Cappoquin (Waterford), Ceapach Choinn, 'Conn's plot of land'.
It is not known who Conn was.

Carbury (Kildare), Cairbre.
The name traditionally refers to Carbery (Cairbre) son of Niall of the Nine Hostages and founder of a royal dynasty in early Irish history.

Cargan (Antrim), Cairgín, 'little rock'.

Carland (Tyrone), Domhnach Carr, 'church on rocky land'.

Carlanstown (Meath), Droichead Chearbhalláin, 'Carlan's bridge'.

Carlingford (Louth), Cairlinn, 'bay of the hags'.
The '-ford' ending of the English name

represents Old Norse *fjórthr*, 'sea-inlet', and the name as a whole derives from that of Carlingford Lough. An earlier Irish name of the lough was *Snámh Aighnech* or *Snámh Each*, 'swimming-ford of the horses'. The settlement of Carlingford itself later became a Viking trading centre. Old Norse *kerling*, meaning 'hag', may here have referred to the three mountain peaks that are locally known as The Three Nuns and that serve as orientation points for ships entering the lough.

Carlow (Carlow), Ceatharlach, 'four lakes'.

There is no trace of the original four lakes here now. They may have been where the rivers Burren and Barrow now meet.

Carnaross (Meath), Carn na Ros, 'cairn of the woods'.

Carndonagh (Donegal), Carn Domhnach, 'cairn of the church'.

The original church here stood where the Protestant church now is.

Carnew (Wicklow), Carn an Bhua, 'cairn of victory'.

There is no cairn here now, although there is one a mile away called Umrygar Moat. Presumably the original has been destroyed.

Carnfree (Roscommon), Carn Fraoich, 'Fraoch's cairn'.

This prominent hill was the traditional place of inauguration of the kings of Connacht, whose palace was at Cruachan. The cairn is still here, some 8 ft (2.4m) high and 15 ft (4.5m) across.

Carnlough (Antrim), Carnlach, 'cairn lake'.

Carnsore Point (Wexford), Ceann an Chairn, 'headland of the cairn'.

The '-ore' ending is Scandinavian, meaning 'sandy point'.

Carnteel (Tyrone), Carn tSiail, 'Shaohal's cairn'.

Carn Tierna (Fermanagh), Carn Tighearnaigh, 'Tierna's cairn'.

Tierna (Tigernach) was the 1st-century king of Ulster who according to tradition is buried beneath the cairn at the top of the hill here.

Carracastle (Mayo), Ceathrú an Chaisil, 'quarter of the stone fort'.

Carraivort (Donegal), Garbhghort, 'rough field'.

Carra Lough, (Mayo), Loch Ceara, 'weir lake'.

Carran (Clare), An Cairn, 'the cairn'.

Carrantuohill, (Kerry), Corrán Tuathail, 'reversed reaping hook'.

This is the highest mountain in Ireland, in Mac Gillicuddy's Reeks. Its name describes the appearance of its curving edge from the Killarney side. Irish *tuathail* means 'turn to the left', 'wrong side', indicating something that is reversed from its normal direction. The curve here is not concave, as on a reaping hook, but convex.

Carraroe (Galway), An Cheathrú Rua, 'the red-coloured quarter'.

Carrick (several), An Charraig, 'the rock'.

Carrickbeg (several), An Charraig Bheag, 'the little rock'.

Carrickblacker (Armagh), Carraig Bhlaicear, 'rock of the Blacker family'.

Carrickboy (Longford), An Charraig Bhuí, 'the yellow rock'.

Carrickcarnan (Louth), Carraig Charnáin, 'rock of the little cairn'.

Carrick Castle (Kildare), Caisleán na Carraige, 'castle of the rock'.

Carrickfergus (Antrim), Carraig Fhearghais, 'Fergus's rock'.

Fergus (Fhearghus) was a kinglet of the Dál Ríada who brought Irish settlements in Scotland under his rule. The place-name really applies to the rock here on which the castle stands.

Carrickmacross (Monahan), Carraig Mhachaire Rois, 'rock of the plain of Ross'.

Carrickmore (Tyrone), An Charraig Mhór, 'the big rock'.

The rock referred to is the natural rock hollow just south-west of the village, where St Columba's well is. The name also occurs elsewhere.

Carrick-on-Shannon (Leitrim), Cora Droma Rúisc, 'weir of the ridge of the bark'.

This is not the usual 'Carrick-' name, but a corruption of *cora*, 'weir', 'dam'. There was formerly a weir across the Shannon here. Irish *rúisc* means 'tree-bark' and here perhaps even implies a vessel of bark, although not, presumably, a boat. A former English version of the present Irish name was 'Carrickdrumrusk'.

Carrick-on-Suir (Tipperary), Carraig na Siúire, 'rock of the (river) Suir'.
The name indicates a large rock in the river-bed here.

Carrig (several), An Charraig, 'the rock'.

Carrigadrohid (Cork), Carraig an Droichid, 'rock of the bridge'.
The castle of this name is east of Macroom, near a bridge over the river Lee, where its ruins can still be seen on a rock here. The castle was destroyed by Cromwell's troops in the mid-17th century.

Carrigafoyle (Kerry), Carraig an Phoill, 'rock of the hole'.
This island in the Shannon is named after a deep hole in the river under the castle.

Carrigaholt (Clare), Carraig an Chabhaltaigh, 'rock of the fleet'.
The name refers to a rock over the bay here where traditionally fleets anchored. The village stands at the mouth of the Shannon.

Carrigahorig (Tipperary), Carraig an Chomhraic, 'rock of the conflict'.
The name must refer to some battle here.

Carrigaline (Cork), Carrig Uí Leighin, 'rock of the descendants of Laighin'.

Carrigallen (Leitrim), Carraig Álainn, 'beautiful rock'.
The name is believed to refer to the rock on which the original church was built.

Carrigans (Donegal), An Carraigín, 'the little rock'.

Carrigaphooca (Cork), Carraig an Phúca, 'rock of the hobgoblin'.
This ruined castle, west of Macroom, stands on a rock over the river Sullane at a point said to be haunted by a 'pooka' or malicious sprite.

Carrigart (Donegal), Carraig Airt, 'craggy rock'.

Carrigatoher (Tipperary), Carraig an Tóchair, 'rock of the causeway'.

Carrigeen (several), Carraigín, 'little rock'.

Carrigkerry (Limerick), Carraig Chiarraí, 'rock of the sheep'.

Carrignavar, (Cork), Carraig na bhFear, 'rock of the men'.
This name suggests a tribal reference.

Carrigogunnell (Limerick), Carraig Ó

gConaill, 'rock of the son of Connell'.
For some time the name was popularly translated as 'candle rock' (as if *Carraig na gCoinneall*), with a consequent legend about a witch lighting a candle nightly here only to be banished eventually by St Patrick.

Carrow (Sligo), An Cheathrú, 'the quarter'.
A 'quarter' was a standard land division of a townland.

Carrowbeg (Mayo), An Cheathrú Bheag, 'the little quarter'.

Carrowdore (Down), Ceathrú Dobhair, 'quarter of (the) water'.

Carrowgowan (Mayo), Ceathrú an Ghabhann, 'quarter of the smith'.

Carrowkeel (several), An Cheathrú Chaol, 'the narrow quarter'.

Carrowmena (Donegal), Ceathrú Meánach, 'the middle quarter'.

Carrowmore (several), An Cheathrú Mhór, 'the great quarter'.
Carrowmore in Sligo is the name of the largest megalithic cemetery in the whole country. The full name of Carrowmore in Mayo is *Ceathrú Mhór Leacan*, 'the great quarter of (the) hillside'.

Carrowreagh (several), Ceathrú Riabhach, 'grey quarter'.

Carryduff (Belfast), Ceathrú Aodha Dhuibh, 'Black Hugh's quarter'.
In a document dated 1623 this name was recorded as *Carowhuduffe alias Carrow-Iduffe alias Carouty-Duffe*.

Carton (Kildare), An Cartún, 'the quarter'.
This word is Anglo-Norman in origin, not Irish.

Cashel (Tipperary), Caiseal, 'circular stone fort'.
This is the famous Rock of Cashel, the main stronghold of the kings of Munster for nine hundred years. The name is also found elsewhere, notably in Galway, where it properly applies to the ring-fort type of burial ground on the hill above the hotel here.

Cashelgarran (Sligo), Caiseal an Gharráin, 'stone fort of the grove'.

Cashelmore (Donegal), An Caiseal Mór, 'the big stone fort'.

Cashen Bridge (Kerry), Droichead an

Chaisín, 'bridge of the (river) Cashen'.

Cashla Bridge (Galway), Droichead Chasla, 'bridge of the sea-inlet'.

Castle Archdale (Fermanagh).

The castle, now in ruins, stands on the east shore of Lower Lough Erne, where it was built by John Archdale of Suffolk in the early 17th century. The original castle was destroyed in 1641, was rebuilt, and was again destroyed in 1689.

Castlebane (several), Caisleán Bán, 'white castle'.

Castlebar (Mayo), Caisleán an Bharraigh, 'Barry's castle'.

The castle belonged to the Barrys after the English invasion, while the town itself was founded at the beginning of the 17th century by John Bingham, ancestor of the earls of Lucan.

Castlebellingham (Louth), Baile an Ghearlánaigh, 'Gernon's homestead'.

The original English name here was 'Garlandstown', from the Anglo-Norman Gernon family of the Irish name. The Gernons were here until the early 17th century, when their estates were confiscated and granted to Henry Bellingham. The castle is now a hotel.

Castleblayney (Monaghan), Baile na Lorgan, 'town of the strip of land'.

Land here was granted by James I to Sir Edward Blayney, governor of Monaghan, on the condition that he built a fort between Monaghan and Newry.

Castlebridge (Wexford), Droichead an Chaisleáin, 'bridge of the castle'.

The bridge is over the river, now called the Castlebridge after the settlement here.

Castlecaldwell (Fermanagh).

The original name of the castle built here in the early 17th century was Castle Hasset, after its owner Francis Blennerhasset. It was sold in 1662 to James Caldwell, who renamed it, and whose family lived here for over two hundred years. The castle is now in ruins.

Castlecaulfield (Tyrone), Baile Uí Dhonnáile, 'town of the descendants of Donnáile'.

The English name is that of Sir Toby Caulfield (or Caulfeild), whose residence here

was built in the early 17th century. The house was burnt down in 1641 and remains in ruins.

Castlecomer (Kilkenny), Caisleán an Chomair, 'castle of the confluence'.

The castle was built here at the time of the Anglo-Norman invasion, and the confluence is that of the river Dinin and a tributary.

Castleconnell (Limerick), Caisleán Uí Chonaill, 'castle of the descendants of Conaing'.

The family name here involved is not that of the O Connells but the 'O Connings', today known as the Gunnings (Irish Ó Conaing). They were the lords of the territory here, and this was their principal castle.

Castlecoole (Fermanagh), Caisleán na Cúile, 'secluded castle'.

The literal meaning of the name is 'castle of the recess' (Irish *cúil*). The mansion here was built in 1748.

Castlecor (Cork), Caisleán na Cora, 'castle of the weir'.

The castle is now in ruins. The name is also found elsewhere, as in Meath.

Castledaly (Galway), Caisleán Uí Dhálaigh, 'castle of the descendants of Daly'.

Castledawson (Derry), An Seanmhullach, 'the old hilltop'.

The name is that of the Dawson family, who held lands here from 1633. The proprietor in the early 18th century was Thomas Dawson, chief secretary for Ireland.

Castlederg (Tyrone), Caisleán na Deirge, 'castle on the (river) Derg'.

The castle was demolished in the Civil War.

Castledermot (Kildare), Díseart Diarmada, 'Dermot's hermitage'.

Dermot (Diarmait) was a grandson of a king of Ulster who founded a monastery here in the 9th century. The 'castle' was the Anglo-Norman one built here in the 12th century. The old English name, representing the present Irish one, was 'Disertdermot'. The round tower of the monastic site still exists.

Castlefinn (Donegal), Caisleán na Finne, 'castle of the (river) Finn'.

Castlegal (Sligo), Caisle Ceala, 'fair fort'.

Castlegregory (Kerry), Caisleán Ghriaire, 'Gregory's castle'.
The 16th-century castle here was built by Gregory Hoare.

Castle Haven (Cork), Gleann Bearcháin, 'Bearchán' valley.
An earlier name was Ballincushlan, from Irish *Baile an Chaisleáin*, 'townland of the castle'.

Castlehill (Mayo), Caorthannán, '(place of) rowan trees'.
There is no castle here, and the English name appears to be a corruption of the Irish.

Castleisland (Kerry), Oileán Ciarraí, 'island of Kerry'.
The castle is a 13th-century one, now ruined.

Castle Island (Mayo), Oileán an Chaisleáin, 'island of the castle'.
The island is in Carra Lough, and has the ruins of an ancient castle.

Castle Kirke (Galway), Caisleán na Circe, 'castle of the hen'.
The castle was built here, on an island in Lough Corrib, by the sons of Rory O Conor, the last king of Ulster, in the 13th century. The site is also known as Hen's Castle, and this name involves a legend about a witch and her hen who built the castle here in a single night.

Castleknock (Dublin), Caisleán Cnucha, 'castle of the hill'.
The remains of the castle can be seen in the grounds of Castleknock College, the boys' school here.

Castlelyons (Cork), Caisleán Ó Liatháin, 'castle of O Lehane'.
The O Lehanes (Irish Ó Liatháin), whose name is here anglicised as Lyons, were said to be descended from Eochy Liathanach, fifth in descent from Oilill Ólum.

Castlemaine (Kerry), Caisleán na Mainge, 'castle of the (river) Maine'.
The former castle here, destroyed by Cromwell's troops, guarded the crossing over the river Maine.

Castlemartyr (Cork), Baile na Martra, 'town of the relics (of the martyrs)'.
The original English name was Bally-

martyr, based on the present Irish name. The castle in now in ruins.

Castlemore (several), An Caisleán Mór, 'the big castle'.

Castlemoyle (several), An Caisleán Maol, 'the dilapidated castle'.
A castle of this name would have been one where stones or materials had been removed for building elsewhere.

Castlepollard (Westmeath), Baile na gCros, 'town of the crosses'.
The present name dates from 1674, when a licence was granted to Walter Pollard to hold a weekly market and two annual fairs here 'at the town of Ballinegrosse alias Rathgrange alias Castle-Pollard'. The first of these three names is an English rendering of the Irish.

Castlerahan (Cavan), Caisleán Rathain, 'castle of the little ring-fort'.

Castlereagh (several), An Caisleán Riabhach, 'the grey castle'.
In many cases the original castle is now in ruins, and in Roscommon there is no trace of the former castle at all.

Castlerock (Derry), Carraig Ceasail, 'castle rock'.
The rocks are two natural ones by the shore here which resemble a castle.

Castleroe (Derry), An Caisleán Rua, 'the red-coloured castle'.

Castleshane (Monaghan), Caisleán an tSiáin, 'castle of the fairy fort'.

Castletown (several), Baile an Chaisleáin, 'town of the castle'.

Castletownbere (Cork), Baile Chaisleáin Bhéarra, 'town of (the) castle of Bear'.
Castletownbere is sheltered by Bear Island.

Castletown Geoghegan (Westmeath), Baile Chaisleán na nGeochagán, 'town of (the) castle of Mac Eochagáin'.
The name refers to a castle here built by the Mac Eochagáins (now usually known as the Geoghegans), who held lands here until the time of Cromwell. The large Anglo-Norman 'motte-and-bailey' here is not the castle referred to.

Castletown House (Kildare), Baile an Chaisleáin, 'townland of the castle'.
This is the largest private house in Ireland, built in the early 18th century.

35

Castletownroche (Cork), Baile Chaisleáin an Róistigh, 'town of Roche's castle'.
The castle here was the stronghold of the Roche family.

Castletownshend (Cork), Baile an Chaisleáin, 'townland of the castle'.
The English name comes from a fort built here in the mid-17th century by the English settler Colonel Richard Townsend. The fort is now in ruins.

Castleventry (Cork), Caisleán na Gaoithe, 'castle of the winds'.
The English rendering of the Irish name appears to be subconsciously linked with the 'vent' of Latin *ventus*, French *vent*, English *ventilate*, and so on.

Castlewellan (Down), Caisleán Uidhilín, 'Uidhilín's castle'.

Causeway (Kerry), An Tóchar, 'the causeway'.

Cavan (Cavan), An Cabhán, 'the hollow'.
The town lies in a hollow, above which rises a round, grassy hill. Irish *cabhán* can mean either of these features. The county took its name from the town.

Cavanacaw (several), Cabhán na gCorr, 'round hill of the chaff'.
The name refers to the custom of winnowing on the top of a hill.

Ceanannus Mór *see* **Kells**.

Cecilstown (Cork).
The name relates to a Lord Cecil whose residence was here.

Celbridge (Kildare), Cill Droichid, 'church of (the) bridge'.
The English name is a half-rendering, half-translation of the Irish. Celbridge is on the river Liffey.

Chanonrock (Louth), Carraig na gCanónach, 'rock of the canons'.
There are underground passages here believed to date from the early Christian period.

Chapelizod (Dublin), Séipéal Iosóid, 'Yseult's chapel'.
The name is traditionally said to derive from that of Yseult, daughter of an Irish king and tragic heroine of the tale 'Tristram and Yseult'. In the Arthurian legend, however, Yseult (or Iseult) is the daughter of a king of Brittany.

Chapeltown (several), Baile an tSéipéil, 'town of the chapel'.

Charlemont (Armagh), Achadh an Dá Chora, 'field of the two weirs'.
The English name comes from the fort built here in the early 17th century by Sir Toby Caulfield (*see* **Castlecaulfield**). It was named after his commander, Charles Blount, 8th Lord Mountjoy, and derives from the first parts of these names. The Irish name refers to the location of Charlemont by the river Blackwater.

Charlestown (several).
The Irish names vary from one place to another, sometimes corresponding to the English (as in Mayo, *Baile Chathail*), but mostly not, so that in Galway the Irish name is *Poll na Muice*, 'pool of the pig', and in Westmeath *Baile na Móna*, 'town of the bog'. The Mayo Charlestown was named after Charles Dillon, who founded it in the 19th century.

Charleville *see* **Ráth Luirc**.

Cheekpoint (Waterford), Pointe na Síge, 'point of the fairies'.
The name is that of a hill near Faithlegg.

Church Island (Antrim, Kerry), Oileán an Teampaill, 'island of the church'.
The Antrim island is on Lough Beg near Toome Bridge, and had an early monastic settlement. (The present ruins are of a later establishment.) There are two islands of the name in Kerry, one on Lough Currane, near Waterville, where the ruins are of the original 6th-century oratory, and the other in the estuary of the Valencia River, where there are also monastic remains.

Churchtown (several), Baile an Teampaill, 'town of the church'.
In Tyrone, the Irish name of Churchtown is *Tulaigh an Iúir*, 'hill of the yew'.

Clabby (Fermanagh), Clabaigh, 'open place'.

Claddagh, The (Galway), An Cladach, 'the sea shore'.
The Claddagh is a district of Galway, on Galway Bay, and is believed to represent the fishing village from which the modern town arose.

Claddaghduff (Galway), An Cladach Dubh, 'the black sea shore'.

Claggan (Donegal), An Cloigeann, 'the skull'.
The name represents a round hill, in this case one here in the land that extends eastward to Inishowenen Head.

Clanabogan (Tyrone), Cluain Uí Bhogáin, 'meadow of the descendants of Bogáin'.

Clandeboye (Down), Clann Aodha Buí, 'descendants of Yellow Hugh (O Neill)'.
Clandeboye House is the 17th-century seat of the marquis of Dufferin and Ava.

Clane (Kildare), Claonadh, 'sloping ford'.
Clane is by the river Liffey.

Clankee (Cavan), Clann an Chaoich, 'descendants of the one-eyed man'.
The reference is to Niall O Reilly, killed in 1256, whose nickname was *caoch* (pronounced approximately 'kee'), 'one-eyed'.

Clanmaurice (Kerry), Clann Muiris, 'descendants of Maurice (Fitzgerald)'.

Clanwilliam (Limerick, Tipperary), Clann Uilliam, 'descendants of William (Burke)'.

Clara (Offaly), Clóirtheach, 'level place'.

Clara Castle (Kilkenny), Caisleán an Chláraigh, 'castle of the level place'.

Clare (Clare), An Clar, 'the level place'.
Other places of the name have the same sense. The literal meaning of Irish *clár* is 'board', 'plank'. Clare, which gave its name to the county, is now Clarecastle (see below).

Clarecastle (Clare), Droichead an Chláir, 'bridge of Clare'.
The location here was originally just 'Clare', at a crossing over the estuary of the river Fergus. (See **Clare**, above.)

Clareen (Offaly), An Cláirín, 'the little plain'.

Claregalway (Galway), Baile Chláir, 'town of (the) plain'.
'Galway' distinguishes this Clare from other places of the name.

Claremorris (Mayo), Clár Chlainne Mhuiris, 'plain of the descendants of Muiris'.

Claretuam (Galway), Clár Thuama, 'plain of Tuam'.
Claretuam is five miles south-west of Tuam.

Clarina (Limerick), Clár Aidhne, 'Aidhne's plain'.

Clarinbridge (Galway), Droichead an Chláirín, 'bridge of the little plain'.
The name could also literally mean 'bridge of the little plank'.

Clashaganny (Roscommon), Clais an Ghainimh, 'hollow of the sand'

Clashmore (Waterford), Clais Mhór, 'big trench'.

Cleenish (Fermanagh), Claon Inis, 'sloping island'.

Clegg (Galway), Claig, 'hollow'.

Cleggan (Galway), An Cloigeann, 'the skull'.
The name indicates a round hill. Compare **Claggan**.

Clementstown (Cavan).
The name is that of the proprietor here, a Colonel Clements.

Clenor (Cork), Claonabhar, 'dark grey meadow'.

Clerihan (Tipperary), Baile Uí Chléireacháin, 'town of the descendants of Clerihan'.
The family name Clerihan (Cléireacháin) means 'clerk' (*cléireach*).

Clifden (Galway), An Clochán, 'the stepping stones'.
The English name appears to be a distortion of the Irish. The basic sense of Irish *cloch* is 'stone', and the name could refer to stone dwellings as well as stepping stones. If the latter, the reference would have been to a way across the river Owenglin. *See also* **Cloghan**.

Cliffoney (Sligo), Cliafuine, 'grove of the hurdles'.

Cliffs of Moher (Clare), Aillte an Mhothair, 'cliffs of the ruin'.
The ruin would be that of a fort of some kind.

Clogh (several), An Chloch, 'the stone (fort)'.

Cloghan (several), An Clochán, 'the stepping stones'.
The name indicates a way across a river or marsh. It could also mean simply 'stone dwelling'. Compare **Cloghane**.

Cloghane (Kerry), An Clochán, 'the stone house'.

Cloghboley (Sligo), Clochbhuaile, 'stony summer pasture'.

Cloghbrack (several), An Chloch Bhreac, 'the speckled stone'.

Clogheen (Tipperary), An Chloichín, 'the little stone (fort)'.

Clogher (several), An Clochár, 'the stony place'.

Clogherhead (Louth), Ceann Chlochair, 'stony headland'.

The half-translated name denotes the headland near this resort.

Cloghermore (Mayo), An Clochar Mór, 'the big stony place'.

Cloghfin (several), Cloch Fhionn, 'white stone (fort)'.

Cloghmore (Down), An Chloich Mhóir, 'the big stone (castle)'.

Cloghoge (several), Cloghóg, 'land full of stones'.

Cloghoula (Cork), Clochbhuaile, 'stony summer pasture'.

Cloghran (Dublin), Clochrán, 'stony place'.

Clogrenan (Carlow), Cloch Grianáin, 'stone (castle) of (the) summer residence'.

Clomantagh (Kilkenny), Cloch Mhantach, 'stone (castle) of Mantagh'.

The name is a nickname, meaning 'toothless' (*manntach*), although here not applied to a person but apparently to a stone circle on a hill here.

Clonakilty (Cork), Cloich na Coillte, 'stone (fort) of the woods'.

Clonalig (Armagh), Cluain an Liag, 'meadow of the standing stone'.

Clonallan (Down), Cluain Áluinn, 'Dallán's meadow'.

The name is said to refer to the 6th-century poet Dallán Forgaill, who composed a lament for Columba.

Clonalvy (Meath), Cluain Ailbhe, 'Ailbhe's meadow'.

Ailbhe is both a woman's and a man's name.

Clonard (several), Cluain Ard, 'high meadow'.

Clonard in Meath, however, derives from *Cluain Ioraird*, 'Iorard's meadow'. Iorard may have been a pagan chief who built the moat that can still be seen here.

Clonaslee (Laois), Cluain na Slí, 'meadow of the road'.

Clonbeg (several), Cluain Bheag, 'little meadow'.

Clonbrock (Galway), Cluain Broc, 'meadow of (the) badgers'.

Clonbullogue (Offaly), Cluain Bolg, 'meadow of bags'.

Presumably bags or sacks were kept or loaded here.

Cloncrew (Limerick), Cluain Creamha, 'meadow of wild garlic'.

Cloncurry (Kildare), Cluain Chonaire, 'Conaire's meadow'.

It is not certain who Conaire was.

Clondalkin (Dublin), Cluain Dolcáin, 'Dolcán's meadow'.

Clonduff (Down), Cluain Dubh, 'black meadow'.

This name has also been interpreted as 'meadow of the ox', from *Cluain Daimh*.

Clone (Wexford), Cluain, 'meadow'.

Clonea (Waterford), Cluain Fhia, 'meadow of deer'.

Clonee (Meath), Cluain Aodha, 'Hugh's meadow'.

Cloneen (Tipperary), An Cluainín, 'the little meadow'.

Clonegall (Carlow), Cluain na nGall, 'meadow of the foreigners'.

That is, a meadow owned by the English.

Clonenagh (Laois), Cluain Eighneach, 'meadow of ivy'.

Clones (Monaghan), Cluain Eois, 'meadow of Eos'.

The name is pronounced in two syllables.

Clonfad (Westmeath), Cluain Fhada Fine, 'long meadow of the family'.

Irish *fine* means 'family', 'tribe', 'community', depending on the size of the group and its nature, and the word was also used of land belonging to this group.

Clonfert (Galway), Cluain Fearta, 'meadow of the grave'.

An ancient ecclesiastical settlement was here, with a monastery founded in the 6th century by St Brendan. The name doubtless refers to the cemetery here.

Clonfinloch (Offaly), Cluain Fionnlocha, 'meadow of the white lake'.

Clongowes (Kildare), Cluain Gabhann, 'meadow of the smith'.

The original Irish is uncertain, and it could also be *Cluain Gamhnach*, 'meadow of the milking cow'. Today the name is that of Clongowes Wood College, in Irish *Coláiste*

Choill Chluana Gabhainn.
Clonhugh (Westmeath), Clann Aodha, '(place of the) descendants of Hugh'.
This is a 'Clon-' name that does not originate from *cluain*, 'meadow'.
Clonkeen (several), Cluain Chaoin, 'pleasant meadow'.
Clonmacnoise (Offaly), Cluain Mhic Nóis, 'meadow of the sons of Noas'.
Noas is said to have been a son of Fiadhach, a chief of the tribe of Dealbhna (Delvin), with his territory located here, It is one of Ireland's most famous early monastic settlements, second only to Armagh.
Clonmahon (Meath), Clann Mathún, '(place of the) descendants of Mahon'.
As with Clonhugh, there is no 'meadow' (*cluain*) involved.
Clonmeen (Cork), Cluain Mhín, 'smooth meadow'.
Clonmel (several), Cluain Meala, 'meadow of honey'.
In some cases the name may have indicated honey from the nests of wild bees, not beehives.
Clonmines (Wexford), Cluain Mathna, 'smooth meadow'.
Clonmona (Tipperary), Cluain Móna, 'meadow of peat'.
Clonmore (several), Cluain Mhór, 'great meadow'.
Clonmult (Cavan, Cork), Cluain Molt, 'meadow of (the) wethers'.
Clonoe (Tyrone), Cluain Eo, 'meadow of (the) yew'.
Clonony (Offaly), Cluain Damhna, 'meadow of (the) families'.
The name may in fact derive from a personal name, so mean 'meadow of Damhna'.
Clonoulty (Tipperary), Cluain an Oltaigh, 'meadow of the Ulsterman'.
Clonsilla (Dublin), Cluain Saileach, 'meadow of willows'.
Clonskeagh (Dublin), Cluain Sciach, 'meadow of whitethorns'.
Clontarf (Dublin), Cluain Tarbh, 'meadow of bulls'.
Clontibret (Monaghan), Cluain Tiobrad, 'meadow of (the) well'.
Clonturk (Dublin), Cluain Torc, 'meadow of (the) boar'.

Clontuskert (Galway), Cluain Tuaiscirt, 'northern meadow'.
Clonwhelan (Longford), Cluain Fhaoláin, 'Faolán's meadow'.
Clonygowan (Offaly), Cluain Uí Ghabhann, 'meadow of the descendants of the smith'.
The name has also been interpreted as 'meadow of the calves', from *Cluain na nGamhan*.
Cloonaddra (Roscommon), Cluain Idir Dhá Áth, 'meadow between two fords'.
Cloonagh (several), Cluain Each, 'meadow of horses'.
Cloonboo (Galway), Cluain Bua, 'meadow of victory'.
This name must refer to a battle here.
Cloondara (Longford), Cluain Dá Ráth, 'meadow of (the) two ring-forts'.
Cloone (Leitrim), An Chluain, 'the meadow'.
Cloonee (Kerry), Cluainí, 'meadows'.
Cloonee in Mayo, however, is from *Cluain Aodha*, 'Hugh's meadow'.
Clooney (Donegal), An Chluanaidh, 'the meadow'.
Cloonfad (Roscommon), Cluain Fada, 'long meadow'.
Cloonfinlough (Roscommon), Cluain Finnlocha, 'meadow of (the) clear lake'.
Cloongullaun (Mayo), Cluain Gallán, 'meadow of standing stones'.
Cloonkeen (Mayo), Cluain Chaoin, 'beautiful meadow'.
Cloonlara (Clare), Cluain Lára, 'meadow of (the) mare'.
Cloonmore (several), Cluain Mhór, 'great meadow'.
Cloonshannagh (Roscommon), Cluain Seancha, 'meadow of (the) fox'.
Cloontuskert (Roscommon), Cluain Tuaiscirt, 'northern meadow'.
Cloonty (several), Cluainte, 'meadows'.
Cloonyquin (Roscommon), Cluain Uí Choinn, 'meadow of the descendants of Quinn'.
Clough (several), An Chloch, 'the stone (castle)'.
Cloughey (Down), Clochaigh, 'stony place'.
Cloughjordan (Tipperary), Cloch Shiurdáin, 'Jordan's stone (castle)'.
Cloughmills (Antrim), Muileann na Cloiche,

'mill of the stone (castle)'.

Cloughoughter (Cavan), Cloch Uachtair, 'upper stone (castle)'.

Clounanna (Limerick), Cluain Eanaigh, 'meadow of (the) marsh'.

Cloverhill (several).

In Sligo, the corresponding Irish name of Cloverhill is *Cnoc na Seamar*, 'hill of the shamrocks'. In Leitrim and Roscommon the Irish name is *Cor Glas*, 'green hill', and in Cavan, Cloverhill is *Droim Caiside*, 'Cassidy's ridge'.

Cloyne (Cork), Cluain, 'pasture'.

An earlier version of the name was *Cluain Uamha*, 'meadow of (the) cave'. The cave can still be seen here.

Coa (Fermanagh), An Cuach, 'the hollow'.

Coachford (Cork), Áthe an Chóiste, 'ford of the coach'.

The Irish name appears to have been devised to match the English, which itself may be a corruption of some other Irish name. The river here is the Lee.

Coad (Cork), Comhad, 'grave'.

Coagh (Tyrone), An Cuach, 'the hollow'.

Coalisland (Tyrone), Oileán an Ghuail, 'island of the coal'.

This is the centre of the Tyrone coalfield, although it has never been profitably worked.

Cóbh (Cork), An Cóbh, 'the cove'.

The Irish word comes from the English. Cóbh, formerly spelt Cove, is noted for its fine harbour. From 1849 to 1922 it was called Queenstown, after Queen Victoria, who paid a royal visit here in the former year.

Colehill (several), Collchoill, 'hazel wood'.

The Colehill in Longford is called *Cnoc na Góla*, 'hill of the passage'.

Coleraine (Derry), Cúil Raithin, 'recess of ferns'.

The name occurs in various forms elsewhere, such as Cooleraine in Limerick, Coolrainy in Wexford, etc.

Colgach (Sligo), Calgach, 'prickly (place)'.

Collinstown (Dublin), Baile Uí Choileáin, 'town of the descendants of Collins'.

Compare the next entry.

Collinstown (Westmeath), Baile na gCailleach, 'town of the nuns'.

Here the Irish name has been assimilated to the English.

Collon (Louth), Collann, '(place of) hazels'.

Collooney (Sligo), Cúil Mhuine, 'recess of (the) thicket'.

Comeragh Mountains (Waterford), Sléibhte an Chumaraigh, 'hills of the confluences'.

Commeen (Donegal), An Coimín, 'the little valley'.

Cong (Mayo), Conga, 'isthmus'.

Cong is on a large isthmus some four miles across between Loughs Mask and Corrib.

Conlig (Down), An Choinleic, 'the flagstone of the hounds'.

This may well be a corrupt name.

Conn, Lough (Mayo), Loch Con, 'pure lake'.

Connagh (Dublin), Conach, '(place of) abundance'.

Connacht '(province of the) Connachta (tribe)'.

The name is still spelt Connaught by some, although this is now regarded as old-fashioned and inaccurate.

Connello (Limerick), Uí Conaill Gabhra, 'territory of the O Connell Gabhra'.

This ancient tribal name ultimately derives from Connell (Conall), the legendary king and warrior who was said to be descended from Oilill Ólum, the famed early king of Munster.

Connemara (Galway), Conamara, 'sea-coast territory of the descendants of Conmac'.

Conmac (Conmacc, Conmhac) was the son of the Ulster warrior Fergus Mac Roy (Fergus mac Róich) in early legendary history, with his territory designated here as 'sea-coast' (Irish *muir*, 'sea') to distinguish it from other lands of members of this tribe. Some prefer to derive the name more realistically from *Cuain na Mara*, 'harbours of the sea'. For a similar tribal name, however, *see* **Larne**.

Connonagh (Cork), Ceannannach, '(place of) white heads'.

The name may refer to hills here.

Connor (Antrim), Coinnire, 'oak wood of the dogs'.

If this interpretation is correct, the name may refer to packs of wild dogs that once lived here.

Connor Pass (Kerry), An Chonair, 'the path'.

Convoy (Donegal), Conmhaigh, 'hound plain'.

Conwal (Donegal), An Chongbháil, 'the establishment'.
The reference is to an ecclesiastical establishment. The two standing stones with crosses here perhaps date from the 7th century.

Cookstown (Tyrone), An Chorr Chríochach, 'the boundary hill'.
The English name comes from Alan Cook, who laid out the long High Street here at the beginning of the 17th century.

Coolagh (Laois), Cúlach, '(place with) corners'.
This name indicates a remote place, one hidden away.

Coolaney (Sligo), Cúil Éanaigh, 'watery secluded place'.

Coolattin (several), Cúil Aitinn, 'secluded place of (the) gorse'.

Coolbanagher (Laois), Cúl Beannchair, 'nook of the pointed hills'.

Coolbawn (Kilkenny, Tipperary), An Cúl Bán, 'the white corner'.

Coolboy (Donegal, Wicklow), An Cúl Buí, 'the yellow secluded spot'.

Coolderry (Monaghan), Cúl Doire, 'nook of (the) oak grove'.

Cooldrumman (Sligo), Cúl Dromman, 'secluded place of (the) little ridges'.

Coole (several), An Chúil, 'the secluded place'.

Coolgrean (Wexford), Cúil Ghréine, 'sunny nook'.

Coolhill (Kilkenny), Cúlchoil, 'secluded wood'.

Coolkenna (Wicklow), Cúil Uí Chionaoith, 'secluded spot of the descendants of Cionaoth'.

Coolock (Dublin), An Chúlóg, 'the little secluded place'.

Coolrain (Laois), Cúil Ruáin, 'nook of red-coloured land'.
The second part of this name may be the personal name Ruan.

Coolroe (Waterford), An Chúil Ruadh, 'the red-coloured secluded spot'.

Coom (Kerry), Com, 'hollow'.

Coos (several), Cuas, 'cave'.

Cootehill (Cavan), Muinchille, 'sleeve'.
The name indicates the contour of some territory here (compare the French name of the English Channel, *La Manche*). The English name relates to the Coote family who gained lands here in the 17th century.

Corballa (Sligo), An Corrbhaile, 'the unusually shaped townland'.

Corclogh (Mayo), Corrchloch, 'round hill of the stones'.

Corcomohide (Limerick), Corca Muichit, 'descendants of Muichet'.
Muichet is said to have been an early disciple of the druids.

Corcomroe (Clare), Corca Mrua, 'descendants of Modhruadh'.
Modhruadh, in early historical legend, was one of the three sons of queen Maeve (Medb) and Fergus (Fearghus).

Corduff (Monaghan), An Chorr Dhubh, 'the black round hill'.

Corglass (Leitrim), Corr Glass, 'green round hill'.

Cork (Cork), Corcaigh, 'marsh'.
The city grew up round a 6th-century monastery founded here on the edge of a marsh. As late as the 18th century the town was intersected by muddy streams, and St Patrick's Street and Grand Parade were built over deep stretches of water where ships loaded and unloaded then.

Corkaguiny (Kerry), Corca Dhuibhne, 'descendants of Duibhne'.
Duibhne was the son of Carbery Musc (Cairbre Músc) in early legend, and so the grandson of the 2nd-century king of Ireland Conary (Conaire).

Corkey (Antrim), Corcaigh, 'marsh'.
This is the same name as that of Cork.

Corlea (Clare), Coir Liath, 'grey round hill'.

Corlough (several), Corlach, 'heron lake'.

Cormeen (Monaghan), Cor Mín, 'smooth round hill'.

Cormorant Island (Westmeath), Cró-Inis, 'hut island'.
The English name may have been partly influenced by the Irish word. The island is on Lough Ennell.

Cornafulla (Westmeath), Corr na Fola, 'round hill of the blood'.

The name presumably refers to a battle here.

Cornakill (Cavan), Corr na Cille, 'round hill of the church'.

Cornamona (Galway), Cor na Móna, 'round hill of the bog'.

Corofin (Clare), Cora Finne, 'Finne's weir'.

Corr (Cavan), Corr, 'round hill'.

Corraun (Mayo), Corrán Acaille, 'sickle shape'.

The name refers to a peninsula here (*Rinn an Chorráin*) and a hill (*Cnoc an Chorráin*).

Corr Castle (Dublin), Caisleán na Coirre, 'castle of the hill'.

Corrib, Lough (Galway/Mayo), An Choirb, 'Oirbsean's lake'.

The name has been corrupted and abbreviated from that of Orbsen (Oirbsean), a legendary hero.

Corrigeenroe (Roscommon), Cairraigín Rua, 'little red-coloured rock'.

Corroy (Mayo), Cor Ráithe, 'red-coloured round hill'.

Corvalley (Monaghan), Cor an Bhealaigh, 'bend of the road'.

Coshlea (Limerick), Cois Sléibhe, '(place at the) foot of (the) mountain'.

The mountains here are the Galties. Irish *cos*, dative *cois*, means basically 'foot', but is used in place-names to indicate a location near or by something else.

Coshma (Limerick), Cois Máighe, '(place by the river) Maigue'.

See **Coshlea**.

Costelloe (several), Casla, 'sea inlet'.

Coumenare, Valley of (Kerry), Com an Áir, 'valley of slaughter'.

There is a local tradition concerning an ancient battle here.

Coumshingaun Lake (Waterford), Loch Com Seangán, 'lake (the) valley of (the) hollow of (the) narrows',

Courtmacsherry (Cork), Cúirt Mhic Shéafraidh, 'residence of the sons of Geoffrey'.

The original Geoffrey would have been a member of an Anglo-Norman family.

Craggagh (Galway), An Chreagach, 'the rocky place'.

Craigavad (Down), Creig an Bháda, 'rock of the boat'.

Craigavad is on Belfast Lough, and if this interpretation is correct there would have been a rock here to which boats were moored at one time.

Craigavon (Armagh).

Craigavon was designated as a New Town in 1965, and took its name from the first prime minister of Northern Ireland, James Craig, Viscount Craigavon.

Craigdoo (Donegal), Creag Dubh, 'black rock'.

Cranagh (Tyrone), An Chrannóg, 'the wooden structure'.

The name suggests a place with plenty of trees.

Cranfield (Antrim), Maigh Chreamhchoille, 'plain of (the) wood of wild garlic'.

The English name is a corruption of the Irish. For a similar distortion see **Crowhill**.

Crannagh (several), Crannach, 'wooden structure'.

This is the same name as for Cranagh.

Cratloe (Clare), An Chreatalach, 'the willow wood'.

Craughwell (Galway), Creamhchaoil, 'wild garlic wood'.

Crawfordsburn (Down), Sruth Chráfard, 'Crawford's stream'.

Crecora (Limerick), Craobh Chomhartha, 'sweet-scented tree'.

Creeslough (Donegal), An Craoslach, 'the gullet lake'.

The name implies that the lake swallows things up.

Creevagh (several), Craobhach, '(place) full of branches'.

Creeve (several), Craobh, '(place by a) densely branched tree'.

Creevy (several), Craobhaigh, '(place) full of branches'.

This is the same name as **Creevagh**.

Creevykeel (Sligo), An Chraobhaigh Chaol, 'the narrow place full of dense trees'.

Cregagh (Belfast), An Chreagaigh, 'the rocky place'.

Cregg (Clare), An Chreag, 'the rock'.

This is the same name as **Carrick** and **Carrig**.

Creggan (several), An Creagán, 'the little rocky place'.

Cregganbaun (Mayo), An Creagán Bán, 'the little white rocky place'.

Cregg Castle (Galway), An Chreag, 'the rock'.

Cremorne (Monaghan), Críoch Moghdhorn, 'territory of the Mughdhorna tribe'.
Mughdhorn, the tribal chief, was the son of Colla, who in early legend was one of the three brothers who conquered Ulster and destroyed the palace of Emania (Emain Macha, or Navan Fort) in the 4th century.

Crettyard (Laois), Crochta Árd, 'high croft'.

Crilly (Tyrone), Crithligh, 'quagmire'.

Croagh (Limerick), Cróch, 'round hill'.

Croaghpatrick (Mayo), Cruach Phádraig, 'St Patrick's hill'.
This is Ireland's 'Holy Mountain', where St Patrick is said to have fasted and lived.

Crockmore (Donegal), An Cnoc Mór, 'the big hill'.

Crolly (Donegal), Croithlí, 'quagmire'.

Cromkill (Antrim), Cromchoill, 'sloping wood'.

Crookhaven (Cork), An Cruachán, 'the little round hill'.
The English name is at least partly a corruption of the Irish. The village does have a well-known harbour, however.

Crookstown (Cork), An Baile Gallda, 'the English town'.
The English name of 'the English town' is based on the surname of its settler. Compare the next entry, however.

Crookstown (Kildare), Baile na Cruaiche, 'town of the rock'.
The English name is a half-translation, half-corruption of the Irish.

Croom (Limerick), Cromadh, 'sloping (place)'.

Crosspatrick (Wicklow), Crois Phádraig, 'Patrick's cross'.
This may not relate directly to St Patrick.

Crossakiel (Meath), Crosa Caoil, 'slender crosses'.
It is possible that the latter part of the name may derive from a personal name such as Caol or Cool.

Crossboy (Sligo), An Chrois Bhuí, 'the yellow cross'.

Crossdoney (Cavan), Cros Domhnaigh, 'cross of (the) church'.

Crossea (Longford), Cros Aodha, 'Hugh's cross'.

Crosserlough (Cavan), Crois ar Loch, 'cross of (the) lake'.

Crossgar (Down), An Chrois Ghearr, 'the short cross'.

Crosshaven (Cork), Bun an Tábhairne, 'river-mouth of the tavern'.
As with Crookhaven, the English name may be based partly on an alternative Irish name of the place, Cros tSeáin, 'John's cross'. But also as with Crookhaven, there is a recognised harbour here on the estuary of the Owenboy River.

Cross Keys (Meath), Carraig an Tobair, 'rock of the well'.
The English name is seen in the Irish form of the same place-name in Antrim, Na hEochracha, 'the keys' The sense seems to be 'keystone', 'cornerstone' rather than an inn name, as might otherwise be the case.

Crossmaglen (Armagh), Crois Mhic Lionnáin, 'cross of the son of Lionnán'.

Crossmolina (Mayo), Crois Mhaoilíona, 'Maoilíona's cross'.

Crossreagh (Cavan), An Chros Riabhach, 'the grey cross'.

Crove (Donegal), Cró Bheithe, 'enclosure of birches'.

Crowhill (Kilkenny), Creamhchoill, 'wild garlic wood'.
The English name is a corruption of the Irish. Compare **Cranfield**.

Crumlin (several), Cromghlinn, 'crooked glen', 'winding valley'.

Crusheen (Clare), Croisín, 'little cross'.

Cuilcagh (Cavan), Cuilceach, 'chalky'.
This mountain, over 2,000 ft (600m) high, has a white face.

Culdaff (Donegal), Cúil Dabhcha, 'secluded place of the sandhills'.
It is possible that the second half of the name is a personal one.

Culkey (Fermanagh), Cuilcigh, 'reedy place'.

Cullahill (Laois, Tipperary), An Chúlcoill, 'the back wood'.

Culleen (several), Na Coillíní, 'the little woods'.

Cullen (several), Cuillinn, 'holly place'.

Cullenwaine (Offaly), Cúil Ó nDubháin, 'secluded place of (the) descendants of Duane'.

Cullybackey (Antrim), Coill na Baice, 'wood of the hollow'.

Culmore (Derry), An Chúil Mhór, 'the big secluded spot'.

Culmullin (Meath), Cúl Muilín, 'corner of (the) mill'.

Cultra (Down), Cúl Trá, 'secluded strand'.
Cultra Manor and the Ulster Folk and Transport Museum are in a park overlooking Belfast Lough.

Cummeenduff (Kerry), An Cúimín Dubh, 'the black river valley'.

Cunningburn (Down), Sruth na gCoinín, 'stream of the rabbits'.
The English name is a part-translation (*sruth*, 'stream', 'burn'), part-corruption of the Irish name. (The former English word for 'rabbit' was 'coney'.)

Currabaha (Tipperary), Cora Bheatha, 'weir of birches'.

Curragh, The (Kildare), An Currach, 'the moor'.
Here the Irish word means 'racecourse', since this type of land is suitable for horses to run over. Elsewhere, the name means simply 'marsh', 'moor'.

Curraghbeg (Kerry), Currach Beag, 'little marsh'.

Curraghboy (Roscommon), An Currach Buí, 'the yellow marsh'.

Curraghmore (Waterford), An Currach Mór, 'the great marsh'.

Curraheen (Tipperary), Curraichín, 'little marsh'.

Curran, The (Antrim), An Currán, 'the crescent'.
The name describes the small curving headland here near Larne.

Curry (several), An Currach, 'the marsh'.
Some places of this name may derive from *cora*, 'weir'.

Curryglass (Cork), An Chora Ghlas, 'the grey marsh'.

Cush (Limerick), An Chois, 'the foot'.
The name implies a place at the foot of a mountain, in this case Slievereagh. See also **Coshlea**.

Cushendall (Antrim), Bun Abhann Dalla, 'mouth of (the) river Dall'.
The English name is based on the alternative Irish *Cois Abhann Dalla*, '(place by the) river Dall'. See **Coshlea** for an explanation of *cois*, and compare **Cushendun**.

Cushendun (Antrim), Bun Abhann Duinne, 'mouth of (the) river Dunn'.
The English name here is based on *Cois Abhann Duinne*, as for Cushendall. See also **Coshlea**.

Cutteen (Waterford), Coitchiann, 'common (place)'.
The name indicates a place held in common, by a community.

D

Daingean (Offaly), An Daingean, 'the fortress'.

The fortress of the name is the medieval one of O Conor Faly. From 1556 to 1920 the village was named Philipstown, after Philip II of Spain, husband of queen Mary, who was reigning at the time of the name change. The king also gave his title to King's County, as Offaly was formerly called.

Dalkey (Dublin), Deilginis, 'thorn island'.

The English name is in fact a Viking one, from Old Norse *dalkr*, 'thorn' and *ey*, 'island'. The first of these words is similar to the Irish (*dealg*), which aided the transition from one language to another. The name properly refers to the island here, with the resort taking its name from this.

Dalystown (Meath), Baile Uí Dhálaigh, 'town of the descendants of Daly'.

Danesfort (Kilkenny), Dún Feart, 'fort of graves'.

The English name is a corruption of the Irish.

Dangan (Meath), An Daingean, 'the fortress'.

This is the same name as Daingean. Not surprisingly, it occurs in a number of other places.

Dargle (Wicklow), Dargail, 'red rock'.

The name is of doubtful meaning, but this interpretation is one of the more likely, from Irish *dearg*, 'red', and *aille*, 'rock'. The reference would be to the colour of the rocks in the bed of this river.

Darragh (Clare), An Darach, 'the place of oaks'.

Deelis (Kerry), Duibhlios, 'black ring-fort'.

Delgany (Waterford), Deilgne, 'thorny place'.

Delphi (Mayo), Fionnloch, 'white lake'.

The origin of the English name is uncertain, although it appears to derive at least partly from the Irish.

Delvin (Westmeath), Dealbhna, '(place of the) descendants of Dealbhaeth'.

According to early legend, there were seven tribes called Dealbhna, all descended from and named after Lughaidh Dealbhaeth, who was the son of Cas Mac Thail, himself the ancestor of the Dalcassians (Dál Cais). The only one to preserve the name was this one.

Derg, Lough (Clare/Galway/ Tipperary), Loch Deirgeirt, 'lake of (the) red eye'.

A legend tells of a king who gave his eye to a wandering poet and afterwards washed his face in this lough, whose waters then ran red with his blood. The true origin probably refers to the colour of a deep point or whirlpool here somewhere, perhaps near where the Shannon flows into it.

Dernish (Clare, Fermanagh, Sligo), Toir-Inis, 'oak island'.

These are three islands respectively in the Shannon, in Upper Lough Erne, and off Milk Haven.

Derradda (Leitrim), Doire Fhada, 'long oak grove'.

Derragh (Cork), Darach, 'place of oaks'.

Derralossary (Wicklow), Doire Lasrach, 'Lassar's oak grove'.

Lassar was a woman saint's name.

Derravarragh, Lough (Westmeath), Loch Dairbhreach, 'lake with an oak plantation'.

In the past, the name has wrongly been interpreted as 'lake of severe judgment', with *dairbhreach*, 'place of oaks' understood to be *daoir*, 'severe' and *bhreath*, 'judgment'.

Derreen (Seveal), Doirín, 'little oak grove'.

Derrinturn (Kildare), Doire an tSoirn, 'oak grove of the kiln'.

Derry see **Londonderry**.

Derrybawn (Wicklow), Doire Bán, 'white oak grove'.

Derrybeg (Donegal), Doirí Beaga, 'little oak groes'.

Derrybrien (Galway), Daraidh Braoin, 'Braon's oak grove'.

Derrycoush (Mayo), Doire an Chuais, 'oak grove of the cave'.

Derrygonnelly (Fermanagh), Doire Ó gConáile, 'oak grove of the descendants of Connolly'.

Derryharney (Fermanagh), Doire Charna, 'oak grove of the descendants of Kearney'.

Derryhivenny (Galway), Doire hAibhne, 'oak grove of (the) river'.

Derrykeevan (Armagh), Doire Chaomháin, 'Caomhán's oak grove'.

Derrykeighan (Antrim), Doire Céigeán, 'Caochán's oak grove'.

Derrylahane (Cavan), Doire Leathan, 'broad oak wood'.
This name is also found elsewhere.

Derrylea (several), Doire Liath, 'grey oak wood'.

Derrylee (Armagh), Doire Lí, 'Lí's oak grove'.

Derrylester (Fermanagh), Doire an Leastair, 'oak grove of the beehive'.

Derrylin (Fermanagh), Doire Loinn, 'Flann's oak grove'.

Derrymore (several), An Doire Mór, 'the big oak grove'.

Derrynacreeve (Cavan), Doir na Cria, 'oak grove of the densely branched trees'.
This interpretation assumes that the last part of the name derives from *craobh*, 'branch', 'tree'.

Derrynane (Kerry), Doire Fhionáin, 'Fionnán's oak grove'.

Derryquay (Kerry), Doir Mhic Aodha, 'oak grove of the son of Hugh'.

Derrytrasna (Armagh), Doire Trasna, 'oblique oak grove'.

Derryvullan (Fermanagh), Doir Mhalán, 'Maelán's oak grove'.

Dervock (Antrim), Dearbhóg, 'little oak grove'.

Desertcreat (Tyrone), Díseart Dá Chríoch, 'hermitage of the two boundaries'.
A number of early churches were on territory boundaries, serving both. It is not clear which boundaries were involved here.

Desertegny (Donegal), Díseart Eigne, 'Egnagh's hermitage'.

Desertmartin (Derry), Díseart Mhártain, 'St Martin's hermitage'.

Desertserges (Cork), An Díseart, 'the hermitage'.
An earlier Irish name has the personal name *Dísirt Saerghusa*, 'Saerghus's hermitage'.

Devenish Island (Fermanagh), Daimhinis, 'ox island'.
The English addition 'island' was made when the main Irish name became meaningless, even though it actually includes the word 'island' (*inis*). The island is in Lough Erne.

Devil's Glen (Wicklow), An Gleann Mór, 'the big valley'.
Another Irish name was *Bun na nEas*, 'bottom of the waterfall'. The river here is the Vartry.

Devil's Mother (Galway), Binn Gharbh, 'rough peak'.
Another Irish name for this mountain was *Machaire an Deamhain*,' 'demon's plain', and the present English name has apparently converted Irish *machaire* to 'mother'. Only the devil could have a mountain as a 'plain'.

Devil's Punch Bowl (Kerry), Poll an Diabhail, 'hole of the devil'.

Dingle (Kerry), An Daingean, 'the fortress'.
A fuller Irish name for Dingle is *Daingean Uí Chúise*, 'fortress of the descendants of Cush'. The final *n* of the Irish name became *l* in the English rendering.

Doagh (Antrim), Dumhach, 'sandhill'.

Doe Castle (Donegal), Caisleán na dTuath, 'castle of the boundaries'.

Dollymount (Dublin), Baile na gCorr, 'town of the herons'.
The English name is a corruption of the alternative Irish name, *Cnocán Doirinne*, with the first word translated as 'mount' and the second giving 'Dolly'.

Donabate (Dublin), Domhnach Bat, 'church of the boat'.
This is a conjectured translation, as the original Irish form is uncertain.

Donagh (several), Domhnach, '(place by a) church'.
A number of names begin with 'Donagh-', and only a small selection is given below.

Donaghadee (Down), Domhnach Daoi, 'church of Diach'.
The last part of this name is uncertain, and this is only a conjectural interpretation.

Donaghcloney (Down), Domhnach Cluana,

'church of (the) meadow'.

Donaghcumper (Kildare), Domhnach Coimir, 'church of (the) confluence'.
Donaghcumper is on the Liffey.

Donaghmore (several), Domhnach Mór, 'big church'.
The Donaghmore in Meath is the site of St Patrick's 'great church' and now has a National Monument status to indicate this.

Donaghmoyne (Monaghan), Domhnach Maighean, 'church of the little plain'.
.This is the traditional interpretation, but it is more likely to derive from *maighean*, 'place', 'ground', indicating a place owned by a particular person or group of people. The given rendering assumes the Irish is based on *mágh*, 'plain'.

Donaghpatrick (Meath), Domhnach Phádraig, 'St Patrick's church'.
The present St Patrick's church here stands on the site of an early monastery.

Donard (Wicklow), Dún Ard, 'high fort'.
There is no fort here now, but there may have been one on the small hill called the Ball Moat, where there are now the ruins of an Anglo-Norman Castle.

Donegal (Donegal), Dún na nGall, 'fort of the foreigners'.
The 'foreigners' were the Danes (the Vikings), who took possession of a primitive fort here in the 10th century. See also **Tir-connell**. The county took the name of the town.

Donegore (Antrim), Dún na gCaradh, 'fort of the heroes'.

Doneraile (Cork), Dún ar Aill, 'fort on a cliff'.
The name has been spelt in a number of ways over the centuries, and in the 17th century alone these spellings were recorded: *Downerahill* (1605), *Donnerayle* (1615), *Donoghraile* (1634), *Donnoughraile* (1663), *Donnoghrayle* (1671). Doneraile is on the river Awbeg.

Donnybrook (Dublin), Domhnach Broc, 'church of St Broc'.

Donohill (Tipperary), Dún Eochaille, 'fort of the yew wood'.

Dooagh (Mayo), Dumha Acha, 'sandbank'.
The Irish name probably represents *dumhach*, with the sense given.

Doochary (Donegal), An Dúchoraidh, 'the black weir'.

Doogary (Cavan), An Dúgharraí, 'the black garden'.

Doohamlet (Monaghan), Dúthamhlacht, 'black graveyard'.
The last part of the name is the same as the place-name Tallaght.

Dooish (Donegal, Tyrone), Dubhais, 'black hill'.

Dooks (Derry), Dumhacha, 'sandhills'.
The Irish name has acquired an English plural 's'.

Doo Lough (Mayo), Dúloch, 'black lake'.

Doon (several), An Dún, 'the fort'.
In many places, traces of the original fort still exist, as at Doon in Limerick.

Doonaha (Clare), Dún Átha, 'fort of the ford'.

Doonamo (Mayo), Dún na mBó, 'fort of the cows'.

Doonan (several), Dúnán, 'little fort'.

Doonbeg (Clare), An Dún Beag, 'the little fort'.

Dooniskey (Cork), Dún Uisce, 'fort of (the) water'.

Dorsey, The (Armagh), Na Doirse, 'the doors'.
This famous earthwork is the largest entrenched enclosure in the whole country.

Douglas (several), Dúglas, 'black stream'.

Down (Down), An Dún, 'the fort'.
The fort of the name is the one of Downpatrick, which gave its name to the county.

Downhill (Derry), Dún Bó, 'fort of cows'.
Downhill is in the parish of Dunboe, which represents the Irish name. The 'hill' of Downhill is seen in the alternative Irish name *Cnoc na Ladhra*, 'hill of the forks'.

Downings (Donegal), Na Dúnaibh, 'the forts'.
The remains of a stone fort can still be seen here, and there were probably others. The '-ings' ending is English, with the 's' denoting the plural. Locally the *g* is not pronounced.

Downpatrick (Down), Dún Pádraig, 'St Patrick's fort'.
The original Irish name of the settlement here was *Dún-dá-leth-glas*, 'fort of the two broken locks'. This became simply *Dún*,

47

then *Dún Pádraig* at the time of the 'discovery' of various relics here, including those said to be of St Patrick, in the late 12th century. The original fort was probably on the site where the Church of Ireland cathedral now is. The town is the source of the county name.

Downs, The (Westmeath), Na Dúnta, 'the forts'.

Dowra (Cavan), An Damhshraith, 'the river meadow of (the) oxen'.

Draperstown (Derry), Baile na Croise, 'town of the cross'.

The 'cross' is that of the ancient church site here, the shrine of St Columba. The present English name was given in 1818 to mark the commercial developments made in the village by the London Drapers Company. The local English name of 'The Cross', of the same origin as the Irish name, is still sometimes used.

Dreenagh (Donegal), Draighnach, 'place of blackthorns'.

Dressogach (Armagh), Dreasógach, 'place of briars'.

Drimnagh (Dublin), Droimeanach, 'place of ridges'.

Drimoleague (Cork), Drom Dhá Liag, 'place of (the) two standing stones'.

Drinagh (Cork, Wexford), Draighneach, 'place of blackthorns'.

Dripsey (Cork), An Druipseach, 'the muddy place'.

Dripsey is on the river Dripsey.

Drishane (Cork), An Driseán, 'the place of brambles'.

Drogheda (Louth), Droichead Átha, 'bridge of (the) ford'.

The English name is a rendering of the Irish. There was a bridge over the river Boyne here as early as the 12th century.

Droichead Nua (Kildare), Droichead Nua, 'new bridge'.

The English name Newbridge is also sometimes used. The river here is the Liffey.

Drom (Tipperary), An Drom, 'the ridge'.

Dromahair (Leitrim), Drom Dhá Thiar, 'ridge of two demons'.

Dromaneen (Cork), An Dromainín, 'the little ridge'.

Dromara (Down), Droim Bearach, 'ridge of (the) heifer'.

Dromard (Sligo), An Droim Árd, 'the high ridge'.

Dromcolliher (Limerick), Drom Collachair, 'ridge of the hazel wood'.

The name is reflected more accurately in an earlier Irish version, *Drom Collchoille*.

Dromdaleague (Cork), Drom Dhá Liag, 'ridge of (the) two standing stones'.

Dromin (several), Dromainn, 'little ridge'. In Louth, Dromin represents Irish *Droim Inge*, 'Ing's ridge'.

Dromineer (Tipperary), Drom Inbhir, 'ridge of the river-mouth'.

Dromineer is on the shores of Lough Derg, near the point where the river Nenagh flows into it.

Dromiskin (Louth), Droim Ineasclainn, 'Ineasclann's ridge'.

Dromkeen (Limerick), Drom Caoin, 'pleasant ridge.'

Drommartin (Kerry), Drom Máirtín, 'Martin's ridge'.

Dromod (Leitrim), Dromad, 'ridge'.

Dromore (several), Droim Mór, 'big ridge'. Dromore in Down is also known as *Druim Mocholmóg*, from its famous 6th-century founder, Mo-Cholmóg, better known as St Colmán.

Dromore West (Sligo), An Droim Mór Thiar, 'the big west ridge'.

There is no 'Dromore East', so Dromore West must relate either to some other ridge east of it or to Sligo itself.

Dromtrasna (Limerick), Drom Treasna, 'cross ridge'.

The name indicates a ridge running obliquely across country.

Drum (several), Drom, 'ridge'.

Drumacoo (Galway), Droim an Chú, 'ridge of the hounds'.

Possibly wild dogs once lived here, although the name could also be a corruption of *Drom Mochua*, 'St Mo-Chua's ridge'.

Drumadoon (Antrim), Droim an Dúin, 'ridge of the fort'.

Drumahoe (Derry), Droim na hUamha, 'ridge of the cave'.

Drumard (several), Drom Árd, 'high ridge'.
Drumbeg (several), Drom Beag, 'little ridge.'
Drumbilla (Louth), Droim Bile, 'ridge of (the) ancient tree'.
Drumbo (Down), Droim Bó, 'ridge of (the) cow'.
Drumbrughas (Cavan, Fermanagh), Drom Brúchais, 'ridge of (the) farmhouse'.
Drumcannon (Waterford), Drom Chonáin, 'ridge of (the) white-faced (cow)'.
If the interpretation is correct, the Irish origin is *ceannann*, that is, *ceann-fhionn*, 'white-faced', a term usually applied to a cow.
Drumcar (Louth), Droim Chora, 'ridge of (the) weir'.
Drumcar is on the river Glyde.
Drumcard (Fermanagh), Droim Ceard, 'ridge of (the) smiths'.
Drumcliffe (Sligo), Droim Chliabh, 'ridge of baskets'.
Drumcolumb (Sligo), Drom Colm, 'St Columba's ridge'.
Drumcondra (Dublin), Droim Conrach, 'Contra's ridge'.
Drumconnick (Cavan), Droim Cunmhaic, 'Conmhac's ridge'.
In early legend, Conmac (Conmhac) was the son of the Ulster warrior Fergus Mac Roy (see **Connemara**).
Drumcree (Westmeath), Droim Cria, 'ridge of cattle'.
Drumcroone (Derry), Droim Cruithean, 'ridge of (the) Picts'.
The Picts inhabited part of the north of Ireland in ancient times, where they were known as *Cruithne*.
Drumcullen (Offaly), Droim Cuileann, 'ridge of holly'.
Drumfadd (Donegal), Druim Fada, 'long ridge'.
Drumfin (Sligo), Droim Fionn, 'fair ridge'.
Drumfree (Donegal), Droim Fraoigh, 'heather ridge'.
Drumgoff (Wicklow), Droim Gaimh, 'ridge of (the) storm'.
This name may well derive from a personal name, and represent Irish *Druim Mhic Eochadha*, 'ridge of the sons of Eochaidh'.

(Irish *Mac Eochaidh* is the modern surname Mac Keogh, or Keogh).
Drumhallagh (Donegal), Droim Shalach, 'ridge of willows'.
Drumgrenaghan (Fermanagh), Droim Gréineacháin, 'Gréinachán's ridge'.
Drumkeen (Donegal), Droim Caoin, 'pleasant ridge'.
Drumkeerin (Leitrim), Droim Caorthainn, 'ridge of rowan trees'.
Drumlane (Cavan), Drom Leathan, 'broad ridge'.
Drumlish (Longford), Droim Lis, 'ridge of (the) ring-fort'.
Drummin (several), An Dromainn, 'the ridge'.
Drummully (Monaghan), Droim Aili, 'ridge of (the) summit'.
Drumnacross (Donegal), Droim na Croise, 'ridge of the cross'.
Drumnakilly (Tyrone), Droim na Coille, 'ridge of the wood'.
Drumnaraw (Donegal), Droim na Rátha, 'ridge of the ring-fort'.
Drumneechy (Derry), Droim Naoise, 'Naoise's ridge'.
Drumquin (Tyrone), Droim Caoin, 'pleasant ridge'.
Drumraney (Westmeath), Droim Raithne, 'ridge of the fern'.
Drumree (Meath), Droim Rí, 'ridge of (the) king'.
Drumroe (Waterford), Droim Ruadh, 'red-coloured ridge'.
Drumshanbo (Leitrim), Droim Seanbhó, 'ridge of (the) old cow'.
The name is said to derive from the resemblance of the ridge here to a cow's back.
Drumsna (Leitrim), Droim ar Snámh, 'ridge of the swimming place'.
The Doon (i.e. fort) of Drumsna is a so-called 'travelling earthwork' one mile long across the Leitrim-Roscommon border. It contains an area of about one square mile in a loop of the Shannon and is believed to have been built to guard river crossings in this region.
Drumsurn (Derry), Droim Sorn, 'ridge of (the) kiln'.

Drung (Cavan), Drong, 'multitude'.
The name probably indicates a tribal meeting-place.

Duagh (Kerry), Dubháth, 'black ford'.
The river here is the Keale.

Dublin (Dublin), Baile Átha Cliath, 'town of (the) ford of (the) hurdle'.
Dublin has two Irish names, since Dublin itself derives from *dubh-linn*, 'black pool'. Both names refer to the river Liffey here, with Baile Átha Cliath being more a historical name, referring to the method used (woven withies) to ford the river, and Dublin more a geographical name, describing the section of the river on which the original settlement was built. It may be significant that the Irish preferred to use the historical name, thus commemorating their feat in fording the river, while the non-Irish world prefer the descriptive name, which is also easier to a non-Celtic tongue. (Baile Átha Cliath might have resulted in an anglicised form 'Ballyclee'.) The name Dublin was recorded by Ptolemy in the 2nd century AD as *Eblana*, and this came to be subsequently used for literary imprints.

Dufferin (Down), Dubhthrian, 'black third'.
A 'third' (Irish *trian*) was a territorial division.

Duhallow (Cork), Dútha Ealla, 'district of (the river) Allo'.
The name of this barony is based on the former name of the river Blackwater.

Duleek (Meath), Damhliag, 'stone church'.
The name denotes the early stone house or church *(daimhliag)* that was founded by St Patrick here and later transferred by him to the care of St Cianán. It is said traditionally to have been the first stone-built church in Ireland. Later, an Augustinian church was built on the site, and finally the present Church of Ireland church.

Dunadry (Antrim), Dún Eadradh, 'middle fort'.
The fort here was the major Irish stronghold on the road between Tara to the south and the ancient territory of Dalriada to the north. It was thus the 'middle' fort between these two places.

Dun Aengus (Galway), Dún Aonghasa, 'Aengus's fort'.
This ancient site is on Inishmore, in the Aran Islands. The name suggests 'Angus' and tourists here usually pronounce it like this name. It should really be pronounced 'Doon Eeneese', however, since it relates to Aonghus, a chief of the Fir Bolg in medieval literary legend.

Dunamase (Laoise), Dún Másc, 'fort of Másc'.
According to tradition, Másc was an ancestor of the Leinster people. The English version of the name should really be 'Dunmask'.

Dunamon (Galway), Dún Iomdhain, 'Iomgan's fort'.
The name relates to the castle here on the river Suck.

Dunboyne (Meath), Dún Búinne, 'Báethán's fort'.

Dunbrody (Wexford), Dún Bróithe, 'Brúide's fort'.

Duncannon (Wexford), Dún Canann, 'Canann's fort'.
It is not known who Canann was, but his fort was probably on the promontory to the west of the village.

Duncormick (Wexford), Dún Chormaic, 'Cormac's fort'.

Dundalk (Louth), Dún Dealgan, 'Dealga's fort'.
The name relates to Castletown Hill to the west of the town, where the great legendary warrior and epic hero Cú-Chulainn is traditionally supposed to have been born. Dealga was said to have been the chief of the Fir Bolg who built the fort. An earlier Irish name of the settlement was *Sraidbaile* (giving English 'Stradbally' elsewhere), 'street-town', that is, a town or settlement consisting of dwellings on a single long street. This distinguished the settlement from *Traghbaile* (or *Baile na Tragha*), which is the present suburb of Seatown (literally 'Strandtown').

Dunderrow (Cork), Dún Darú, 'fort of the oak plain'.
The fort is still here, half a mile south of the village.

Dunderry (Meath), Dún Doire, 'fort of the oak grove'.

Dundonald (Down), Dún Dónaill, 'Dónall's fort'.
The fort can be seen near the Church of Ireland parish church.
Dundrum (several), Dún Droma, 'fort of the ridge'.
Dunfanaghy (Donegal), Dun Fionnachaidh, 'fort of (the) white field'.
Dungannon (Tyrone), Dún Geanainn, 'Geanann's fort'.
There is no record or local tradition as to where the fort might have been.
Dungarvan (Waterford), Dún Garbháin, 'Garbhán's fort'.
Dungivan (Derry), Dún Geimhin, 'fort of (the) hide'.
If this is the correct interpretation, hides or skins may have been stored here.
Dungloe (Donegal), An Clochán Liath, 'the grey stepping stones'.
The grey rocks of this small fishing port are still here as a natural feature. The English name represents Irish *Dún Gloir*, 'fort of (the) noise', said to derive from a fair transferred here.
Dungourney (Cork), Dún Guairne, 'Guairne's fort'.
Dunhill (Waterford), Dúnaill, 'fort of (the) cliff'.
The name probably refers to the rock on which Dunhill Castle now stands, so that this is the site of the original fort.
Dunkerrin (Offaly), Dún Cairin, 'Caire's fort'.
Dunkettle (Cork), Dún Cathail, 'Cahill's fort'.
Dunkineely (Donegal) Dún Cionnaola, 'Cionnaola's fort'.
The fort is at the western end of the village.
Dunkitt (Kilkenny), Dún Cuit, 'Ceat's fort'.
Dún Laoghaire (Dublin), Dún Laoghaire, 'Laoghaire's fort'.
Laoghaire is said to have been a 5th-century high king of Ireland and a disciple of St Patrick. Dún Laoghaire (once anglicised as 'Dunleary') was known as Kingstown from 1821 to 1920, this name commemorating a visit by King George IV in the former year on his way back to England after a state invitation to Dublin.
Dunleer (Louth), Dún Léire, 'Léire's fort'.

Dunlewy (Donegal), Dún Lúiche, 'Lughaidh's fort'.
Dunloe (Kerry), Dún Lóich, 'fort of (the river) Loe'.
Dunluce (Antrim), Dún Libhse, 'palace'.
Dunluce Castle, now in ruins, is near the Giant's Causeway. The interpretation of the name, which is conjectural, derives from *dún-lios*, a combination of *dún*, 'fort', used adjectivally, and *lios*, the word normally translated as 'ring-fort'. Perhaps the best rendering would be 'fortified residence'.
Dunmore (several), Dún Mór, 'big fort'.
The Galway Dunmore takes its name from the large fort that belonged to Turloch Mór O Conor, the 12th-century high king and king of Connacht.
Dunmore East (Waterford), Dún Mór, 'big fort'.
Remains of the fort still exist here at this port on the western side of Waterford Harbour. There is no 'Dunmore West', so that 'East' doubtless refers to the location of the resort east of Waterford.
Dunmore Head (Kerry), Ceann an Dúin Mhóir, 'headland of the big fort'.
This is the most westerly point of Ireland, and an excellent site for the fort that can still be seen here on the tip of the Dingle Peninsula.
Dunmurry (Antrim), Dún Muirígh, 'Muiríoch's fort'.
Dunnamanagh (Tyrone), Dún na Manach, 'fort of the monks'.
Dunquin (Kerry), Dún Chaoin, 'pleasant fort'.
Dunsandle (Galway), Dún Sandail, 'Sandal's fort'.
Dunsany (Meath), Dún Samhnaí, 'Samhnach's fort'.
Dunseverick (Antrim), Dún Sobhairce, 'Sobhairce's fort'.
Dunshaughlin (Meath), Dún Seachlainn, 'St Seachnal's fort'.
Seachnal, or Secundinus, was the 5th-century saint who came to help St Patrick in his missionary work. His church was on or near the site of the present Protestant church.
Dunsink (Dublin), Dún Sinche, 'Sineach's

fort'.

Dunsoghly (Dublin), Dún Sachaille, 'Sochaille's fort'.

Duntryleague (Limerick), Dún Trí Liag, 'fort of (the) three standing stones'.
There is no fort here now. Perhaps there once was on the site of the present parish church. The fort was said to have been built for Cormac Cas, son of Oilill Ólum (see **Connello**), and the three stones were those that covered his grave.

Durrow (several), Darú, 'oak plain'.

Dysart (several), An Díseart, 'the hermitage'.
The many places so called are spelt Dysart or Dysert, amongst others, from Irish *díseart*.

Dysert O Dea (Clare), Díseart Uí Dheá, 'O Dea's hermitage'.
This ancient monastic site was founded by St Tóla, the 8th-century bishop of Clonard.

E

Eask, Lough (Donegal), Loch Iasc, 'fish lake'.

Easky (Sligo), Iascaigh, 'abounding with fish'.
Easky has a good angling reputation even today on the river Easky.

Eden (Antrim), An tÉadan, 'the face'.
The sense here is 'hill-slope', 'hill-brow'.

Edenderry (Offaly), Éadan Doire, 'hill-brow of the oak grove'.
The hill of the name is probably the one south of the town on which Blundell's Castle stands, or else perhaps Carrick Hill to the north.

Edenduffcarrick (Antrim), Edan Dubh Carrige, 'hill-brow of (the) black rock'.
The better known name of Edenduffcarrick is Shane's Castle, so called after Shane (Seán) O Neill of Clandeboye. (See also **Randalstown**.)

Edentinny (Leitrim), Éadan Tine, 'hill-brow of fire'.

Edergole (Fermanagh), Eadar Ghabhal, '(place) between (river) forks'.
This is the same name as Addergoole.

Edgeworthstown (Longford), Meathas Troim, 'frontier of (the) elder tree'.
The village is also known as Mostrim, an anglicised version of the Irish name. The English Edgeworth family settled here in the 16th century, making their home at Edgeworthstown House.

Eglinton (Derry), An Magh, 'the plain'.
The English name comes from Archibald Montgomerie, 13th earl of Eglinton, who was lord lieutenant of Ireland in 1858, the year when the name was changed from 'Muff', (i.e. *An Magh*) to avoid confusion with the larger Muff nearby in Donegal. The earl's title comes from Eglinton Castle, near Irvine, Scotland.

Eglish (several), An Eaglais, 'the church'.
This name is found more in the north, corresponding to Aglish in the southern half of Ireland.

Eighter (Cavan), Íochtar, 'lower (area)'.
The Irish word that gives this name can also mean 'northern'.

Eliogarty (Tipperary), Éile Uí Fhogartaigh, '*Éile* of the descendants of Fogarty'.
Éile was a tribal name, derived from its ancestor Éile, who in ancient folk history was descended from Cian, son of Oilill Ólum (see **Connello**).

Elphin (Roscommon), Ail Finn, 'rock (of the) clear (spring)'.
According to tradition, St Patrick founded a church here near a spring flowing from under a large stone or rock (*aill*).

Emain Macha (Armagh), Eamhain Mhacha.
The second part of the name is that of the legendary queen and goddess Macha, who is said to be buried here and whose name also appears in that of Armagh. The first word has been fancifully interpreted as 'neck brooch' (*eo*, 'brooch' and *muin*, 'neck'), referring to a tale in which Macha indicated the site where the fort was to be built by piercing the ground with her brooch. The actual meaning of the word is obscure, however. The ancient site here, the crowning place of the kings of Ulster for some six hundred years before the 4th century AD, is also known as Navan Fort. This is a corruption of *Eamhain* preceded by the Irish definite article *an*. (The name of Navan in Meath, however, has quite another origin.) Emain Macha also appears in older texts in its latinised form of *Emania*.

Emania see **Emain Macha**.

Emlagh (several), Imleach, 'borderland', 'land by a lake'.

Emlaghdauroe (Galway), Imleach Dá Ghruadh, 'lakeland of (the) two cows'.

Emly (Tipperary), Imleach, 'borderland'.
This is the same name as Emlagh. Emly is said to have been founded by St Ailbhe in the 5th century here on the edge of a lake which has now been drained. The full Irish name of the village is *Imleach Iobhair*, 'lakeland of (the) yew tree'.

Emlygrennan (Limerick), Imleach Draighnigh, 'lakeland full of blackthorns'.

According to some, the name is a corruption of *Bile Ghroidhnín*, 'Grynan's ancient tree'. The English spelling of the name, however, suggests an origin in *Imleach Grianain*, 'lakeland of (the) summer house'. Either way, the name may have been influenced by that of Emly, only a few miles away across the border in Tipperary.

Emyvale (Monaghan), Scairbh na gCaorach, 'shallow (place) of the sheep'.
The English name represents Irish *Uí Méith Tíre*, 'descendants of the rich land', with English 'vale' added.

Enagh (several), Eanach, 'marsh'.

Enfield (Meath), An Bóthar Buí, 'the yellow road'.
The English name was originally 'Innfield' ('inn by the field'), but was renamed Enfield by the railway company, apparently as this was regarded as more 'correct'.

Ennereilly (Wicklow), Inbhear Dhaoile, 'mouth of the (river) Dael'.
The river is now known as the Redcross.

Ennis (Clare), Inis, 'island'.
Ennis is on the river Fergus which itself contains several small islands. The name also means 'riverside land', and either interpretation would do for this location.

Enniscrone (Sligo), Inis Crabhann, 'riverside land of the ridge of the river'.
The earlier spelling of the Irish name was *Inis Screobhainn*, understood as *inis eascra abhann*, literally 'island of (the) esker of (the) river'. But this sense looks like an attempt to give a meaning to a meaningless name. The first part of the name, however, is certainly *inis*, 'island', 'riverside land'.

Enniskean (Cork), Inis Céin, 'Cian's riverside land'.
An alternative interpretation of this name could be 'beautiful riverside land', from *Inis Caoin* (*caoin*, 'beautiful', 'pleasant'). The personal name seems more likely, however.

Enniskerry (Wicklow), Áth na Sceire, 'ford of the reef'.
This is not an 'Ennis-' name like those above and below. Perhaps 'reef' here implies a rough or rocky crossing over the river Cookstown here.

Enniskillen (Fermanagh), Inis Ceithleann, 'Cethlenn's island'.
In early legend, Cethlenn (or Ceithleann) was the wife of Balor of the Great Blows, the Fomorian pirate. The town is certainly on an island at the upper end of the Lower Lough Erne. The Inniskilling Fusiliers, the British army regiment, take their name from Enniskillen, where they were raised in 1689. (The regiment is now part of the Royal Irish Rangers.)

Ennisnag (Kilkenny), Inis Snaig, 'riverside land of (the) woodpecker'.
Irish *snag* is the name of a number of birds and creatures, with its main sense as 'snail'. It may be an attempt here to give a meaningful interpretation for an obscure name.

Ennistymon (Clare), Inis Díomáin, 'Díomán's riverside land'.

Erne, Lough (Fermanagh), Loch Éirne, 'lake of the Erni'.
The lough has a tribal name. The Erni or Ernai were said to be a Fir Bolg people who lived on the plain that was here before the lake covered it.

Errigal (Donegal), An Earagail, 'the oratory'.
This mountain, like many others, may well have had an oratory or hermitage on it.

Errigal Keeroge (Tyrone), Aireagal Dachiaróg, 'St Dachiaróg's oratory'.

Esk, Lough (Donegal), Loch Eascach, 'lake of fish'.

Esker (several), An Eiscir, 'the esker'.
An esker is a sandy ridge or line of hills, or a ridge of gravel or sand in a river.

Eskeragh (several), Eiscrach, 'place of eskers'.
See **Esker**.

Esnadarragh (Fermanagh), Ais na Darach, 'place of the oak wood'.
Irish *ais* has a number of meanings, from 'hill' or 'fort' to 'recess' or simply 'place'.

Estersnow (Roscommon), Díseart Nuadhain, 'St Nuadha's hermitage'.
The English name, suggesting 'Easter snow', is a corruption of the Irish.

Eyeries (Cork), Na hAoraí, 'the rising ground'.
The ground in fact starts to rise here up to the Slieve Miskish range, south and east of

Eyeries. An English 's' has been added as a plural to correspond to the Irish.

Eyrecourt (Galway), Dún an Uchta, 'fort of the bank'.

The English name comes from the Eyre family who held lands here in the 17th century. The second part of the Irish name (which has been anglicised as 'Donanaghta') comes from *ucht*, 'breast'.

F

Fad, Lough (Donegal), Loch Fada, 'long lake'.

Faha (several), Faithche, 'lawn', 'sports field', 'exercise green'.

Fahan (Donegal), Fathain, 'grave'.
The name refers to the monastic site here with a graveyard. Compare **Fahan** (Kerry).

Fahan (Kerry), Fán, 'slope'.
Compare **Fahan** (Donegal).

Fair Head (Antrim), An Bhinn Mhór, 'the great headland'.
The English name is misleading, since it derives as a part translation, part corruption of the Irish alternative name *Rinn an Fhir Léith*, 'Grey Man's Point'.

Fairyhouse (Meath), Brú Sí, 'fairy house'.

Fairymount (Roscommon), Mullach na Sí, 'hill of the fairies'.

Falcarragh (Donegal), An Fál Carrach, 'the rough hedge'.

Falls (Belfast), Tuath na bhFál, 'enclosed land'.
Literally, 'land of the enclosures', with English plural 's' added.

Fall of Doonass (Clare/Limerick), Eas Danainne, 'Danann's waterfall'.

Fanad (Donegal), Fanad, 'sloping ground'.
Fanad Head is at the end of the Fanad peninsula.

Farahy (Cork), Fairche, 'parish'.

Farney (Monaghan), Fearnmhuighe, 'place of alders'.

Farran (Cork), An Fearann, 'the land'.

Farrancassidy (Fermanagh), Fearann Uí Chaiside, 'land of the descendants of Caiside'.

Farranfore (Kerry), An Fearann Fuar, 'the cold land'.

Fassadinan (Kilkenny), Fasach an Deighnín, 'wasteland of the (river) Dinin'.

Feakle (Clare), An Fhiacail, 'the tooth'.
The name refers to some natural feature here, such as a rock.

Feeagh, Lough (Mayo), Loch Fiadhach, 'woody lake'.

Feeard (Clare), Fíodh Árd, 'high wood'.

Feenagh (several), Fíonach, 'woody (place)'.

Feeny (Derry), Na Fíneadha, 'the woods'.

Feighcullen (Kildare), Fíodh Cuileann, 'holly wood'.

Fenagh (several), Fíonacha, 'woody (places)'.
There are no trees now at Fenagh in Leitrim, and other once densely wooded places of the name may also have lost their trees, usually by clearing.

Fenit (Kerry), An Fhianait, 'the wild place'.

Fenor (Wexford), Fionnúir, 'white field'.

Feohanagh (Limerick), An Fheothanach, 'the place of thistles'.

Ferbane (Offaly), An Féar Bán, 'the white grass'.

Fermanagh, Fear Manach, '(place of the) men of Monach'.
This is a tribal name, referring to the leader, Monach. The tribe had to flee from their native Leinster after murdering the son of its king. Some settled in the county of Down, others settled by Lough Erne, where they gave their name to the territory there (the present county).

Fermoy (Cork), Mainistir Fhear Maí, 'monastery of (the) men of (the) plain'.

Ferns (Wexford), Fearna, 'elder trees'.
As in some other names, the Irish plural has been rendered by an English 's'.

Ferrard (Louth), Fir Árda, 'men of (the) height'.
The 'height' is Slieve Bregh.

Ferrycarrig (Wexford), Glascharraig, 'grey rock'.
The first half of the English name relates to the former ferry across the mouth of the river Slaney here. The second half represents Irish *carraig*, 'rock', 'crag'. On top of the rock can be seen the keep of what must once have been a superb Anglo-Norman castle.

Fertagh (Kilkenny), Feartach, 'place of graves'.
According to some, the graves were those of sheep that had died of distemper here.

Fethard (several), Fiodh Árd, 'high wood'.
Fethard in Tipperary was once surrounded
by forests.

Fews (Armagh, Waterford), Feadha,
'woods'.
Once again, an English plural 's' has been
added, to represent the Irish plural (*feadha*
is the plural of *fiodh*). Compare **Ferns**.

Fiddown (Kilkenny), Fiodh Dúin, 'wood of
(the) fort'.

Fieries (Kerry), Na Foidhrí, 'the woods'.

Finaghy (Antrim), An Fionnachadh, 'the
white field'.

Finglas (Dublin), Fionnghlas, 'clear
stream'.
The name refers to a holy well here, the
'Fair Rill', once famous for its apparent
cure of eye diseases. Finglas became a
health resort in the 19th century.

Finn, Lough (Donegal), Loch Finne, 'clear
lake'.
Legend derives the name from a woman
called Finna who drowned in the lake in a
vain attempt to rescue her wounded
brother Fergoman.

Finnea (Westmeath), Fiodh an Átha, 'wood
of the ford'.
The ford would have been over the river
Inny here, surrounded by trees.

Finnihy River (Kerry), An Fhinnithe, 'the
clear stream'.

Fintona (Tyrone), Fionntamhnach, 'fair
arable field'.

Fintown (Donegal), Baile na Finne, 'town of
the (river) Finn'.

Fintragh Bay (Donegal), Bá Fionntrá, 'bay
of the white strand'.

Finvoy (Antrim), An Fhionnbhoith, 'the
white cottage'.
An alternative spelling of the Irish name is
Fionnmhagh, which would mean 'fair
plain'.

Fir Mount (Longford), Cnoc na Giuise, 'hill
of the firs'.

Fivemiletown (Tyrone), Baile na Lorgan,
'town of the shank'.
The English name is said to describe the
location of the village approximately five
miles from Clabby, Clogher and Colebrooke. The lands here where it was
founded in the early 17th century were

originally known as 'Ballynacoole', 'townland of the recess'.

Flannery Bridge (Galway).
This bridge across the Kilkerrin Estuary
was built, to replace an older bridge, in the
late 19th century, and was named after the
Reverend T. J. Flannery, parish priest of
Carna, to mark his friendship with the chief
secretary for Ireland (later prime minister),
Lord Balfour.

Flesk (Kerry), An Fhleisc, 'the rod'.
The sense of this river name is not clear.

Florence Court (Fermanagh), Mullach na
Seangán, 'height of the ants'.
The English name of this Georgian mansion, seat of the earls of Enniskillen, comes
from that of its original owner, Lord
Mount Florence, created Earl of Enniskillen in 1784. An alternative Irish name
for the location is *Gort na Caillighe*, 'field
of the hag'.

Foil (several), Faill, 'cliff'.

Fontstown (Kildare), Baile Fant, 'Fant's
town'.
This is presumably based on an Anglo-
Norman family name.

Fore (Westmeath), Baile Fhobhair, 'townland of (the) spring'.
The 'spring' is the water that rises in the
valley here by the old church of St Fechin.

Forlorn Point (Wexford), Crois Fearnóg,
'elder tree cross'.
The English name appears to be a corruption of the Irish, with *n* becoming *l*.

Formil (Meath), Formaoil, 'round hill'.

Forth (Carlow, Wexford), Fotharta, 'people
of Fothart'.
According to historical legend, Fothart was
the brother of Conn of the Hundred
Battles, ancestor of the kings of Ireland,
and he and some of his descendants settled
in the territory that is now the two counties
of Carlow and Wexford.

Four Knocks (Meath), Fuarchnoc, 'cold
hill'.
The English name, misleadingly suggesting 'four hills', is a corruption of the Irish.

Foxfield (Leitrim), Cnocán an Mhada Rua,
'little hill of the fox'.
Irish *madadh ruadh* literally means 'red
dog'.

Foxhall (Mayo), Poll na tSionnaigh, 'hole of the fox'.
Irish *poll* seems to have been corrupted to English 'hall'.

Foyle (several), Faill, 'cliff'.
All the Foyles are rivers, with 'cliff' doubtless indicating their source. Lough Foyle is named after the river Foyle that flows into it, with the river itself formed at Lifford by the confluence of the Finn and the Mourne.

Foynes (Limerick), Faing, 'western boundary'.
It is not clear which boundary is meant, although Foynes is on the Shannon estuary which itself forms the boundary between Limerick and Clare.

Freaghill (several), Fraoch-Oileán, 'heathy island'.

Many small islands off the west coast have this name.

Freshford (Kilkenny), Achadh Úr, 'fresh field'.
This name implies 'clean land'. The English name is a mistranslation of the Irish, with *achadh*, 'field', taken to be *áth*, 'ford'.

Frosses (Donegal), Na Frosa, 'the showers'.
Frosses is in south-west Donegal, close to Donegal Bay, where it has no hills to protect it from driving rain from the direction of the Atlantic.

Funcheon (Cork), An Fhoinnsean, 'the (river of) ash trees'.

Furness (Kildare), Fornocht, 'bare hill'.

Fussough (Tipperary), Fosach, 'sheltered (place)'.

G

Galbally (Limerick), An Gallbhaile, 'the foreigner's townland'.
The 'foreigner' here is English, and probably the Anglo-Norman Fitzgeralds, who settled here early. The name exists elsewhere, for example in Tyrone and Wexford.

Gallen (Offaly), Mainistir Ghailline, 'monastery of Gallen'.
Gallen Priory here is said to derive its name from Gallen of the Britons (Galline na mBretan), a chief whose own name has been translated as 'Dishonoured Spear'. The monastery itself, of which nothing remains above ground, was founded in the 5th century here by St Canoc.

Gallow (Meath), Galamh, 'place of standing stones'.

Galtee Mountains (Tipperary/Cork), Na Gaibhlte, 'the mountains of (the) woods'.

Galway (Galway), Gaillimh, 'stony (river)'.
The town, like the river at whose mouth it stands, takes its name from the stony or rocky locality in which it is set. The county of Galway is named after the town.

Garinish (Cork), Garinis, 'near island'.
Garinish is in Bantry Bay, south-west of Glengarriff, and is closer to the shore than Sheelane Island.

Garran (several), Garrán, 'grove'.

Garranard (Mayo), Garrán Ard, 'high grove'.

Garranekinnefeake (Cork), Garrán Chinféic, 'Kinnefeake's grove'.
The family who gave their name to this place came from Glamorganshire.

Garranes (Cork), Na Garraín, 'the groves'.

Garretstown Strand (Cork), Trá Ghearóid, 'Garrett's strand'.

Garrison (Fermanagh), An Garastún, 'the garrison'.
The garrison here was a former outpost of the fort at Belleek.

Garry (Antrim), Garraí, 'garden'.

Garry Castle (Offaly), Garraí an Chaisleáin, 'garden of the castle'.
The name refers to the Mac Coghlan castle,

near Banagher, now in ruins.

Garryduff (several), Garraí Dubh, 'black garden'.

Garrymore (several), Garraí Mór, 'big garden'.

Garryspillane (Limerick), Garraí Uí Spealáin, 'garden of the descendants of Spealán'.

Garryvoe (Cork), Garraí Bhoithe, 'garden of the cottage'.

Gartan (Donegal), Gartán, 'little garden'.

Garvagh (several), Garbhachadh, 'rough field'.

Garvaghy (Tyrone), Garbhachadh, 'rough field'.
This is the same name as **Garvagh**.

Garvarry (Fermanagh), Garbhaire, 'rough land'.

Gearha (Kerry), Gaortha, 'wooded valley'.

Geashill (Offaly), Géisill, 'place of swans'.
Presumably the swans were on a lake by the castle here, or on the upper reaches of the Tullamore River.

Geneva (Waterford).
This former village, also known as New Geneva, takes its name from Geneva in Switzerland. An attempt was made at the end of the 18th century to found a settlement here for craftsmen and academics from Geneva. The enterprise failed, however, and the colony buildings were turned into a military barracks.

Giant's Causeway, The (Antrim), Clochán an Aifir, 'stepping stones of the giant'.
The alternative Irish name for this famous landmark is *Clochán na bhFórmorach*, 'stepping stones of the Fomorians'. This refers to the legendary giant sea rovers whose causeway it was said to be. Another legend tells how Finn Mac Cool (Finn mac Cumaill), the great hero of Irish popular tradition, built a bridge across to Scotland from here to vanquish a mighty rival.

Gibbing's Green (Cork), An Tuar Mór, 'the big bleaching green'.

Gibbstown (Meath), Baile Ghib, 'Gibb's town'.

Gilford (Down), Áth Mhic Ghiolla, 'ford of the sons of Gilla'.

Gill, Lough (Leitrim/Sligo), Loch Gile, 'lake of brightness'.

Gilnahirk (Down), Cill Ó nDearca, 'church of the descendants of Dearc'.
This is a doubtful interpretation, as is another sometimes found — '(hillbrow of the) gillie of the horn'.

Girley (Meath), Greillighe, 'mire', 'trampled land'.

Glack (Donegal), Glaic, 'hollow'.

Glanbehy Bridge (Kerry), Droichead Ghleann Beithe, 'bridge of (the) birch glen'.

Glandore (Cork), Cuan Dor, 'Dor's harbour'.

Glanerdalliv (Kerry), Gleann Ardtalaimh, 'glen of (the) high land'.

Glanleam (Kerry), Gleann Léime, 'glen of (the) leap'.
Glanleam is on Valentia Island, below the highest hill of Jeokaun Mount.

Glanmire (Cork), Gleann Maghair, 'Maghar's glen'.

Glantane (several), An Gleanntán, 'the little glen'.

Glanworth (Cork), Gleannúir, 'watery glen'.
Glanworth is on the river Funshion.

Glasdrummond (Down), An Ghlasdromainn, 'the green ridge'.

Glashaboy (Cork), An Ghlaise Bhuidhe, 'the yellow stream'.
The stream is also known as Glamire, and this village is on it.

Glasheen (several), Glaisín, 'little stream'.

Glaslough (Monaghan), Glasloch, 'grey lake'.
Glaslough is on the lough of the same name. The place is sometimes spelt Glasslough.

Glasnevin (Dublin), Glas Naíon, 'stream of the infants'.
The origin of this name is not clear, if it does indeed derive from *naoidhe*, 'infant' (genitive plural *naoidhin*). Perhaps the second word is a personal name.

Glassan (Westmeath), Glasán, 'little stream'.

Glasthule (Dublin), Glas Tuathail, 'Tuathal's stream'.

Glen (several), An Glean, 'the valley'.

Glenade (Leitrim), Gleann Éada, 'Éada's glen'.

Glenagarey (Dublin), Gleann na gCaorach, 'glen of the sheep'.

Glenamaddy (Galway), Gleann na Madadh, 'glen of the curs'.

Glenamoy (Mayo), Gleann an Muaidhe, 'glen of the (river) Moy'.

Glenariff (Antrim), Gleann Aireamh, 'glen of (the) arable land'.

Glenarm (Antrim), Gleann Arma, 'glen of (the) army'.
The name perhaps refers to some battle or military gathering here.

Glenavuddig (Cork), Gleann an Bhodaigh, 'glen of the churls'.
The 'churls' would have been labourers here.

Glenavy (Antrim), Lann Abhaigh, 'church of (the) dwarf'.
The legend runs that when St Patrick had built a church here, he left it in the charge of his disciple Daniel, who was nicknamed 'Dwarf' for his small stature. The name is thus not a 'glen' name, like those above and below.

Glen Ballyemon (Antrim), Gleann Bhaile Éamainn, 'glen of Éamann's homestead'.

Glenbane (Tipperary), Gleann Bán, 'white glen'.

Glenbeigh (Kerry), Gleann Beithe, 'valley of (the river) Beigh'.

Glenbrook (Cork), Leaca Rua, 'red slope'.
The English name appears to be a corruption of the Irish.

Glencam (Cork), An Ghleann Cam, 'the winding glen'.

Glencar (Kerry), Gleann Chárthaigh, 'Carthac's glen'.
Compare **Glencar Lough** (Leitrim/Sligo).

Glencar Lough (Leitrim/Sligo), Loch an Chairthe, 'lake of the standing stone'.

Glencloy (Antrim), Gleann Claidhe, 'glen of (the) fences'.
Irish *claidhe* often implies a stone fence.

Glencolumbkille (Donegal), Gleann Cholm Cille, 'St Columba's valley'.
There is a strong association here with St Columba, although all ecclesiastical remains here are later than the 6th century.

Glencorrib (Mayo), Gleann Coirb, 'glen of (the river) Corrib'.

Glencree (Wicklow), Gleann Críothaigh, 'quaking glen'.
The name implies a quagmire.

Glencullen (Dublin), Gleann Cuileann, 'glen of holly'.

Glendalough (Wicklow), Gleann Dá Loch, 'valley of (the) two lakes'.
This famous beauty spot and ancient monastic site has two lakes called Upper Lake and Lower Lake. The Glendalough in Galway has the same Irish name, but there it means 'valley of the lakes' (*da* is 'of the', not 'two').

Glendine (several), Gleann Doimhin, 'deep glen'.

Glendowan (Donegal), Gleann Domhain, 'deep glen'.
This mountain range was presumably named after one of its own 'deep glens'.

Glenduff (Limerick), Gleann Dubh, 'black glen'.

Glendun (Antrim), Gleann Duinne, 'valley of (the river) Dunn'.

Glenealy (Wicklow), Gleann Fhaidle.
It is difficult to give a meaningful interpretation of this name.

Gleneask (Sligo), Gleann Iasc, 'glen of (the) fish'.

Gleneely (Donegal), Gleann Daoile, 'Daol's glen'.

Glenfarne (Leitrim), Gleann Fearna, 'glen of elder trees'.

Glengarriff (Cork), An Gleann Garbh, 'the rugged valley'.
The glen here is a noticeably craggy one.

Glengavlen (Cavan), Gleann Ghaibhle, 'glen of (the) fork'.
Glengavlen is near the source of the Shannon between the mountains of Slieve Anierin and Cuilcagh.

Glengormley (Antrim), Gleann Ghormlaithe, 'Gormley's glen'.

Gleninagh (Clare), Gleann Eidhneach, 'glen of (the) ivy'.

Glenisland (Mayo), Gleann Aoláin, 'Aolán's glen'.
The English name has been influenced by the word 'island'.

Glenkeen (Mayo), Gleann Caoin, 'pleasant glen'.

Glenlossera (Mayo), Gleann Lasrach, 'Lasrach's glen'.

Glenmacnass (Wicklow), Gleann Log an Easa, 'glen of (the) hollow of the waterfall'.

Glenmalure (Wicklow), Gleann Maolúra, 'Maolúra's glen'.

Glenmore (several), An Gleann Mór, 'the big valley'.

Glennaghevlagh (Galway), Gleann na nGeimhleach, 'glen of the prisoners'.
This name appears to refer to some historic incident.

Glennanean (Mayo), Gleann na nÉan, 'glen of the birds'.

Glenoe (Antrim), Gleann Eo, 'glen of (the) yew'.

Glen of the Downs (Wicklow), Gleann Dá Ghura, 'glen of (the) two ridges'.
The English name appears to be a rendering of another Irish name, *Gleann na nDún*, 'glen of the forts'.

Glenosheen (Limerick), Gleann Oisín, 'Oisín's glen'.
Oisín, whose name is usually anglicised as Ossian, was the legendary son of Finn Mac Coole (Finn mac Cumaill).

Glenquin (Limerick), Gleann Chuinn, 'glen of (the) hollow'.
The interpretation assumes the second word of the Irish name to represent *cúm*.

Glenroe (Limerick), An Gleann Rua, 'the red-coloured glen'.

Glenshane (Derry), Gleann Seáin, 'Seán's glen'.

Glenshesk (Antrim), Gleann Seirc, 'glen of (the) sedges'.

Glenstal (Limerick), Gleann Státhail, 'Státhal's glen'.

Glentane (Galway), Gleanntán, 'little glen'.

Glentavraun (Mayo), Gleann tSamhráin, 'Samhrán's glen'.

Glenties (Donegal), Na Gleannta, 'the glens'.
Glenties stands at the head of two picturesque glens, and the rivers Owenea and Stracashel meet here. Once again, the Irish plural is represented by an English 's'.

Glenveagh (Donegal), Gleann Bheatha, 'glen of (the) birches'.

Glenwhirry (Antrim), Gleann an Choire,

'glen of the whirlpool'.

The whirlpool must be in the Glenwhirry River itself, or in one of its tributaries (perhaps at a point where the two meet).

Glin (Limerick), An Gleann, 'the valley'.

Glin is on the estuary of the Shannon, but takes its name from the valley to the south of it (Glencorby).

Glynn (Antrim, Carlow). An Gleann, 'the glen'.

Gobbins, The (Antrim), Na Gobáin, 'the points of land'.

The Gobbins are a run of basaltic cliffs on Island Magee.

Gola (several), Gola, 'river forks'.

The name represents a confluence, or the locality there, from Irish *gabhal*, plural *gaibhle*.

Golden (Tipperary), An Gabhailín, 'the little fork'.

The 'little fork' is in the river Suir here, where the waters divide for a short distance.

Golden Vale (Tipperary), Machaire Méith na Mumhan, 'rich plain of Munster'.

This is an unusual name, since it is meaningful on two levels. First, it denotes the fertile valley here north of the Galtee Mountains, through which flow the river Suir and other rivers. (It has an alternative name of Golden Vein in this sense.) Second, it is this same plain, or part of it, round the village of Golden.

Goleen (several), An Góilín, 'the little inlet'.

Goresbridge (Kilkenny), An Droichead Nua, 'the new bridge'.

The English name comes from the family name of the first landowner here, Colonel John Gore. The bridge is over the river Barrow.

Gorey (Wexford), Guaire, 'sandbank'.

The name could also mean 'wooded' (*guaireach*).

Gormanston (Meath), Baile Mhic Gormáin, 'homestead of the sons of Gormán'.

Gort (Galway), An Gort, 'the field'.

Gortaclare (Tyrone), Gort an Chláir, 'field of the plain'.

Gortahill, (Cavan), Gort an Choill, 'field of the wood'.

Gortahork (Donegal), Gort an Choirce, 'field of the oats'.

Gortavoy (Tyrone), Gort an Mhaí, 'field of the plain'.

Gorteen (several), Goirtín, 'little field'.

Gorteeny (Galway), Goirtíní, 'little fields'.

Gortgranagh (Tyrone), Gort Greanach, 'sandy field'.

This name could also mean 'grain field', from *gráinne*.

Gortin (several), An Goirtín, 'the little field'.

This is the same name as Gorteen.

Gortmore (several), Gort Mór, 'big field'.

Gortnagarn (Tyrone), Gort na gCarn, 'field of the cairns'.

Gortnaskeagh (Leitrim), Gort na Sceach, 'field of the whitethorns'.

Gortreagh (Tyrone), An Gort Riabhach, 'the striped field'.

Gortroe (Cork), Gort an Rú, 'field of the rue'.

This is the interpretation of the Irish as it stands, but it may well originally have meant simply 'red field' (*gort ruadh*).

Gougane Barra (Cork), Guagán Barra, 'Finnbarr's rocky cave'.

The name is that of a mountain lake, and according to legend, St Finnbarr founded a monastery here in the 7th century. St Finnbarr's Well is at the entrance to the causeway that leads to an island in the middle of the lake.

Goul (several), An Gabhal, 'the fork'.

Gouldavoher (Limerick), Gabhal Dá Bhóthar, 'fork of the two roads'.

Gouldavoher is still at a point where two minor roads fork north and south to the south-west of Limerick.

Goulnacappy (Kerry), Gabhal na Ceapaighe, 'fork of the plot of land'.

Gowlan (several), Gabhlán, 'little fork'.

Gowran (Kilkenny), Gabhrán, 'place of goats'.

Irish *gabhar* could also mean 'horse', and this may be the sense here.

Gracehill (Antrim), Baile Uí Chinnéide, 'homestead of the descendants of Kennedy'.

The English name derives from the Moravian settlement established here in the mid-18th century, and was thus chosen for its religious associations.

Graigue (several), An Ghráig, 'the village'. This name is found almost exclusively in the Republic.

Graiguenamanagh (Kilkenny), Gráig na Manach, 'village of the monks'.
The village is well known for its Cistercian monastery founded in the early 13th century and known as Duiske Abbey (from the little Dubh Uisge or 'black water' stream here).

Grallagh (several), An Ghreallach, 'the mire'.

Granabeg (Wicklow), Greanach Bheag, 'little gravelly place'.

Granagh (Limerick), Greanach, 'gravelly place'.

Grange (several), An Ghráinseach, 'the grange'.

Grangegeeth (Meath), Gráinseach na Gaoithe, 'grange of the wind'.

Grangemockler (Tipperary), Gráinseach Mhóicléir, 'Mockler's grange'.

Gransha (Down), An Ghráinseach, 'the grange'.
This is the same name as Grange, denoting a granary.

Greagh (Monaghan), Gréach, 'level moorland'.

Great Island (Cork), An tOileán Mór, 'the big island'.
Great Island is the island on which Cóbh stands.

Greenane (several), An Grianán, 'the summer dwelling place'.
The literal sense of the name is 'sunny spot', from *grian*, 'sun'. In some cases the name had a metaphorical sense 'elevated place', 'important place', so can be rendered as 'royal seat' where appropriate.

Greencastle (Antrim), Cloch Mhic Coisteala, 'castle of the sons of Costello'.
There are other Greencastles in the country, all with different Irish names, such as Greencastle, Donegal (*An Caisleán Nu*, 'the new castle') and Greencastle, Derry (*Teampull Maol*, 'bare church').

Greengates (Caval), Na Geataí Uaine, 'the green gates'.

Greenoge (several), Grianóg, 'sunny little spot'.

Grevine (Kilkenny), Gairbhín, 'rough place'.

Greyabbey (Down), An Mhainistir Liath, 'the grey monastery'.
The monastery is a small Cistercian abbey here, founded at the end of the 12th century.

Greystones (Wicklow), Na Chlocha Liatha, 'the grey stones'.

Grianan of Aileach (Donegal), Grianán Ailigh, 'Aileach's summer residence'.

Groomsport (Down), Port an Ghiolla Ghruama, 'port of the gloomy servant'.
The English name is a corruption of the Irish, which itself appears to relate to some personal name.

Guitane, Lough (Kerry), Loch Goiteán, 'lake of (the) little boat'.

Gulladuff (Derry), An Ghuala Dhubh, 'the black hill-shoulder'.

Gurranebraher (Cork), Garrán na mBráthar, 'grove of the friars'.

Gurteen (several), Goirtín, 'little arable field'.

Gurtymadden (Galway), Gort Uí Mhadáin, 'field of the descendants of Madden'.

Gweebarra (Donegal), Gaoth Barra, 'Barra's tide-inlet'.
Gweebarra Bridge here spans the Gweebarra River where it flows into Gweebarra Bay. The 'tide-inlet' is that of this river, whose valley is one of the longest in Donegal.

Gweedore (Donegal), Gaoth Dobhair, 'water inlet'.

Gyleen (Cork), An Gaibhlín, 'the little inlet'.

H

Hacketstown (Carlow), Baile Haicéid, 'Hacket's town'.

The name probably comes from that of an Anglo-Norman settler here, possibly Haket de Ridelesford, named in a 13th-century deed, or another member of his family. (This particular man gave his name to Ballyhacket, 8 miles (13km) west of Hacketstown.)

Hamiltonsbawn (Armagh), Bábhún Hamaltún, 'Hamilton's enclosure'.

The 'bawn' or enclosure (fortification), was built here by John Hamilton in 1619 but was almost entirely destroyed in the Rebellion of 1641.

Harryville (Antrim), Baile Éinrí, 'Henry's homestead'.

The English name also occurs as Henryville, and must derive from a settler or landowner here. An earlier Irish name was *An Baile Caol*, 'the narrow townland'.

Hazelwood (Sligo), An tEanach, 'the marsh'.

The English name may translate an earlier Irish name (which could have been *Collchoill*).

Headford (Galway), Áth Cinn, 'ford of the peak'.

This literal interpretation does not make sense for such a low-lying place. Perhaps 'Head' is a personal name, translated into Irish from the English, or even the other way round (i.e. from Ceann).

Heathfield (Mayo), Achadh Fraoigh, 'field of heather'.

Helen's Bay (Down), Cuan Héilin, 'Helen's bay'.

The Helen of the name is Helen Sheridan, Countess of Dufferin, wife of the fourth baron Dufferin and Clandeboye, whose residence was at Clandeboye here in the first half of the 19th century. Helen's Tower here is also named after her.

Hen's Castle (Galway), Caisleán na Circe, 'castle of the hen'.

This is the alternative name of **Castle Kirke** (*which see*).

Herbertstown (Limerick), Baile Hiobaird, 'Herbert's townland'.

Hill of Down (Meath), Cnoc an Dúin, 'hill of the fort'.

The English name has been only half translated from the Irish.

Hillsborough (Down), Cromghlinn, 'winding valley'.

The English name derives from that of Sir Moyses Hill, the army officer who obtained lands here in the early 17th century. An alternative Irish name is *Buirgéis Hill*, 'Hill's borough'.

Hollywood (Wicklow), Cillín Chaoimhín, 'St Kevin's little church'.

The English name may have originated as 'holy wood', since there are a number of sites associated with St Kevin here, including St Kevin's Bed (i.e. his hermitage) and formerly St Kevin's Chair, Cave and Well. A 13th-century document, moreover, gives the name in Latin as *Sanctus Boscus*, 'holy wood'.

Holycross (Limerick), Baile na gCailleach, 'town of the nuns'.

Holycross (Tipperary), Mainistir na Croiche, 'monastery of the cross'.

This is Holy Cross Abbey, founded in the 12th century and named after a relic of the True Cross said to have been preserved here.

Holywood (Down), Árd Mhic Nasca, 'height of Nasca's sons'.

The English name means what it says, and like Hollywood in Wicklow, was named *Sanctus Boscus* by the Normans. The reference is probably to the 7th-century church of St Laisrén here. The original Irish name here was 'Ballyderry' ('townland of the oak wood').

Hook Head (Wexford), Rinn Dubháin, 'St Dubhán's headland'.

The English name appears to have originated through a 'translation' of the saint's name as if it was the ordinary word *dubhán*, 'hook'. This happens to be a suitable name for a headland, since it can denote the con-

64

tour of the coastline.

Horn Head (Donegal), Corrán Binne, 'crescent of (the) peak'.

This descriptive name is apt in either English or Irish for this headland.

Horse and Jockey (Tipperary), An Marcach, 'the jockey'.

This is an inn name, with the Irish a shortened version of the English. An earlier Irish name was *Baile na Pairce*, 'townland of the pasture'.

Horseleap (Westmeath), Baile Átha an Urchair, 'homestead of (the) ford of the throw'.

The English name derives from a modern legend regarding a leap on his horse made here by Hugh de Lacy over the moat of the now vanished Ardnurcher Castle when being pursued by his enemies. The castle name appears to be a corruption of the Irish name of the village, with *áth*, 'ford', becoming *ard*, 'height'. Certainly 'ford' suits the location here much better. Irish *urchar* means 'cast', 'throw', 'shot', and perhaps relates to some historic event here, as the English name may. On the other hand the English name, if it is not itself a corruption, could be simply descriptive for a point where the stream here could be ridden across on horseback.

Hospital (Limerick), An tOspidéal, 'the hospital'.

The name refers to the house of the Knights Hospitallers, founded here in the early 13th century. Kenmare Abbey, now ruined, was built on the site of the house.

Howth (Dublin), Binn Éadair, 'Éadar's peak'.

This is a Viking name, representing Old Norse *hofuth*, 'headland'. Éadar is the name of a legendary hero associated with it.

Humewood (Wicklow), Coill an Bhuitléaraigh, 'Butler's wood'.

A deed of 10/11 March 1708 granted Butlerswood and its lands to William Hume of Hacketstown, and the name was changed accordingly in English some time in the middle of the 18th century. The Irish name, which dates from the 13th century, relates to the Anglo-Norman owner of the land here, Theobald Walter (i.e. the latter name rendered as 'Butler').

Hyne, Lough (Cork), Loch Oighin, 'lake of (the) whirlpool'.

The 'H' of the name is not pronounced locally.

I

Idrone (Carlow), Uí Dróna, '(island of the) descendants of Dróna'.

According to historical legend, Dróna was fourth in descent from Cahirmore (Cathaír Már), who is said to have reigned over Leinster in the 1st century.

Illaunmore (Tipperary), An tOileán Mór, 'the big island'.

Illauntannig (Kerry), Oileán tSeanaigh, 'St Seanach's island'.

Imaal, Glen of (Wicklow), Uí Máil, '(glen of the) descendants of Mal'.

Mal was said to have been the brother of Cahirmore (see **Idrone**).

Inagh (Clare), Eidhneach, 'place of ivy'.

Inagh, Lough (Galway), Loch Eidhneach, 'ivy lake'.

Inch (several), An Inis, 'the island'.

This name could also mean 'riverside meadow', or simply indicate land that was like an 'island' in bogland. In Donegal, Inch was formerly an island in Lough Swilly, but is now joined to the mainland as a result of drainage works here. The Irish names of some of the places called Inch also include the personal name of an individual associated with it, so that in Wexford, for example, Inch is *Inis Mocholmóg*, 'St Mo-Cholmóg's riverside meadow'.

Inchagoill (Galway), Inis an Ghoill, 'island of the foreigner'.

The full name of this island in Lough Corrib is *Inis an Ghoill Cráibhthigh*, 'island of the devout foreigner'. This is said to have been Lugnat (Lugnaed), the pilot of St Patrick, who spent his life in prayer on the shore of Lough Mask, just north of here.

Inchbofin (Westmeath), Inis Bó Finne, 'island of (the) white cow'.

Inch Castle (Kildare), Caisleán na hInse, 'castle of the riverside meadow'.

Inch Castle, now ruined, is 3 miles (4.8km) east of Athy by a small river.

Inchicore (Dublin), Inse Chór, 'Guaire's riverside meadow'.

Inchicore is in Dublin city where Islandbridge is today, with Inchicore Road

here to preserve the name.

Inchicronan, Lake (Clare), Loch Inse Chrónáin, 'lake of (the) island of St Crónán'.

Inisclothran (Westmeath), Inis Clothrann, 'Clothra's island'.

Inishannon (Cork), Inis Eonáin, 'Eonán's riverside land'.

Inishannon is on the river Bandon.

Inishargy (Down), Inis Cairge, 'island of the rock'.

The rising land where the church stands here was at one time surrounded by marshes.

Inishbeg (several), Inis Bheag, 'little island'.

Most places of the name are genuine islands, either off the coast or in lakes or rivers.

Inishbofin (Donegal, Galway), Inis Bó Finne, 'island of (the) white cow'.

This is the same name as Inchbofin (Westmeath). The two islands mentioned here are not the only ones of the name. Inevitably, legends have arisen concerning enchanted white cows that appear out of the water as a symbol of regeneration or fertility. The many islands of Ireland have always been the source of legend and mysticism.

Inishcarra (Cork), Inis Cara, 'island of (the) leg'.

The reference seems to be to a bend of the river Lee here, opposite its confluence with the Bride.

Inishcealtra (Clare), Inis Cealtrach, 'island of churches'.

Inishcealtra is also known as Holy Island and Island of the Churches, for its many monastic remains and ruined churches.

Inisheer (Galway), Inis Oírr, 'eastern island'.

Inisheer is the farthest east of the three Aran Islands.

Inishfree (Donegal), Inis Fraoigh, 'island of heather'.

Inishfree is in Inishfree Bay, south-west of Gweedore Bay. Yeats's 'Lake Isle of Inisfree', which has the same meaning, is in Lough Gill, in Sligo.

Inishglora (Mayo), Inis Gluaire, 'island of brightness'.

This is a small rocky island off the west coast of the Mullet peninsula.

Inishkeen (Monaghan), Inis Caoin, 'pleasant riverside meadow'.

This village is on low-lying land by the river Fane, west of Dundalk.

Inishkeeragh (several), Inis Caorach, 'island of sheep'.

Islands of this name would have been used as pasturelands for sheep in the summer.

Inishlounaght (Tipperary), Inis Leamhnachta, 'riverside meadow of new milk'.

The name indicates good grazing land.

Inishmaan (Galway, Mayo), Inis Meáin, 'middle island'.

In Galway, Inishmaan is the middle of the three Aran Islands. In Mayo, the island is in Lough Mask, where it is the largest, surrounded by smaller islands.

Inishmacsaint (Fermanagh), Inis Muighe Samh, 'island of (the) plain of sorrel'.

The name has been corrupted to suggest a personal or tribal name.

Inishmore (several), Inis Mhór, 'big island'.

This is the largest of the Aran Islands, in Galway, where its Irish name is Árainn Mhór, 'big Aran'. There is another well known Inishmore at the northern end of Upper Lough Erne, in Fermanagh.

Inishmurray (Sligo), Inish Muirígh, 'Muiríoch's island'.

Inishowen, (Donegal), Inis Eoghain, 'Eoghan's island'.

In early historical legend, Eoghan (Eogan, often anglicised as Owen), was the son of Niall of the Nine Hostages.

Inishtioge (Kilkenny), Inis Tiog, 'Teoc's riverside meadow'.

Inishtioge is on low-lying pastureland by the river Nore.

Inishtooskert (Kerry), Inis Tuaisceart, 'northern island'.

Inishtooskert is to the north of Great Blasket Island.

Inishturk (Mayo), Inis Toirc, 'island of boars'.

Inis Patrick (Dublin), Inis Phádraig, 'St Patrick's island'.

This is one of the rock islands that gave their name to Skerries.

Innisfallen (Kerry), Inis Faithleann, 'Faithlenn's island'.

This is a small wooded island on Lough Leane.

Inver (Donegal), Inbhear, 'estuary'.

Inver is located where the Eany River enters Inver Bay, an inlet of the larger Donegal Bay.

Ireland, Éire, 'land of Éire'.

The name of Ireland is not quite the same as that of England or Scotland, which are both named directly after their people ('land of the Angles', 'land of the Scots'). The Irish people got their name from the country's name, not the other way round. Irish Éire itself probably means 'western', related to modern Irish iarthar, 'west'.

Ireland's Eye (Dublin), Inis Mac Neasáin, 'island of the sons of Neasán'.

The current Irish name refers to a prince of the royal family of Leinster. An earlier Irish name was Inis Ereann, 'Eria's island', this being the name of a woman who is said to have built a church here in the 7th century. However, her name was taken to be the genitive of Éire (Ireland), and 'Eye' represents Old Norse ey, 'island'. Thus the present English name of this island evolved, suggesting, as it turned out, a rather poetic approach to the eastern 'face' of Ireland.

Irvinestown (Fermanagh), Baile an Irbhinigh, 'Irvine's town'.

The English name derives from the Irvine family of Castle Irvine (now Necarne Castle). An earlier English name for the settlement was Lowtherstown.

Isertkelly (Galway), Díseart Cheallaigh, 'Kelly's hermitage'.

The Irish name has lost its initial 'D' in the English version.

Islandmagee (Antrim), Oileán Mhic Aodha, 'island of the sons of Hugh'.

The 'island' is actually a low peninsula extending north from Whitehead and ending by Larne. The Irish name is interpreted literally, although the place is said by some to have belonged at one time to the Scottish family Magee.

Island Mahee (Down), Inis Mochaoi, 'St Mochaoi's island'.

The island is in Strangford Lough, and on it are ruins of an early monastery said to have been founded by St Mochaoi in the 5th century.

Iverk (Kilkenny), Uibh Eirc, '(place of the) descendants of Erc'.

Iveruss (Limerick), Uibh Rosa, '(place of the) descendants of Rosa'.

J

Jamestown (Leitrim), Baile Shéamais, 'James's town'.
The name is that of James I, who gave the village a charter of incorporation in 1621.

Jamestown (Laois), Baile Thaidhg Dhuibh, 'Black Tadhg's town'.
There are other places of this name, all referring to a James (or perhaps an Irishman named Séamus).

Jenkinstown (Kilkenny), Corclach, 'pointed stone'.
The Irish name of Jenkinstown in Louth is the same as the English, *Baile Sheinicín*. Jenkin or Jenkins is the family name of the landowner or settler at these places.

Jerpoint Abbey (Kilkenny), Cnoc Sheireapúin, 'Jerpoint hill'.
The name is that of the Cistercian abbey founded here in the late 12th century with what appears to be a French or Norman name.

Jigginstown (Kildare), Baile Shigín, 'Jiggin's homestead'.
This is not a village but a mansion, now ruined, built in the first half of the 17th century for entertaining Charles I. Jiggin or Jiggins is a family name.

Johnstown (several).
There are a number of places so called, named after an English person called John or an Irishman called Eoin or Seaan (and in some cases with the English place-names translated from an Irish name such as 'Ballyowen' or 'Ballyshan'). In certain instances the John is a church dedication (St John's church). The Irish forms of this name vary, but are often *Baile Eoin* or *Baile Sheáin*. Only after careful local research is it often possible to establish who the particular John or Seán was. The Johnstown west of Arklow in Wicklow, for example, is probably named after a man called John English who held the lease of Killahurler church here in the 15th century.

Jonesborough (Armagh), Baile an Chláir, 'town of the plain'.

Jordan's Castle (Down), Caisleán Shiurdán, 'Jordan's castle'.

Joyce's Country (Galway), Dúiche Sheoigheach, 'Joyce's district'.
The Joyces came to Galway from Wales in the 13th century, and the descendants of the original family group still live here. The first word of the Irish name is *dúthaigh*, 'native land', 'country'.

K

Kanturk (Cork), Ceann Toirc, 'head of the boar'.

The name seems to refer to the outline of a hill near here, resembling a boar's head.

Katesbridge (Down), Droichead Cháit, 'Kate's bridge'.

This is apparently the woman's name Kate rather than a family name. Perhaps the bridge was named after her by her husband or father.

Keadeen (Wicklow), Céidín, 'little plateau'.

The name is a diminutive of *céide*, 'course', 'flat-topped hill', belying the fact that Keadeen is actually a mountain over 2,000 ft (600m) high. Compare **Keadue**.

Keadew (Donegal), An Céide, 'the green'.

This is the Irish word whose diminutive gave the name of Keadeen.

Keadue (Roscommon), Céideadh, 'flat-topped hill'.

The name is exactly the same as that of Keadew, and the word (*céide*) also gave, in its diminutive from, the name of Keadeen, another mountain. See also **Keady**.

Keady (Armagh), An Céide, 'the flat-topped hill'.

The name of this river and town is exactly the same as that of Keadew and Keadue. Keady is on high ground near the Monaghan border. See also **Keadeen** (which although a diminutive is the name of a much higher place).

Kealkill (Cork), An Chaolchoill, 'the narrow wood'.

Keam Bridge (Cork), Droichead na Céime, 'bridge of the pass'.

The 'pass' is the narrow valley of the river Bride here, near Glenville.

Keel (Mayo), An Caol, 'the narrow place'.

Keel is on the west coast of Achill Island between Keel Lough and the sea.

Keeloges (several), Na Caológa, 'the narrow places'.

Keelty (several), Coillte, 'woods'.

Keem (Mayo), An Choim, 'the pass'.

Keem is on a narrow stretch of lowland on the west coast of Achill Island, below the mountain of Croaghaun.

Keenagh (Longford), Caonach, 'mossy place'.

Keenaght (Derry), Ciannachta, '(land of the) descendants of Cian'.

In legendary history, Cian (Cúldub, 'of the dark hair') was the son of Oilill Ólum (see **Connello**). His descendants were called *Ciannachta*, 'the people of Cian'.

Keimaneigh, Pass of (Cork), Céim an Fhia, 'pass of the deer'.

Kells (several), Na Cealla, 'the cells'.

The name, with its English plural 's', refers to monastic cells. The important places so called are Kells in Meath (also known as Ceanannas Mór, Cenlis Mór, or Kenlis, 'head fort'), from which ancient place came the famous Book of Kells, and Kells in Kilkenny, whose full name is Kenlis Osraighe (*Ceanannas Osrai*), 'head fort of Ossory'.

Kelly's Grove (Galway), Garrán Uí Cheallaigh, 'grove of the descendants of Kelly'.

Kenbane (Antrim), Cinn Bán, 'white headland'.

The chalk cliffs north-west of Ballycastle here are strikingly white. The name is also spelt Kinbane and appears on many maps in its English form of White Head.

Kenmare (Galway), Neidín, 'little nest'.

The English name represents Irish *ceannmara*, 'sea head', referring to the location of the town at the highest point reached by the tide on the estuary of the Kenmare River. Compare other names beginning Ken- and Kin-.

Kensalebeg (Waterford), Cionn tSáile Beag, 'small sea headland'.

The second part of the name is Irish *sáile*, 'sea-water'.

Kentstown (Meath), Baile Cheant, 'Kent's town'.

Kerry, Ciarraí, '(land of the) descendants of Ciar'.

In early legend, Ciar was the son of King Fergus and Queen Maev. His descendants are said to have taken territory to the west of Abbeyfeale, with their name passing to it.

Kerrykeel (Donegal), An Cheathrú Chaol, 'the narrow quarter'.

Kesh (several), An Cheis, 'wicker causeway'. The name is Irish *ceas* or *cis*, 'wicker basket', here used to make a crossing over a stream, small river, marsh or the like. In one or two cases, such as in Fermanagh, the name has passed to the stream itself.

Keshcarrigan (Leitrim), Ceis Charraigín, 'wicker causeway of the little rock'. The causeway is said to have been constructed out of brambles and clay, not far from a large limestone rock here.

Kilbaha (Clare, Kerry), Cill Bheathach, 'church of (the) birch wood'.

Kilbarrack (Dublin), Cill Bharróg, 'St Barróg's church'.

Kilbarron (Donegal), Cill Barráin, 'St Barrán's church'. The name of Kilbarron in Tipperary has the same origin.

Kilbarry (Cork, Waterford), Cill Barra, 'St Barr's church'.

Kilbeg (several), Cill Bheag, 'little church'. In many places this name almost certainly means 'little wood' (from *Coill Bheag*), all the more as most church names include the personal name of the saint to whom they are dedicated.

Kilbeggan (Westmeath), Cill Bheagáin, 'St Beagán's church'. The name of this village comes from the monastic church founded here, perhaps in the 7th century, by St Beagán (Beccanus). The site of this may be the mound at the Church of the Relic, half a mile south of Kilbeggan on the road to Tullamore.

Kilbehenny (several), Coill Bheithne, 'birch wood'.

Kilberry (Kildare, Meath), Cill Bhearaigh, 'St Bearach's church'.

Kilbolane (Cork), Cill Bholáin, 'St Bolán's church'.

Kilbonane (Kerry), Cill Bhonáin, 'St Bonán's church'.

Kilbreedy (Limerick), Cill Bhríde, 'St Brigid's church'.

Kilbride (several), Cill Bhríde, 'St Brigid's church'. In pagan mythology, Brigid (Brigit, Bríd), was the goddess of poetry and mother of the three craftsman gods, Brian, Liuchar and Uar. Later, Brigid was the name of several saints, the most famous being St Brigid of Kildare. The same place-name, with the same meaning, is found in Scotland.

Kilbrittain (Cork), Cill Briotáin, 'St Briotán's church'.

Kilbroney (Down), Cill Brónaí, 'St Brónach's church'. Brónach was a virgin martyr.

Kilcar (Donegal), Cill Charthaigh, 'St Carthach's church'. Carthach was a 6th-century bishop.

Kilcash (Tipperary), Cill Chais, 'Cass's church'.

Kilcavan (Wexford), Cill Caomhán, 'St Kevin's church'. St Kevin (Cáemgen, Caoimhín) was the abbot and founder of Glendalough.

Kilchreest (Galway), Cill Chríost, 'Christ's church'.

Kilclare (several), Coill an Cláir, 'wood of the plain'. There is no wood now at Kilclare in Offaly.

Kilclief (Down), Cill Cleuthe, 'church (made) of wattles'.

Kilclooney (Donegal), Cill Cluana, 'church of (the) meadow'. The grouped portal graves of the original church are still here.

Kilcock (Kildare) Cill Choca, 'St Coca's church'. St Coca is said to have been the aunt of St Patrick, and head of the monastery here at the end of the 5th century.

Kilcogy (Cavan), Cill Chóige, 'St Cóige's church'.

Kilcolgan (Galway), Cill Cholgáin, 'St Colga's church'.

Kilcolman (several), Cill Cholmáin, 'St Colmán's church'. There were very many saints of this popular name, which in origin is a diminutive of Columba.

Kilcommon (several), Cill Chuimín, 'St Comán's church'

Kilconnell (Galway), Cill Chonaill, 'St Conall's church'. St Conall is said to have been appointed bishop by St Patrick. The site of the original monastery here is still used as a cemetery.

Kilcoo (Down), Cill Chua, 'St Cua's church'.

Kilcoole (Wicklow), Cill Chomghaill, 'St Comgall's church'.

Kilcooley (Tipperary), Cill Chúile, 'church of (the) secluded place'.

Kilcormac (Offaly), Cill Chormaic, 'St Cormac's church'.

Kilcoman (Limerick), Cill Chomáin, 'St Comán's church'.

Kilcrea (Cork), Cill Chré, 'Créde's church'. There are a number of women of this name in Irish history and legend.

Kilcrohane (Cork), Cill Crócháin, 'St Cróchán's church'.

Kilcullen (Kildare), Cill Chuillinn, 'church of (the) slope'.

This is a disputed name, which could also mean 'St Cuilleann's church', 'church of the holly' or even 'church of the wood'. The interpretation 'slope' does suit the topography here, however.

Kilcummin (several), Cill Chuimín, 'St Cuimín's church'.

In Mayo, the original 7th-century church is still here at Kilcummin.

Kilcurry (Louth), Cill an Churraigh, 'church of (the) marsh'.

Kildalkey (Meath), Cill Dealga, 'Delga's church'.

This name appears to relate to Delga, the Firbolg chief who is said to have built the church at Dundalk.

Kildare (Kildare), Cill Dara, 'church of (the) oak'.

The name refers to the traditional location of St Brigid's cell here, where she is said to have established a nunnery (with two houses, one for men, one for women) in a pagan sacred grove.

Kildavin (Carlow), Cill Damháin, 'St Damhán's church'.

Kildemock (Louth), Cill Dhíomóg, 'St Déamóg's church'.

Kildermody (Waterford), Cill Diarmada, 'St Diarmaid's church'.

Kildimo (Limerick), Cill Díoma, 'St Díoma's church'.

Kildorrery (Cork), Cill Dairbhre, 'church of (the) oaks'.

Kildownet (Mayo), Cill Damhnait, 'St Damhnait's church'.

This is a woman's name.

Kildrum (several), Cill Droma, 'church of (the) ridge'.

Kilfane (Kilkenny), Cill Pháin, 'St Pán's church'.

Kilfenora (Clare), Cill Fhionnúrach, 'Fionnúir's church'.

In legendary history Fionnúir was the daughter of Oilill Ólum, the famed early king of Munster, and Maeve (Medb), queen of Connacht.

Kilfergus (Limerick), Cille Fhearghasa, 'St Fergus's church'.

Kilfinane (Limerick), Cill Fhíonáin, 'St Fíonán's church'.

Kilfithmone (Tipperary), Cill Fiodh Mughaine, 'church of (the) wood of (the) bog'.

Kilflynn (Kerry, Limerick), Cill Flainn, 'Flann's church'.

Kilfrush (Limerick), Cill Frois, 'Fros's church'.

Kilgarvan (several), Cill Gharbháin, 'St Garbhán's church'.

Kilglass (several), Cill Ghlais, 'grey church'.

Kilgobbin (Dublin), Cill Ghobáin, 'St Gobán's church'.

Kilgobnet (Waterford) Cill Ghobnait, 'St Gobnait's church'.

This name is a feminine form of Gobán (see **Kilgobbin**).

Kilgolagh (Cavan), Cill Ghabhlach, 'forked church'.

The name suggests a church built in two distinct halves, or a church with a double cross or other exterior feature.

Kilgowan (Kildare), Cill Ghabhann, 'church of (the) smith'.

Kilgreany (Waterford), Cill Ghréine, 'Grian's church'.

Kilhefernan (Tipperary), Cill Ifearnáin, 'Ifearnán's church'.

Kilkea (Kildare), Cill Chathaigh, 'Cathach's church'.

Kilkeary (Tipperary), Cill Chéire, 'St Ciar's church'.

Kilkee (Clare), Cill Chaoi, 'St Caoi's

church'.

Kilkeedy (Clare, Limerick), Cill Caoide, 'St Caoide's church'.

Kilkeel (Down), Cill Chaoil, 'church of (the) narrow (place)'.

Kilkeel is on the river Aughrim by the sea, south of the Mourne Mountains.

Kilkelly (Mayo), Cill Cheallaigh, 'St Ceallach's church'.

Kilkenny (Kilkenny), Cill Chainnigh, 'St Cainneach's church'.

The name is often anglicised as Kenneth, this being the 6th-century Irish monk who worked in the Hebrides and western Scotland before founding a monastery here. The original church may have been on the site of the present St Canice's Cathedral (Church of Ireland) on top of the hill here.

Kilkearan (several), Cill Chiaráin, 'St Ciarán's church'.

Kilkinlea (Limerick), Cill Chinn Shléibhe, 'church of (the) head of (the) mountain'.

Kilkinlea is near the head of the valley of the river Feale, where it is surrounded by hills on three sides.

Kilkishen (Clare), Cill Chisín, 'church of (the) little wicker causeway'.

Kilkishen is almost insulated by a series of small lakes. See also **Kesh.**

Kill (several), An Chill, 'the church'.

Killadeas (Fermanagh), Cill Chéile Dé, 'church of (the) Culdees'.

There was a chapel here belonging to the Culdees of Devenish. The Culdees (literally 'companions of God') were a group of monastic reformers of the 8th century.

Killadysert (Clare), Cill an Dísirt, 'church of the hermitage'.

The hermitage here was that of St Murthaile.

Killala (Mayo), Cill Ala, 'church of St Ala'.

The site of the original church traditionally founded here by St Patrick is now occupied by the Protestant Cathedral.

Killaloe (Clare, Kilkenny), Cill Dalua, 'St Dalua's church'.

St Dalua (or Do-Lua, or Mo-Lua) founded an early monastery in both places in the 6th century. In Killaloe, Clare, the original oratory was on Friar's Island but was removed to the Roman Catholic church

here in 1929 when the island was submerged under the Shannon hydroelectric scheme.

Killaloo (Derry), Coill an Lao, 'wood of the calf'.

Killamery (Kilkenny), Cill Lamhraí, 'Lamhrach's church'.

Killan (Offaly), Cill Anna, 'St Anne's church'.

Killane (Antrim), Cill Anna, 'St Anne's church'.

Killanne (Wexford), Cill Áine, 'Áine's church'.

Killanummery (Leitrim), Cill an Iomaire, 'church of the ridge'.

Killard (Clare), Cill Árd, 'high church'.

Killare (Westmeath), Cill Áir, 'church of slaughter'.

If this is a correct interpretation, the reference is presumably to a battle, or burial ground for battle or other victims.

Killarga (Leitrim), Cill Fhearga 'St Fearga's church'.

Killarney (Kerry), Cill Airne, 'church of (the) sloes'.

There are a number of other places of the name, with the same meaning. However, Killarney in Wicklow, near Bray, has a name that apparently means 'church of bishop Sáráin', as early records of the name show (*Kilescosather* in the early 13th century, representing modern Irish *cill easpuig Sáráin*).

Killary Bay (Galway/Mayo), Caoláire, 'narrow sea-inlet'.

Killary Harbour is a long sea-inlet at the head of which is Leenane.

Killashandra (Cavan), Cill na Seanrátha, 'church of the old ring-fort'.

The original church was built inside the ring-fort, which still partly exists here.

Killashee (Kildare, Longford), Cill na Sí, 'church of the fairy hill'.

It is possible that Killashee has a name meaning 'St Ausaille's church', referring to the saint (also known as Auxilius), who was a bishop and contemporary of St Patrick.

Killaspugbrone (Sligo), Cill Easpog Bróin, 'church of bishop Brón'.

Bishop Brón (or Bronus) was a disciple of St Patrick.

Killaspuglonane (Clare), Cill Easpog Fhlannán, 'church of bishop Flannán'.

Killavally (several), Coill an Bhaile, 'wood of the townland'.

In a few cases the 'Kill-' may be 'church', and the 'townland' (*baile*) may actually have originally been 'road', 'way' (*bealach*).

Killavullen (Cork), Cill an Mhuilinn, 'church of the mill'.

Killea (Derry), Cill Fhéich, 'Fiach's church'.

In Tipperary, Killea is Cill Shléibhe, 'church of (the) mountain'.

Killead (Antrim), Cill Éad, 'Faod's church'.

Killeagh (Cork, Meath), Cill Ia, 'Ia's church'.

Killeany (Clare, Galway), Cill Éanna, 'St Eany's church'.

Killeavy (Armagh), Cill Shléibhe, 'church of (the) mountain'

Killeavy is near Slieve Gullion.

Killeedy (Limerick), Cill Íde, 'St Íde's church'.

St Íde (Ita) was a virgin saint who founded a nunnery here in the 6th century.

Killeen (several), An Cillín, 'the little church'.

Of the many names thus, most have this sense, but some almost certainly mean 'little woods' (*Coillíní*)

Killeenagh (Waterford), An Cillíneach, 'the place of the little church'.

This name refers to Killeenagh Burial Ground, on a low hill about six miles southeast of Waterford.

Killeentierna (Kerry), Cillín Tiarna, 'St Tiarnach's little church'.

Killeevan (Monaghan), Cill Laobháin, 'St Laobhán's church'.

Killeglan (Meath), Cill Dhéagláin, 'St Deaglán's church'.

This is the Irish name (and the English version of it) for Ashbourne, where traditionally the church was founded by St Deaglán (Declan).

Killeigh (Offaly), Cill Aichidh, 'church of (the) field'.

Killelton (Kerry), Cill Eiltín, 'St Eiltín's church'.

Killen (Tyrone), Cillín, 'little church'.

Killenaule (Tipperary), Cill Náile, 'St Náile's church'.

Killenure (Tipperary), Cuilan Iúir, 'secluded spot of (the) yew'.

This is therefore not a 'church' name, like most beginning 'Kill-'.

Killerig (Carlow), Cill Eirc, 'St Earc's church'.

Killeshin (Laois), Cill Uiseán, 'St Oisín's church'.

Killester (Dublin), Cill Easra, 'St Easra's church.'.

Killeter (Tyrone), Coill Íochtair, 'lower wood'.

Here 'Kill-' is not *cill*, 'church', but *coill*, 'wood'.

Killimer (Clare), Cill Iomaí, 'St Iomar's church'.

Killimor (Galway), Cill Íomhar, 'St Íomhar's church'.

Killinaboy (Clare), Cill Iníne Baoith, 'church of (the) daughters of Baoth'.

Killinchy (Down), Cill Dhúinsí, 'St Dúinseach's church'.

This is a woman's name.

Killiney (Dublin), Cill Iníon Léinín, 'church of the daughters of Léinín'.

Killinick (Wexford), Cill Fhionnóg, 'St Finneóg's church'.

Killinure (Armagh), Cill an Iúir, 'church of the yew'.

Killisk (Wicklow), Cill Uisce, 'church of (the) water'.

A small stream still runs by the ruins of the old church here.

Killmannock (Wexford), Cill Manach, 'church of (the) monks'.

Killoe (Longford), Cill Eo, 'church of the yews'.

Kill of the Grange (Dublin), Cill na Gráinsí, 'church of the grange'.

The church here is dedicated to St Fintan.

Killone (Clare), Cill Eoin, 'St John (the Baptist)'s church'.

The church here was built for Augustinian nuns near the end of the 12th century.

Killongford Bridge (Waterford), Droichead Poll na Cloiche Gile, 'bridge of (the) pool of the bright stone'.

The English name appears to derive from Irish *Cill Longphuirt*, 'church of the fort'.

Killorglin (Kerry), Cill Orglan, 'Orgla's

church'.

Killough (Down, Tipperary), Cill Locha, 'church of (the) lake'.

In Down, Killough is on Killough Bay, which forms a sheltered harbour here.

Killowen (Down), Cill Eoin, 'St John (the Baptist)'s church'.

Killukin (Roscommon), Cill Eimhicín, 'St Eimhicín's church'.

Killure (several), Cill Iubhair, 'church of (the) yew'.

Yew trees were often planted near churches, as they have been elsewhere in Britain.

Killursa (Galway), Cill Fhursa, 'St Fursa's church'.

St Fursa is said to have built an abbey on a small island on Lough Corrib near here.

Killybegs (several), Na Cealla Beaga, 'the little churches'.

Perhaps a more accurate interpretation is 'the small monastic cells'. The Irish plural is represented by English 's'.

Killyclogher (Tyrone), Coillidh Chlochair, 'wood of (the) stony place'.

Killycluggin (Cavan), Cill an Chloigín, 'church of the little bell'.

Killycolpy (Tyrone), Coill an Cholpa, 'wood of the bullock'.

Killyfassy (Cavan), Coillidh Fásaigh, 'wood of (the) wilderness'.

Killygarry (Cavan), Coillidh Ghearra, 'short wood'.

Killygordon (Donegal), Coill na gCuirridín, 'wood of the horsetail grasses'.

Perhaps the first word of the name is really Irish *cúil*, 'secluded place', not *coill*.

Killykergan (Derry), Coill Uí Chiaragáin, 'wood of the descendants of Ciaragáin'.

Killylea (Armagh), Coillidh Léith, 'grey wood'.

Killyleagh (Down), Cill Ó Laoch, 'church of (the) descendants of (the) heroes'.

Killynaher (Cavan), Cill an Athar, 'church of the father'.

Killyon (Meath, Offaly), Cill Liain, 'Líadaine's church'.

This is a woman's name.

Kilmacanogue (Wicklow), Cill Mocheanóg, 'St Mochonóg's church'.

Kilmacduagh (Galway), Cill Mhic Duach, 'church of (the) son of Duach'.

The 'son of Duach' was St Colmán, of the royal race of Connacht, who founded the church here in the 6th century.

Kilmacow (Kilkenny), Cill Mochua, 'St Mo-Chua's church'.

Kilmacreehy (Clare), Cill Mhic Creithe, 'church of (the) sons of Creithe'.

Kilmacrenan (Donegal), Cill Mhic Réanáin, 'church of (the) sons of Éanán'.

The English name should really be 'Kilmacnenan', and the Irish *Cill Mhic nÉnáin*.

Kilmacthomas (Waterford), Coil Mhic Thomáisín, 'wood of (the) sons of little Thomas'.

Kilmaine (Mayo), Cill Mheáin, 'middle church'.

The church is in the middle of the Plains of Ellertrin.

Kilmainham (Dublin), Cill Mhaighneann, 'Maighne's church'.

The church here may have stood in the old churchyard where there is now just a high cross. The final '-ham' of the name seems to have appeared under the influence of English names with this ending.

Kilmakilloge (Kerry), Cill Mochilleóg, 'St Mocheallóg's church'.

Compare **Kilmallock**.

Kilmalkedar (Kerry), Cill Maolchéadair, 'St Maolchéadar's church'.

Kilmallock (Limerick), Cill Mocheallóg, 'St Mocheallóg's church'.

St Mocheallóg (Mo-Cheallóg) founded the church or monastery here in the 7th century. He is the same saint as in the name of Kilmakilloge.

Kilmanagh (Kilkenny), Cill Mhanach, 'church of (the) monks'.

Kilmanahan (Waterford), Cill Mainchín, 'St Mainchín's church'.

This saint's name means 'little monk'.

Kilmeaden (Waterford), Cill Mhíodáin, 'St Míodán's church'.

Kilmeedy (Limerick), Cill Míde, 'St Íde's church'.

This is the same saint as for Killeedy. Her name is generally common in Limerick.

Kilmessan (Meath), Cill Mheasáin, 'St Measán's church'.

Kilmichael (Cork), Cill Mhichíl, 'St

Michael's church'.

Kilmihill (Clare), Cill Mhichíl, 'St Michael's church'.

Kilmore (several), An Cill Mhór, 'the big church'.

There are almost a hundred places with this name, which in some cases may represent 'big wood', not 'big church', (i.e. from *coill*, not *cill*). In Kilmore, Armagh, the Church of Ireland church is on the site of the original 'big church', and the round tower of the old church is enclosed within the square walls of the present one.

Kilmore Quay (Wexford), Port na Cille Móire, 'harbour of the big church'.

An alternative Irish name for Kilmore Quay is *Cé na Cille Móire*.

Kilmovee (Mayo), Cill Mobhí, 'St Mobhí's church'.

Kilmuckridge (Wexford), Cill Mhucraise, 'St Mochraise's church'.

Kilmurry (several), Cill Mhuire, 'St Mary's church'.

Kilmurvey (Galway), Cill Mhuirbhigh, 'church of the sandy shore'.

Kilmurvey is on Inishmore, in the Aran Islands.

Kilnalag (Galway), Coill na Lag, 'wood of the hollows'.

Kilnaleck (Cavan), Cill na Leice, 'church of the flagstones'.

Kilnamanagh (several), Cill na Manach, 'church of the monks'.

In some cases, the name will mean 'wood of the monks', indicating the secluded location of the church or monastery.

Kilnamona (Clare), Cill na Móna, 'church of the bog'.

Kilnaraha (Cork), Cill na Rátha, 'church of the ring-fort'.

Kilnasaggart (Armagh), Cill na Sagart, 'church of the priests'.

This is one of the earliest securely dated Christian monuments in Ireland, known to have been established in the early 8th century.

Kilnavert (Cavan), Cill na bhFeart, 'church of the graves'.

Kilpatrick (several), Cill Pádraig, 'St Patrick's church'.

Kilpedder (Wicklow), Cill Pheadair, 'St

Peter's church'.

Kilquane (Kerry, Limerick), Cill Cúán, 'St Cuán's church'.

Kilrane (Wexford), Cill Ruáin, 'church of (the) ferns'.

Kilrea (Derry), Cill Ria, 'red-coloured church'.

Kilree (Kilkenny), Cill Rí, 'king's church'.

Kilreekill (Galway), Cill Rícill, 'St Richil's church'.

Kilronan (several), Cill Rónáin, 'St Rónán's church'.

Kilroot (Antrim), Cill Rua, 'red-coloured church'.

The church here is said to have been founded by St Colmán in the 6th century. The colour referred to would probably have been that of the soil here.

Kilross (Donegal, Tipperary), Cill Ros, 'church of (the) wood'.

Kilruddery (Wicklow), Cill Ruairí, 'church of (the) wanderers'.

Early forms of this name, such as *Kilrotheri* in the early 13th century and *Kilrothery* in the 16th, suggest that the Irish origin is *cill rothaire* or *cill ruathaire*, from *ruathaire* 'vagrant', 'wanderer', perhaps implying roving missionaries or pilgrims. However, this origin is not certain, and the latter half of the name may well be a personal name such as Ruairí.

Kilrush (Clare), Cill Rois, 'church of the peninsula'.

Kilrush is at the head of a natural harbour, to the north of a small headland (now a departure point for steamers to Scattery Island).

Kilsallagh (several), Coill Salach, 'willow tree wood'.

Kilsaran (Louth), Cill Saráin, 'St Sarán's church'.

Kilshanny (Clare), Cill Seanaigh, 'St Seanach's church'.

Kilsheelan (Tipperary), Cill Síoláin, 'Síolán's church'.

Kilskeer (Meath), Cill Scíre, 'St Scíre's church'.

Scíre is a woman's name. Compare **Kilskeery**.

Kilskeery (Tyrone), Cill Scíre, 'St Scíre's church'.

Kiltartan (Galway), Cill Tartain, 'Tartan's church'.

Kiltealy (Wexford), Cill Téile, 'St Síle's church'.
Síle is a woman's name, often anglicised as Sheila. Compare **Kilteel**.

Kilteel (Kildare), Cill tSíle, 'St Síle's church'.

Kiltegan (Wicklow), Cill Téagáin, 'St Téagán's church.
The name was first recorded in the 13th century, but as in so many 'church' names, nothing is known about the saint associated with it.

Kiltennanlea (Clare), Cill tSeanán Léith, 'St Seanán the Grey's church'.
The saint's nickname (*liath*) means 'grey-headed'.

Kilternan (Dublin), Cill Tiarnáin, 'St Tiarnán's church'.

Kiltimagh (Mayo), Coillte Mach, 'wood of (the) plain'.

Kiltoom (Roscommon), Cill Tuama, 'church of (the) burial mound'.

Kiltubbrid (Leitrim), Cill Tiobrad, 'church of (the) well'.

Kiltullagh (several), Cill Tulach, 'church of (the) little hill'.

Kilturk, (Wexford), Coill Torc, 'wood of (the) boars'.

Kiltybegs (several), Coillte Beaga, 'little woods'.
The Irish plural is represented by the English 's'.

Kiltyclogher (Leitrim), Coillte Clochair, 'woods of (the) stony place'.

Kilwaterway (Waterford), Cill Uachtar Muighe, 'church of (the) upper plain'.
In the English name, 'water' is a corruption of Irish *uachtar*, 'upper'. For a further comment on this, see also **Waterford**.

Kilworth (Cork), Cill Uird, 'church of (the) order'.
Irish *órd* (genitive *úird*) means not only 'order' in the general sense, but 'religious order', as in this name.

Kinalea (Cork), Cineál Aodha, '(place of the) descendants of Aodh'.
Aodh (often anglicised as Hugh), is said to have been the father of Fáilbhe Fland, king of Munster in the 7th century.

Kinalmeaky (Cork), Cineál mBéice, '(place of the) descendants of Bece'.

Kinard (several), Cinn Áird, 'high hill'.

Kinawley (Fermanagh), Cill Náile, 'St Náile's church'.
St Náile (Natalis), was the 6th-century abbot of Devenish. The English version of the name has lost the final 'l' of *cill* (which could have given a more accurate name as 'Kilnawley').

Kincasslagh (Donegal), Cionn Caslach, 'head of (the) inlet'.
The name accurately describes the location of Kincasslagh in The Rosses, west of Loughanure. There is another Kincasslagh only a few miles away, west of Mullaghderg Lough.

Kincun (Mayo), Ciona Con, 'head of (the) hound'.
The name probably refers to the outline of a hill here.

Kindrum (Donegal), Cionn Droma, 'head of (the) ridge'.

Kingarrow (Donegal), Cionn Garbh, 'rough head'.

Kinghill (Down), Cnoc an Rí, 'hill of the king'.

Kingscourt (Cavan), Dún an Rí, 'fort of the king'.

Kinlough (Leitrim), Cionn Locha, 'head of (the) lake'.
Kinlough is near the head of Lough Melvin.

Kinnegad (Westmeath), Ceann Átha Gad, 'head of (the) ford of (the) points'.
The reference is probably to the sticks of willow or other branches used to ford the stream here.

Kinneigh (Cork), Ceinn Eich, 'head of (the) horse'.
The name may refer either to the outline of a hill here, like a horse's head, or to a hill where horses were kept.

Kinnitty (Offaly), Cionn Eitigh, 'Eitach's head'.
According to legend, the place is so called since the head of Eitach, an early Irish princess, was buried here.

Kinsale (Cork), Cionn tSáile, 'head of (the) sea'.
Kinsale is on the estuary of the river Ban-

don at approximately the highest point reached by the tide. See also **Kenmare** and **Kensalebeg**.

Kinure (Cork), Cinnabhair, 'head of (the) yew'.

Kinvara (Galway), Cinn Mhara, 'head of (the) sea'.
Kinvare is a small tidal port at the head of an inlet of Galway Bay. Its name has exactly the same sense as that of Kenmare.

Kinvoy (Leitrim), Ceann an Mhaí, 'head of the plain'.

Kippure (Wicklow), Cip Iubhair, 'stumps of yew'.
This is the traditional interpretation of the name of this mountain, but it is almost certainly incorrect, since earlier spellings of the name show it as *Kippmore*, and in any case yew trees are hardly likely to have given the name of a mountain over 2,000 ft (600m) high. The name thus probably derives from *cíop* (*cíob*), 'course mountain grass', 'sedge', together with *mór*, 'big', so that overall it can give the meaning 'great place of coarse grass'. This is an accurate description of the land here.

Kircubbin (Down), Cill Ghobáin, 'St Gobán's church'.

Kiskeam (Cork), Coiscéim na Caillí, 'footstep of the hag'.
This is almost certainly a folk origin of the name, whose precise meaning is unclear.

Knappagh (several), Cnapach, 'place full of small hills'.

Knappogue (Clare), An Chnapóg, 'the hillock'.

Knightstown (Kerry), Baile an Ridire, 'town of the knight'.
This is the 'capital' of Valentia Island, named after its former proprietor, the Knight of Kerry who lived at the demesne of Glanleam to the west of Knightstown. The Knights of Kerry were the Fitzgeralds. Subsequently, Glanleam passed to Lord Mounteagle.

Knock (several), An Cnoc, 'the hill'.

Knockacappel (Kerry), Cnoc an Chapaill, 'hill of the horse'.

Knockaderry (Limerick), Cnoc an Doire, 'hill of the oak wood'.

Knockainy (Limerick), Cnoc Áine, 'Áine's

hill'.
According to legend, Áine was a famous banshee who was goddess of the elfmound here, daughter of the elfin Fer Í ('yew man') and unwilling lover of Oilill Ólum, the famous early king of Munster.

Knockalough (Clare), Cnoc an Locha, 'hill of the lake',
The village is by Knocka Lough, itself named after the hill (which is named after the lake).

Knockanillaun (Mayo), Cnoc an Oileáin, 'hill of the island'.

Knockaraha Bridge (Waterford), Droichead Chnoc na Ráithe, 'bridge of (the) hill of the ring-fort'.

Knockaraven (Fermanagh), Cnoc an Riabháin, 'hill of the swarthy person'.
This is a literal interpretation of the Irish name as it stands, but is probably a corruption of the true origin.

Knockavilla (several), Cnoc an Bhile, 'hill of the ancient tree'.
The 'ancient tree' (*bile*) would have been a sacred or historic one, often by a fort or a holy well. The English name is also spelt to end in '-e' or '-y'.

Knockboy (several), Cnoc Buidhe, 'yellow hill'.

Knockbrack (several), An Cnoc Breac, 'the speckled hill'.

Knockbrandon (Wexford), Cnoc Breánainn, 'St Brendan's hill'.

Knockbridge (Louth), Droichead an Chnoic, 'bridge of the hill'.
The river here is the Fane.

Knockcloghrim (Derry), Cnoc Clochdhroma, 'hill of (the) stony ridge'.

Knockcosgrey (Westmeath), Cnoc Uí Choscraigh, 'hill of the descendants of Coscraigh'.

Knockcroghery (Roscommon), Cnoc an Chrochaire, 'hill of the hangman'.
To the east of the village is a mound that was used as a place of execution.

Knockduff (Cavan), An Cnoc Dubh, 'the black hill'.

Knockeen (Waterford), An Cnoicín, 'the little hill'.

Knockglass (Galway), Cnoc Glas, 'green hill'.

KYLEMORE

Knocklayd (Antrim), Cnoc Laethid, 'broad hill'.
Knocklofty (Tipperary), Cnoc Lochta, 'hill of (the) shelf', 'shelving hill'.
Knocklong (Limerick), Cnoc Loinge, 'hill of (the) house'.
According to tradition, Cormac mac Airt, king of Tara, camped here with his army when he invaded Munster in the 3rd century.
Knockmahon (Waterford), Cnoc Machan, 'hill of (the river) Mahon'.
Knockmany (Tyrone), Cnoc Meánach, 'middle hill'.
The hill is midway in a range of hills and mountains that runs across Tyrone from Enniskillen in the south-west to Pomeroy in the north-east.
Knockmaroon (Dublin), Cnoc Mhaolruáin, 'Maolruan's hill'.
Knockmealdown Mountains (Waterford), Cnoc Mhaoldonn, 'hill of Maol Duin'.
The Irish name is that of the single mountain that gives the whole range its name. The personal name, which may mean 'warrier of the fort', has also been given as Maoldomhnach, meaning 'servant of the church'.
Knockmore (several), An Cnoc Mór, 'the big hill'.
Most of the 'big hills' are in fact mountains.
Knockmoy (Galway), Cnoc Muaidhe, 'Muaidh's hill'.
Knockmoyle (several), An Cnoc Maol, 'the bare hill'.
Knockmoyleen (Mayo), Cnoc an Mhaolín, 'hill of the small rise'.
Knocknaboley (Clare), Cnoc na Buaile, 'hill of the summer pasture''.
Knocknacarry (Antrim), Cnoc na Cora, 'hill of the weir'.
This name could also be Irish Cnoc na Carraige, 'hill of the rock'.
Knocknacroohy (several), Cnoc na Cruaiche, 'hill of the cross'.
The Irish word croch also means 'gallows', and this may be the sense for some of these places, where the hill was a place of execution.
Knocknageehy (Cork), Cnoc na Gaoithe, 'hill of the wind'.

On some older maps this hill is marked as 'Mount Zephyr'.
Knocknageragh (Tipperary), Cnoc na gCaorach, 'hill of the sheep'.
Knockagore (several), Cnoc na nGabhar, 'hill of the goats'.
Knocknahoe (several), Cnoc na hUamha, 'hill of the cave'.
Knocknahorn (Tyrone), Cnoc na hEorna, 'hill of the barley'.
Knocknanuss (Cork), Cnoc na nOs, 'hill of the deer'.
Knocknarea (Sligo), Cnoc na Ria, 'hill of the executions'.
Compare **Ardnaree**.
Knochninny (Fermanagh), Cnoc Ninnidh, 'St Ninnidh's hill'.
Knockrath (Wicklow), Cnoc Rátha, 'hill of (the) ring-fort'.
Knockroe (several), Cnoc Rua, 'red hill'.
Knockrush (Roscommon), Cnoc an Rois, 'hill of the wood'.
Knocksouna (Limerick), Cnoc Samhna, 'hill of November celebrations'.
The Samhain (said to derive from samhfhuin, 'summer's-end') was first a pagan then a Christian celebration to mark the end of the harvest and the opening of the winter season, which lasted until May. It began in November and was associated with much activity from the fairies. In Christian terms it corresponds to All-Hallowtide.
Knockstackin (Antrim), Cnoc an Staicín, 'hill of the stake'.
Knocktemple (Cork), Magh Leamha, 'plain of elms'.
The English name means 'hill of the church'.
Knocktopher (Kilkenny), Cnoc na Tóchair, 'hill of the causeway'.
Traces of an ancient causeway can still be seen here crossing the marshy valley.
Knopoge (Clare), An Chnapóg, 'the little hill'.
Kyle (several), An Choill, 'the wood'.
Many Kyles are 'the church', from cill. Only local knowledge will show which is appropriate, or an examination of early spellings of the name.
Kylemore (several), An Choill Mhóir, 'the

79

big wood'.

In some cases, this name will mean 'the big church' (like Kilmore), but at Kylemore Abbey in Galway, for example, the 'big wood' can still be clearly seen on the lower slopes of the mountains to the north of Kylemore Lough.

L

Laban (Galway), Lábán, 'mire', 'dirt'.
Labasheeda (Clare), Leaba Shíoda, 'Síoda's grave'.
Labba (several), Leaba, 'bed', 'grave'.
Labbacallee (Cork), Leaba Caillí, 'grave of (the) hag'.
This is a famous prehistoric tomb, known locally in English as 'The Hag's Bed'.
Labbamolaga (Cork), Leaba Molaga, 'St Molaga's grave'.
The monastery here was founded by St Molaga in the 7th century.
Lack (Fermanagh), An Leac, 'the flagstone'.
Lackabaun (Kerry), Leaca Bhán, 'white hillside'.
Lackagh (several), Leacach, 'place of flagstones'.
Lackamore (Tipperary), An Leaca Mhór, 'the great hillside'.
Lackan (several), Leacain, 'hillside'.
Lackareagh (Clare), Leaca Riabhach, 'grey hillside'.
Ladysbridge (Cork), Droichead na Scuab, 'bridge of the brooms'.
Both names are rather unclear. The Irish name may suggest that brooms or brushes were kept on or under the bridge. If the English name were 'Ladyswell' the reference would be to the Virgin Mary. Possibly the bridge is named after a local lady.
Lady's Island (Wexford), Oileán Muire, 'Mary's (i.e. Our Lady's) island'.
Lady's Well is on the mainland near this peninsula on Lady's Island Lough.
Lagan (Donegal), An Lagán, 'the small hollow'.
Perhaps the river Lagan had (or still has) a little pool or hollow somewhere along its course. The name is found for rivers elsewhere.
Laghey Corner (Tyrone), Cúinne na Laithí, 'corner of the mire'.
Laght (several), Leacht, 'grave', 'monument', 'tomb'.
Laghtgeorge (Galway), Leacht Seoirse, 'George's tomb'.
It is not clear who George was.

Lagore (Meath), Loch Gabhair, 'lake of horses'.
Lahard (Kerry), Leath Árd, 'half-height'.
The name implies a gradual, easy slope.
Lahardane (Mayo), Leathardán, 'half-hill'.
As with Lahard, the name implies an easy ascent.
Lahinch (Clare), An Leacht, 'the grave'.
The name has also been interpreted as 'half-island' (*leath-inis*), i.e. peninsula, presumably referring to the headland north of Lahinch. But similarly the 'grave' name also appears in its longer Irish form of *Leacht Uí Chonchúir*, 'O'Connor's grave'.
Lambay (Dublin), Reachrainn.
The 'English' name is in fact a Norse one, meaning 'lamb island'. Lambay was doubtless a place of pasture for ewes when they were about to lamb. The Irish name is difficult to interpret with any certainty.
Lambeg (Antrim), Lann Bheag, 'little church'.
Lanesborough (Longford), Béal Átha Liag, 'ford-mouth of (the) standing stones'.
The Irish name gave English 'Ballyleague' as the original name of the place before Charles I granted a charter creating the manor of Lanesborough, apparently named after the English landowner here.
Laois
This county name, formerly anglicised as Leix, means '(place of the people of) Lugaid Laígne', who was granted lands here after he had driven invading forces from Munster. From 1556 to 1920, Laois was called Queen's County, after Queen Mary.
Laracor (Meath), Láithreach Cora, 'place of (the) weir'.
Laracor is by the river Boyne.
Laragh (several), Láithreach, 'place', 'site'.
The Irish word implies a place of some significance, even if only local, such as a special building or its ruins, a battle site, or a sanctuary.
Laraghbryan (Kildare), Láithreach Briúin, 'Bryan's (house) site'.

81

Largy (several), An Leargaidh, 'the hillside'.

Larne (Antrim), Latharna, '(territory of the) people of Lathair'.

According to early historical legend, Lathair was one of the twenty-five children of Hugony the Great (Ugaine Mór), a prechristian monarch of Ireland. Each child was granted an equal share of the country, but only Lathair's land survives with the name of its possessor. The name thus originally denoted a much larger territory than that of the present town. For a similar tribal name, see **Connemara**.

Latteragh (Tipperary), Leatracha, 'wet hillsides'.

Laughil (several), Leamhcoill, 'elm wood'.

Laune (Kerry), An Leamhain, 'the elm river'.

Laurencetown (Galway), Baile Shíl Anmach, 'town of (the) race of Anmchaid'.

The English name refers to a landowner here, perhaps an Anglo-Norman.

Lavagh (several), Leamhach, 'place of elms'.

Lavaghery (Armagh), Leamh-Mhachaire, 'elm plain'.

Lavey (Cavan), Leamhaigh, 'place of elms'.

Laytown (Meath), An Inse, 'the island'.

Laytown is a coastal resort, so a better interpretation would be 'waterside land'. An alternative Irish name is *Port na hInse*, 'island port'. The English name must derive from a landowner or settler here called Lay.

Leamanch (Clare), Léim an Eich, 'leap of the horse'.

The name must indicate some local incident or legend. Compare **Horseleap**.

Leamore (Offaly), Liath Mór, 'big grey place'.

Leap (Cork), An Léim, 'the leap'.

The name properly belongs to a gorge or ravine here, which was said to have been a favourite resort of outlaws who could escape here by a 'leap' across. A local saying ran, 'Beyond the Leap, beyond the law'. There are other places of the name, for example The Leap (*An Léim*) in Wexford.

Lecale (Down), Leath Chathail, 'Cathal's half'.

Cathal was a chief here in the early 8th century, and this district was his 'half' or territory.

Lecarrow (several), An Leithcheathrú, 'the half quarter'.

A 'quarter' was a measure of land, and this name denotes a 'half' portion of it.

Leck (Donegal), Leac, 'flagstone'.

This is the same name as Lack, indicating a flat-faced rock or a place with a solid level surface.

Leckanvy (Mayo), Leac Ainbhe, 'Ainbhe's flagstone'.

Leckaun (Leitrim), An Leacán, 'the hillside'.

Leckpatrick (Tyrone), Leic Pádraig, 'St Patrick's flagstone'.

Leenane (Galway), An Líonan, 'the shallow sea-bed'.

Leenane is on the upper reaches of the Killary Harbour.

Legacurry (several), Lag an Choile, 'hollow of the cauldron'.

Irish *coire* is here used in the sense 'whirlpool'.

Legan (Longford), Liagán, 'little hollow'.

Legananny (Down), Lag an Eanaigh, 'hollow of the marsh'.

Leggs (Fermanagh), Na Laig, 'the hollows'.

As often happens, the Irish plural is here represented by an English 's'.

Leglands (Tyrone), Leithghleann, 'halfglen'.

This is the same name as Leighlin, with an unjustified English 's' added.

Lehinch (several), Leithinse, 'half-island', 'peninsula'.

Leighlin (Carlow), Leithghlinn, 'half-glen'.

This is a river, and the name must describe some natural feature or formation in it.

Leighlinbridge (Carlow), Leithghlinn an Droichid, 'half-glen of the bridge'.

Leighlinbridge is on the river Barrow, and 'half-glen' here refers to the original location of the place on the valley side of the river, not the hill side, that is, to the west, towards Oldleighlin. The ten-arch bridge was built in the 14th century.

Leighmoney (Cork), Liathmhuine, 'grey thicket'.

Leinster, Laighin, 'place of the Lagin people'.

This ancient tribal name is that of the Celtic people who came to Ireland in perhaps the

3rd century BC, led by their legendary ancestor Labraid Longsech. Their own name may derive from a word related to modern Irish *laighean*, 'spear'. The place-name of this province has the '-ster' ending also seen in Munster and Ulster. This is now thought to be a combination of Old Norse genitive (possessive) *s* and Irish *tír* 'land', 'district'.

Leitrim (several), Liatroim, 'grey ridge'.
The county name is that of the village, close to the river Shannon, which marks the county border. The 'ridge' would be the rising ground east of Leitrim.

Leixlip (Kildare), Léim an Bhradáin, 'leap of the salmon'.
The 'English' name is actually Norse, from Old Norse *leax*, 'salmon' and *hlaup*, 'leap'. The name describes the point where salmon were able to leap up the cataract on the river Liffey here (now replaced by a specially constructed fish pass).

Lemanaghan (Offaly), Liath Manacháin, 'St Manchán's grey place'.

Lemybrien (Waterford), Léim Uí Bhriain, 'O Brien's leap'.
If this is not a corrupt name, it probably derives from some local legend.

Lenamore (Longford), An Léana Mór, 'the big swampy meadow'.

Leopardstown (Dublin), Baile an Lobhar, 'townland of the sick'.
The name may indicate a former isolation site for people suffering from some infectious disease. The English name is a corruption of the Irish.

Lerrig (Kerry), Leirg, 'hillside'.

Letter (several), An Leitir, 'the wet hillside'.

Letterbreen (Fermanagh), Leitir Bhrúin, 'Brúin's wet hillside'.

Letterbrick (Donegal, Mayo), Leitir Bhric, 'Breac's wet hillside'.
This name could also mean 'hillside of badgers', from Irish *broc*, genitive *bruic*.

Letterfinish (Kerry), Leitir Fionnuisce, 'hillside of clear water'.

Letterfrack (Galway), Leitir Fraic, 'Frac's hillside'.

Lettergow (Galway), Leitir Ghaba, 'wet hillside of the smith'.

Letterkenny (Donegal), Leitir Ceanainn,
'wet hillside of the O Cannons.'

Lettermacaward (Donegal), Leitir Mhic an Bhaird, 'wet hillside of (the) sons of the bard'.
The second half of the name gave the modern surname Mac Ward.

Lettermore (several), Leitir Móir, 'big wet hillside'.

Lettermullan (Galway), Leitir Mealláin, 'Meallán's wet hillside'.

Levitstown (Kildare), Baile Luibhéid, 'Levit's townland'.
Levit is an Anglo-Norman family name.

Leyny (Sligo), Luighne, '(place of the) descendants of Lugaid'.
Lugaid Laigne was the legendary ancestor of the O Mores and related families.

Liffey (Wicklow/Dublin), An Life.
The origin of the name of the well known river is obscure. It is not *leath*, 'broad'.

Liffock (Derry), Leitóg, 'little half'.
The 'half' here is a measure of land.

Lifford (Donegal), Leifear, 'side of (the) water'.
The name is really a territorial one, indicating the land on the west bank of the river Foyle, where Lifford is, as against land on the opposite (east) bank, where Strabane is. The letter *d* has been added by association with English 'ford'.

Legoniel (Belfast), Lag an Aoil, 'hollow of the line'.
The 'line' is a stratum of cretaceous chalk here. The name was originally 'Bally-legaile', and is nothing to do with the family name O Neill, as sometimes stated.

Limavady (Derry), Léim an Mhadaidh, 'leap of the dog'.
The name originally related to the site of a former castle here overhanging a deep glen two miles south up the valley of the river Roe. If not a corruption, the name must refer to a local legend.

Limerick (Limerick), Luimneach, 'bare area of ground'.
The name is related to modern Irish *lom*, genitive *luim*, 'bare place', with the *n* of the word becoming *r*, and would have originally applied to the land by the lower reaches of the river Shannon. The 'bare' sense can be understood both literally and

83

as denoting an unprotected or vulnerable location. The county name comes from the town.

Lisbane (Down), An Lios Bán, 'the white ring-fort'.

Lisbealad (Cork), Lios Béalaid, 'ring-fort of (the) pass'.

Lisbellaw (Fermanagh), Lios Béal Átha, 'ring-fort of (the) ford-mouth'.

Lisbellaw is just east of an area of streams, lakes and rivers between Upper and Lower Lough Erne.

Lisburn (Antrim), Lios na gCearrbhach, 'ring-fort of the gamblers'.

The Irish name refers to the old fort sites north-east and south-west of the town where 'outlaws' used to play at cards and dice. At one time, there was thick woodland here, which would have concealed their activity. The former English name of Lisburn was Lisnagarvey, which is a version of the Irish. Some time in the 17th century, this was superseded by the present name, which outwardly appears to derive from English 'burn', but this is unlikely and hardly suitable for the river Lagan here. (Any reference to a fire here is hardly worth considering, although this is the popular explanation, alluding to the great blaze of 1641.) The name Lisburn is almost certainly entirely Irish, and although *Lios na Bearman* ('ring-fort of the gap') is perhaps a possible source, a much more likely origin is *Lios na Bruidhne*, 'ring-fort of the fairy palace' or 'ring-fort of the mansion'. Irish *bruidhean* (genitive *bruidhne*) is found in other place-names, such as Bryanmore and Bryanbeg in Westmeath.

Liscannor (Clare), Lios Ceannúir, 'Ceannúr's ring-fort'.

Liscarney (Mayo), Lios Cearnaigh, 'Cearnach's ring-fort'.

Liscarroll (Cork), Lios Cearúill, 'Cearúl's ring-fort'.

Liscarton (Meath), Lios Cartáin, 'Cartán's ring-fort'.

Lisclogher (Meath), Lios Clochair, 'ring-fort of (the) stony place'.

Liscloon (Tyrone), Lios Claon, 'sloping ring-fort'.

Liscolman (Antrim, Wicklow), Lios Chol-máin, 'Colmán's ring-fort'.

In Wicklow, an earlier name of Liscolman was 'Lismacolman' (recorded in the early 13th century as *Lismacluman*), so a more accurate interpretation here would be 'ring-fort of the sons of Colmán'.

Lisdoonvarna (Clare), Lios Dúin Bhearna, 'ring-fort of the gapped fort'.

Since two kinds of fort are involved in this name, it might be preferable to render *lios* as 'enclosure'. A 'gapped' fort is one that is dilapidated and of uneven or broken appearance. This particular one is to the left of the road from Lisdoonvarna to Ballyvaghan.

Lisdowney (Kilkenny), Lios Dúnadhaigh, 'Dúnadach's ring-fort'.

Lisduff (Laois), An Lios Dubh, 'the black ring-fort'.

Lisfinny (Waterford), Lios Finín, 'Finín's ring-fort'

Finín was an early 7th-century king of Munster.

Lisgoole (Fermanagh), Lios Gabhal, 'ring-fort of (the) fork'.

Lisheen (several), Lisín, 'little ring-fort'.

Lislap (Tyrone), Lios Leapa, 'ring-fort of (the) grave'.

Lislaughtin (Kerry), Lios Lachtín, 'ring-fort of St Lachtín'.

This is the name of Lislaughtin Abbey (now ruined) near Ballylongford.

Lislea (several), Lios Liath, 'grey ring-fort'.

Lislevane (Cork), Lios Leamháin, 'ring-fort of the elm tree'.

Lismore (Waterford), Lios Mór, 'big ring-fort'.

The famous monastery here was founded in the 7th century by St Carthach, and the *lios*, or enclosure, was built round it. Today the remains of the fort can be seen as a flat-topped mound a mile east of the town. There are several other places of the name.

Lismullin (Meath), Lios na Mhuilinn, 'ring-fort of the mill'.

Lisnadill (Armagh), Lios na Daille, 'ring-fort of the blindness'.

This literal interpretation of the name may be a corruption of some other word.

Lisnagarvey see **Lisburn**.

Lisnageer (Cavan), Lios na gCaor, 'ring-fort

of the berries'.

Lisnagreeve (Monaghan), Lios na gCraobh, 'ring-fort of the branches'.

Lisnagry (Limerick), Lios na Graí, 'ring-fort of the horse-stud'.

Lisnagunogue (Antrim), Lis na gCuinneog, 'ring-fort of the churns'.
Possibly churns or pails were filled or kept here.

Lisnamuck (Derry), Lios na Muc, 'ring-fort of the pigs'.

Lisnarick (Fermanagh), Lios na nDaróg, 'ring-fort of the little oaks'.

Lisnaskea (Fermanagh), Lios na Scéithe, 'ring-fort of the shield'.
If this is a true reading of the name, the reference must be to the hill fort and mound north-east of Lisnaskea which traditionally was the inauguration site of the Maguires.

Lispole (Kerry), Lios Póil, 'Paul's ring-fort'.

Lisryan (Longford), Lios Riain, 'Rian's ring-fort'.

Liss (Galway), Lios, 'ring-fort'.

Lissadill (Sligo), Lios an Daill, 'ring-fort of the blind man'.
If this is the true origin of the name, the reference must be to some local incident or legend.

Lissan (several), Leasán, 'little ring-fort'.

Lissaniska (several), Lios an Uisce, 'ring-fort of the water'.
The name usually indicated a fort by a river or lake, so that Lissaniska in Mayo, for example, is on the river Moy.

Lisselton (Kerry), Lios Eiltín, 'Eiltín's ring-fort'.

Lissonuffy (Roscommon), Lios Ó nDubhthaigh, 'ring-fort of the descendants of Dubhthach'.
The personal name gave the modern family name O Duffy.

Lissoughter (Galway), Lios Uachtair, 'upper ring-fort'.

Lissoy (Westmeath), Lios Eo, 'fort of (the) yew tree'.
This name has also been interpreted as 'ring-fort of (the) cave' (*Lios Uaimhe*). Today Lissoy is usually known as Auburn.

Lissycasey (Clare), Lios Uí Chathasaigh, 'ring-fort of the descendants of Cathasach'.

The personal name gave the modern family name O Casey.

Listellian (Donegal), Lios Tealláin, 'Teallán's ring-fort'.

Listowel (Kerry), Lios Tuathail, 'Tuathal's ring-fort'.

Little Ash (Louth), An Fhoinseog Bheag, 'the little ash tree'.

Little Island (Cork), An tOileán Beag, 'the little island'.
Little Island is not quite an island but a peninsula extending south into Lough Mahon.

Lixnaw (Kerry), Leic Snámha, 'flagstone of the swimming (place)'.
Perhaps swimmers wishing to cross the river Brick dived into it from the large flat rock here.

Lohort (Cork), Lubhghort, 'kitchen garden'.
The name denotes a vegetable garden or orchard attached to a fort or castle here.

Londonderry (Derry), Doire, 'oak grove'.
There are many places in Ireland called 'Derry' (*Doire*), and it soon becomes necessary to distinguish an individual name in some way, usually by adding a second word. In the case of Londonderry, the first distinguishing addition was *Calgach*, a personal name. This was recorded in the 7th century as *Daire-Calgaich*, 'Calgach's oak wood'. Meanwhile, St Columba had established a monastery here in the 6th century, and the name now became 'Derry-Columcille' (*Doire Choil Chille*), 'St Columba's oak wood'. Finally 'London' was added to Derry in 1609 when James I granted a charter for a settlement here by merchants from London. Today the name is often used in its shorter original form of Derry, and this is now recognised by the Post Office. The original oak wood survived for several hundred years after the location was first named here. The county name (also often shortened today) derives from that of the town.

Longfield (Tipperary), Leamhchoill, 'elm tree wood'.
The English name is a corruption of the Irish, both here and wherever else it occurs.

Longford (Longford), An Longfort, 'the fortress'.

The English name suggests a 'long ford', but the Irish (from *longphort*, literally 'house-fort') shows the true origin. Longfort was once the site of a fortress of the O Farrells, but no trace of it remains today. The name Longford exists elsewhere. The county name came from the town.

Longfordpass (Tipperary), Coill an Longfoirt, 'wood of the fortress'.

Longstone (Kildare), An Chloc Fhada, 'the long stone'.

This is the name of the ring-fort of Longstone Rath, three miles east of Furness. It is remarkable for its pillar stone, which is 16½ ft (4.95m) high.

Loo Bridge (Kerry), Droichead Lua, 'bridge of (the river) Lua'.

Loop Head (Clare), An Lúb, 'leap head'.

The name is a Norse modification (Old Norse *hlaup*, as in Leixlip) of English 'Leap Head', in Irish *Léim Chonchuillinn*, 'Cú-Chulainn's leap'. A legend tells how this great warrior and hero was pursued by a woman named Mal, and to escape her leapt from this cape on to a rock in the sea. She sprang after him, so he leapt back to the mainland. In endeavouring to do likewise, Mal fell short and drowned in the stormy waves.

Lorum (Carlow), Leamhdhrom, 'elm ridge'.

Loughan (several), Lochán, 'small lake'.

Loughanavally (Westmeath), Lochán an Bhealaigh, 'little lake of the road'.

Loughanure (Donegal), Loch an Iúir, 'lake of the yew'.

Loughbeg (Cork), Loch Beag, 'small lake'.

Loughbeg is on a shallow arm of Cork Harbour.

Loughbrickland (Down), Loch Bricleann, 'Briccriu's lake'.

The *r* of the personal name has become *l* and in the English name *d* has been added by association with 'land'.

Loughcrew (Meath), Loch Craoibhe, 'lake of (the) brannches'.

Loughcutra (Galway), Loch Cútra, 'Cútra's lake'.

Loughermore (Derry), Luchair Mhór, 'large district of reeds'.

Loughgall (Armagh), Loch gCál, 'Cál's lake'.

Loughill (several), Leamhchoill, 'elm wood'.

Loughinisland (Down), Loch an Oileáin, 'lake of the island'.

The lough of this name, east of the village of Loughinisland, has an island with the ruins of three ancient churches.

Loughlinstown (Dublin), Baile Uí Lochlainn, 'townland of the descendants of Loughlin'.

Loughrea (Galway), Baile Locha Riach, 'town of (the) grey lake'.

The town takes its name from the lough.

Loughros (Donegal), Luacharos, 'rushy headland'.

Loughros Point here on the west coast has given its name to Loughros More Bay to the north of it, and Loughros Beg Bay to the south. As their respective names indicate, the former bay is the larger (*mór*) and the latter the smaller (*beag*).

Louisburgh (Mayo), Cluain Cearbán, 'Carbán's meadow'.

The English name commemorates the capture of Louisburg, Nova Scotia, in 1758. The name was given by Henry Browne, uncle of the first marquis of Sligo, who was present.

Loup (Derry), An Lúb, 'the loop'.

The name indicates a secluded place in a river bend, the angle of a hill, or the like.

Louth (Louth), Lú, 'plain'.

The full name of Louth is *Lubhadh*, recorded earlier in a more meaningful form as *Lughmhaigh*. The latter half of this is *magh*, 'plain', but the first half cannot be satisfactorily explained. It does not appear to be a personal name. The county took its name from the village, which has the ruins of a once important monastic site.

Lowtown (Down), Baile Íochtair, 'lower town'.

Lowtown lies below the mountains that rise to the summit of Slieve Croob.

Lucan (Dublin), Leamhcán, 'place of elms'.

Lugatemple (Mayo), Log an Teampaill, 'hollow of the church'.

Lugnaquilla (Wicklow), Log na Coille, 'hollow of the wood'.

Some sources suggest the name may mean 'hollow of the woodcock', from *coileach*, 'cock', 'male bird'. The interpretation given above, however, seems the most likely.

Lukeswell (Kilkenny), Tobar Lúcáis, 'Luke's well'.

Lumcloon (Offaly), Lomchluain, 'bare meadow'.

Lurga (Mayo), An Lorgain, 'the strip of land'.

Irish *lorgan* literally means 'shin', usually denoting a long, low hill.

Lurgan (several), An Lorgain, 'the strip of land'.

Lurganboy (Leitrim), An Lorgain Bhuí, 'the yellow strip of land'.

Lurraga (several), Lorga, 'strip of land'.

Lusk (Dublin), Lusca, 'cave'.

According to traditional history, bishop Cuindid who founded the monastery here in the 5th century was buried in the cave that gave its name to the place.

Lusmagh (Offaly), Lusmágh, 'plain of herbs'.

Lynally (Offaly), Lann Eala, 'church of Eala'.

The church here was founded in the late 6th century by St Colmán Eala (or Elo), whose distinguishing name is said to come from a wood near here.

Lynn (Westmeath), Lann Mhic Luacháin, 'Mac Lúacháin's church'.

The church here is said to have been founded in the late 6th century by St Colmán mac Lúacháin.

Lyracrompane (Kerry), Ladhar an Chrompáin, 'fork of the creek'.

Lyre (several), An Ladhar, 'the fork'.

The name usually indicates a division of a river or stream, or of a valley.

Lyrenageeha (Cork), Ladhair na Gaiothe, 'fork of the wind'.

M

Maam Bridge (Galway), An Mám, 'the mountain pass'.

Maam Bridge lies at the head of the extreme north-west reach of Lough Corrib between two mountain ranges. The bridge is over Joyces River here. See also **Maam Cross**.

Maam Cross (Galway), An Teach Dóite, 'the burnt house'.

Maam Cross is five miles south of Maam Bridge at the crossroads of the T71 and L100. Its Irish name refers to some local incident here.

Maas (Donegal), An Más, 'the thigh'.

The name refers to a long hill here. See also **Mace**.

Mace (several), Mas, 'thigh', 'long low hill'.

Mac Gillycuddy's Reeks (Kerry), Na Cruacha Dubha, 'the black peaks'.

The mountains here were a place of refuge for the powerful sept of the Mac Gilly-cuddys, whose descendant still bears the title of 'Mac Gillicuddy of the Reeks'. ('Reeks' means 'ridges', 'crests'.)

Macollop (Waterford), Maigh Cholpa, 'Colpa's plain'.

Macosquin (Derry), Maigh Choscáin, 'Coscán's plain'.

Macroom (Cork), Maigh Chromtha, 'crooked plain'.

Magh Adair (Derry), Maigh Adhair, 'Adhar's plain'.

Maghera (several), Machaire, 'plain'.

Maghera in Derry has the full Irish name of *Machaire Rátha*, 'plain of the ring-fort'. Originally it was known as *Ráth Lúraigh*, 'Lúrech's ring-fort'. Lúrech was an obscure saint whose 'grave' is said to be at the low mound lying about 40 yards (36m) west of the church here.

Magheraboy (several), Machaire Buidhe, 'yellow plain'.

Magheracloone (Monaghan), Machaire Cluana, 'plain of (the) meadow'.

Magherafelt (Derry), Machaire Fíolta, 'plain of Fíolta'.

A fuller Irish name here is *Machaire Teach Fíolta*, 'plain of (the) house of Fíolta'.

Magheralin (Down), Machaire Lainne, 'plain of (the) church'.

A fuller Irish name is *Machaire Laine Rónáin*, 'plain of St Rónán's church'. This was St Rónán Fin, who founded the monastery here in the 7th century. The site, now a National Monument, is by the remains of the parish church.

Magheramena (Fermanagh), Machaire Meadhónach, 'middle plain'.

Magheramore (Wicklow), Machaire Mór, 'great plain'.

Magheramorne (Antrim), Machaire Morna, 'Morna's plain'.

Magherareagh (Clare), Machaire Riabhach, 'grey plain'.

Magherasaul (Down), Machaire Sabhail, 'plain of (the) barn'.

Magheraveely (Fermanagh), Machaire Mhílic, 'plain of (the) low ground'.

Maghery (Donegal), An Machaire, 'the plain'.

Magilligan (Derry), Aird Mhic Giollagáin, 'Mac Gilligan's height'.

The name properly applies to Magilligans Point, on Lough Foyle.

Maguire's Bridge (Fermanagh), Droichead Mhic Uidhir, 'Maguire's bridge'.

The Maguires (Mac Guires) were the leading sept of Fermanagh.

Magunihy (Kerry), Magh gCoinchinn, 'plain of the O Conkins'.

Mahee Island (Down), Inis Mochaoi, 'St Mochaoi's island'.

The island is in Strangford Lough, and Nendrum here was founded by St Mochaoi, a disciple of St Patrick.

Maigue (Limerick), An Mháig, 'the (river of the) plain'.

Malahide (Dublin), Mallach Íde, 'Íde's hill-top'.

This is a controversial name. Some sources claim the name derives from a 'John de la Hyde', who was here in the 13th century. Others relate the name of this river to that of Malahide Bay, which was also known as

Maol Domhnain, 'whirlpool of the Firdomnainn' (said to mean 'men of the deep pits' and to be a group of Firbolg). This itself gave the local name 'Muldowney' for the mouth of the river — which again is said to be connected with the name of the Meadow Water here at the estuary (now more commonly known as the Broad Meadow Water).

Malin Head (Donegal), Málainn, 'brow'.

Malin More (Donegal), Málainn Mhóir, 'big brow'.

Mallaranny (Mayo) An Mhala Raithní, 'the hill brow of (the) ferns'.

Mallow (Cork), Mala, 'plain of the Ealla'.
The brief Irish name represents *Magh Eala*, with Eallo (or Allo, or Allow) the former name of the stretch of the river Blackwater as it flows through the town here. Compare **Dunhallow**.

Malone (Antrim), Má Lón, 'plain of elms'.
The Irish name appears to be a corruption of *Magh Leamhna*.

Manorcunningham (Donegal), Mainéar Uí Chuinneagáin, 'Cunningham's manor'.
A grant of 1629 refers to a 'James Cunningham Esquire' who 'created the Manor of Fort Connyngham'. An alternative Irish name for the place is *An Machaire Mór*, 'the great plain'.

Manorhamilton (Leitrim), Cluainín, 'little meadow'.
The full Irish name is *Cluainín Uí Ruairc*, 'O Rourke's little meadow'. The English name derives from that of Sir Frederick Hamilton, to whom lands were granted here by Charles I.

Mansfieldtown (Louth).
The present name is a corruption of the original Anglo-Norman family name, as shown by historic records: *Villa Maundevyle* in 1294, *Maundeville's town* in 1297, and *Maundeuileston* in 1316. 'Mandeville' has thus become 'Mansfield'.

Manulla (Mayo), Magh Nulla, 'Fionnalbha's plain'.
The personal name has been distorted and abbreviated out of recognition in the modern Irish and English place-name.

Marble Hill (Donegal), Cnoc an Mharmair, 'marble hill'.

The name is said to be a corruption of 'Marble Hall', a former demesne here.

Marino (Dublin), Marino.
The name is that of Marino House here, built for James Caulfield, fourth viscount Charlemont, in the latter half of the 18th century, and itself apparently named after the Italian town of Marino, while at the same time suggesting a seaside location.

Markethill (Armagh), Cnoc an Mhargaidh, 'hill of the market'.

Martinstown (Antrim, Limerick), Baile Uí Mháirtín, 'Martin's town'.

Maryborough See **Port Laoise**.

Maryville (Tipperary), Teach Mháire, 'Mary's house'.
The name is that of a house here.

Mashanaglass (Cork), Maigh Seanghlaise, 'plain of (the) old stream'.

Massereene (Antrim), Coill Ultach, 'Ulster wood'.
The English name represents the Irish for 'hill of the queen', from *más*, 'thigh' (so 'long hill') and *ríoghan* (genitive *ríoghna*), 'queen'. The name is that of the demesne of Antrim Castle.

Massford (Down), Áth an Aifrinn, 'ford of the mass'.
The name presumably indicates a ford where an open air mass was celebrated. Compare **Mass Fort**.

Mass Fort (Down), Dún an Aifrinn, 'fort of the mass'.
The name is that of an ancient fortification near Kilkeel where mass was celebrated when it was an offence to do so in church. See also **Massford**.

Maum. See **Maam**.

Maumturk Mountains (Galway), Mám Torc, 'pass of (the) boars'.
The mountain range is named after the pass that runs between the peaks of Maumturkmor and Letterbrickaun, north-west of Maam Bridge. The name is also spelt Maamturk.

Mayglass (Wexford), Maigh Ghlas, 'green plain'.

Maynooth (Kildare), Maigh Nua, 'Nuadu's plain'.
Nuadu Necht was said to be the legendary ancestor of Leinstermen.

Mayo (Mayo), Maigh Eo, 'plain of (the) yew trees'.
Mayo's original full Irish name was *Maigheó na Sacsan*, 'yew tree plain of the Saxons', referring to the English monks who settled here in the 7th century. The county name comes from that of the abbey, now in ruins, near the village of Mayo. The name is fairly common elsewhere. (See for example **Mayobridge**.)

Mayobridge (Down), Droichead Mhaigh Eo, 'bridge of (the) plain of (the) yew trees'.
The bridge takes the present B7 road over a small stream here.

Maze, The (Armagh), An Má, 'the plain'.
The name is found elsewhere, with the Irish version often as *An Maigh*.

Meath, An Mhí, 'the middle (place)'.
Meath was the fifth and final province of Ireland to be established, the others being Connacht, Leinster, Munster and Ulster. Its name was recorded in the 9th century as *Mide*, this referring to its location between Ulster to the north, Connacht to the west, and Leinster to the south. The original Meath covered an area at least as extensive as that of the present counties of Meath and Westmeath, and the present county of the name came into existence only in the 13th century.

Meelick (several), Míleac, 'place by water'.
Most places of the name are on or near a river. Meelick in Galway is on the Shannon.

Meenacahan (Donegal), Mín Mhac Catháin, 'mountain pasture of the sons of Cathán'.

Meenaclady (Donegal), Mín na Claodaí, 'mountain pasture of the (river) Clady'.

Meenagorp (Tyrone), Mín na gCorp, 'mountain pasture of the corpses'.
The name apparently refers to a graveyard for the victims of a battle or fatal disease.

Meenaneary (Donegal), Mín an Aoire, 'mountain pasture of the shepherd'.

Meencarrigagh (Donegal), Mín Charraigeach, 'rocky mountain pasture'.

Mellifont (Louth), An Mhainistir Mhór, 'the great monastery'.
The famous abbey here was founded in the first half of the 12th century as the first Cistercian abbey in Ireland. The founders were Irish novice monks who had been to Clairvaux in France, and the abbey (and its riverside site) were based on this. The name, from Latin *Fons Mellis*, means 'source of honey'. The abbey is now in ruins.

Melvin, Lough (Fermanagh/Leitrim), Loch Meilghe, 'Meilghe's lake'.
Meilghe is the name of a legendary ruler here.

Merrion (Dublin), Muirfin, 'seashore land'.
Merrion is on the south shore of Dublin Bay.

Middleton (Wexford), An Baile Láir, 'the middle town'.
The village of Middleton is on the coast just south of Courtown, and is perhaps named for its location approximately halfway between Cahore Point to the south and Kilmichael Point to the north.

Middletown (Donegal), Na Machaireacha, 'the plains'.
Middletown is the middle of the lowlands here, west of Gweedore.

Midleton (Cork), Mainistir na Corann, 'monastery of the weir'.
Midleton is the middle of a stretch of low-lying country here in south-east Cork, approximately halfway between Carrigtohill and Castlemartyr.

Milehouse (Wexford), Teach an Mhíle, 'mile house'.
A 'mile house' is a house a mile from a town or village, usually by a milestone. In this case, Milehouse is a mile from Enniscorthy, now on the L30 road.

Milestone (Tipperary), Cloch an Mhíle, 'the milestone'.
Milestone is at a crossroads (today of the T19 and L34) approximately halfway between Nenagh and Tipperary.

Milford (several), Áth an Mhuilinn, 'ford of the mill'.
In some cases the Irish name is different, so that in Donegal, for example, Milford is *Baile na nGallóglach*, 'town of the gallowglasses' (i.e. of the armed soldiers).

Millbrook (Antrim), Sruthán an Mhuilinn, 'stream of the mill'.

Mill Brook (Meath), Béal Átha na gCeannai, 'ford-mouth of the merchants'.

Milleens (Kerry), Meillíní, 'little hills'.
The English name has an 's' to represent the Irish plural.

Millisle (Down), Oileán an Mhuilinn, 'island of the mill'.
Millisle has the only complete windmill in the country, dating from the late 18th century.

Millstreet (Cork, Waterford), Sráid an Mhuilinn, 'street of the mill'.
'Street' here means a village with one central street.

Milltown (several), Baile an Mhuilinn, 'town of the mill'.
There are very many places of this name, often several in one county, indicating the abundance of rivers and streams in Ireland and the importance of the mill in the economy of the country. See also **Milford**.

Milltown Malbay (Clare), Sráid na Cathrach, 'village of the stone fort'.
This small town and resort overlooks Mal Bay.

Milltownpass (Westmeath), Bealach Bhaile an Mhuilinn, 'road of (the) town of the mill'.
The 'pass' here is the Pass of Kilbride, not a mountain pass but simply the main road (now the T4) from Kinnegad to Kilbeggan. (Compare the name of **Tyrrellspass** on the same road.)

Minerstown (Down), Baile na Mianadóirí, 'town of the miners'.
An alternative Irish name for Minerstown is *An Rinn Mhór*, 'the great headland', referring to Ringmore Point (the same name anglicised), east of the village.

Mitchelstown (Cork), Baile Mhistéalai, 'Mitchel's homestead'.
The name was recorded in the late 13th century as *Villa Michel*, and was apparently named after the Welsh-Norman landowner here, Mitchel Condon.

Moate (Westmeath), An Móta, 'the mound'.
The name refers to the large ring-fort or motte that lies south-west of the village and is known as Moatgrange ('little Grace's mound', said to be named after a Munster princess).

Mocollop (Waterford), Magh Colpa, 'plain of (the) cattle'.

Modeshil (Tipperary), Magh Deisil, 'southern plain'.

Mogeely (Cork), Maigh Dhíle, 'Éile's plain'.

Moher Cliffs. See **Cliffs of Moher**.

Mohill (Leitrim), Maothail, 'soft land'.

Moig Cross (Limerick), Crois na Má, 'cross-road of the plain'.
Moig Cross is on the main road (now the L28) from Shanagolden to Ardagh, at a point where it is crossed by a minor road.

Moira (Down), Maigh Rath, 'plain of (the) ring-forts'.
This is the popular interpretation of the name, but the Irish is almost certainly corrupt and the true origin therefore uncertain.

Monagay (Limerick), Móin an Ghé, 'bog of the goose'.
The name refers to the wild geese here near Newcastle West.

Monaghan (Monaghan), Muineachán, '(place of) little thickets'.
The town gave its name to the county.

Mona Incha (Tipperary), Móin na hInse, 'bog of (the) island'.
Mona Incha Abbey is two miles from Roscrea where it was founded on land that was formerly an 'island' in surrounding bog.

Monard (Tipperary), An Mhóin Árd, 'the high bog'.

Monasteranenagh (Limerick), Mainistir an Aonaigh, 'monastery of the assembly'.
The 'assembly' was probably an ancient fair here. The monastery is now in ruins.

Monasterboice (Louth), Mainistir Bhuithe, 'St Buite's monastery'.
St Buite is said to have founded the monastery here in the 6th century, although the site was probably a sacred place already before he arrived here. Little is known about St Buite.

Monasterevan (Kildare), Mainistir Eimhín, 'St Eimhín's monastery',
St Eimhín was perhaps a contemporary of St Patrick. The monastery no longer exists, but its former site is that of Moore Abbey.

Monasteroris (Offaly), Mainistir Fheorais, 'Feora's monastery'.

Monea (Fermanagh), Maigh Niagh, 'plain of heroes'.

Moneen (Clare), Móinín, 'small bog'.

Money (several), Muine, 'grove', 'shrubbery'.

Moneygall (Offaly), Muine Gall, 'grove of (the) foreigners'.

The 'foreigners' here would have been the English.

Moneyglass (Antrim), An Muine Glas, 'the green grove'.

Moneylea (Westmeath), Muine Liath, 'grey grove'.

Moneymore (several), Muine Mór, 'big grove'.

Moneyneaney (Derry), Móin na nIonadh, 'bog of the wonders'.

This interpretation assumes that the last part of the name comes from Irish *iongnadh*, 'surprise', 'wonder'. If it does, there should be a local explanation for the name.

Monivea (Galway), Muine Mheá, 'grove of (the) mead'.

Doubtless mead was brewed here at one time.

Monkstown (several), Baile an Mhanaigh, 'townland of the monk'.

The Irish version of the name is usually the same as this, although for Monkstown, the suburb of Dublin, the Irish is *Carraig Bhréanainn*, 'Brendan's rock'.

Montiaghs (Armagh), Móinteacha, 'boggy place'.

Mooghaun (Clare), An Múchán, 'the underground passage'.

This is the name of the ancient stone fort in the grounds of Dromoland Castle, and describes one of its features.

Mooncoin (Kilkenny), Móin Choinn, 'Caidhn's bog'.

Moone (Kildare), An Mhaoin, 'the possession'.

This is Moone Abbey, whose full Irish name is *Maon Choluim Cille*, 'St Columba's gift'. The abbey itself is now long ruined, as is Moone Castle, but the name is preserved in the village here and in Moone Abbey House.

Moore Park (Cork), Baile Uí Mhaolmhordha, 'Moore's town'.

More Castle (Cork), An Caisleán Mór, 'the big castle'.

Morgallion (Meath), Machaire Gaileang, 'plain of the Mór Gailenga'.

The Mór Gailenga ('great Gailenga') were the tribe whose leader is said to have given his name to Gallen.

Mornington (Meath), Baile Uí Mhornáin, 'homestead of the descendants of Mornáin'.

This is the Mornington that gave the title of the Earl of Mornington who was the elder brother of the Duke of Wellington. He in turn gave the name of Mornington Crescent in London.

Moroe (Limerick), Maigh Rua, 'red-coloured plain'.

Mosney (Meath), Má Mhuireadha, 'Muirid's plain'.

Mostrim. See **Edgeworthstown.**

Mothel (Waterford), Maothail Brógán, 'soft land'.

Mountallen (Roscommon), Cnoc an Chaisleáin, 'hill of the castle'.

Mount Bellew (Galway), An Creagán, 'the rocky ground'.

Mountcharles (Donegal), Móin Séarlas, 'Charles's bog'.

An alternative Irish name here is *Tamhnach an tSalainn*, 'field of the salt'. There is no bog here, however, and the Irish name appears to be a corruption of the English.

Mountgarrett (Wexford), Móta Gairéad, 'Gairéad's castle'.

Irish *móta* can mean both 'moat' and 'mound', and is also the word for a moated dwelling or fortification.

Mount Juliet (Kilkenny), Garrán an Bhaltúnaigh, 'Walton's grove'.

An alternative English name for Mount Juliet was Jerpointchurch, alluding to Jerpoint Abbey, and 'Juliet' appears to be a corruption of 'Jerpoint', influenced by the other personal names that usually form the latter half of a 'Mount' name.

Mountmellick (Laois), Móinteach Mílic, 'bog land of (the) water meadows'.

Mountmellick is practically surrounded by the river Owenass.

Mountnorris (Armagh), Achadh na Cranncha, 'field of the place of trees'.

The English name derives from the fort built here in the latter half of the 16th century by Sir John Norris to protect the pass between Armagh and Newry.

Mount Nugent (Cavan), Droichead Uí Dhálaigh, 'bridge of the descendants of Daly'.

Mountrath (Laoise), Maighean Rátha, 'bog of the ring-fort'.
The first word of the Irish name appears to represent *móin*, 'bog', with this providing the bogus English 'Mount'.

Mountsandel (Derry), Dún Dá Bheann, 'fort of (the) two peaks'.
The ancient fort here is now just a large mound. The 'peaks' or 'tops' are those of the promontory here south of Coleraine overlooking the river Bann. The English 'mount' is the fort.

Mountshannon (Clare), Baile Uí Bheoláin, 'Boland's homestead'.
According to one theory, the English name was borrowed from the demesne of Mount Shannon in Limerick, which is actually by the river Shannon.

Mourne Abbey (Cork), Mainistir na Móna, 'monastery of the bog'.
English 'Mourne' is a version of Irish *móin*, 'bog'.

Mourne Mountains (Down), Beanna Boirche, 'peaks of Boirche'.
The English name derives from the Mughdhorna tribe, whose leader was Mughdhorn and who also gave their name to Cremorne. The Irish name is traditionally said to refer to a shepherd who looked after the royal cattle of Ulster here on the mountains in the 3rd century.

Movanagher (Derry), Má Bheannchair, 'plain of (the) place of peaks'.
The peaks would be the mountains west of here.

Movilla (Down), 'plain of the ancient tree'.

Moville (Donegal), Maigh Bhile, 'plain of the ancient tree'.
This is the same name as Movilla.

Moy (Tyrone), An Maigh, 'the plain'.

Moyacomb (Wicklow), Magh Dá Chon, 'plain of (the) two dogs'.
This is the traditional interpretation of the name, but the last word of the Irish is almost certainly a corruption of *chonn*, 'heads', referring to hills or peaks nearby.

Moyaliff (Tipperary), Magh Ailbh, 'Ailbhe's plain'.

Moyard (Galway), Maigh Árd, 'high plain'.

Moyarget (Antrim), Maigh Airgid, 'plain of silver'.
It is not clear what the 'silver' is here. Perhaps the latter half of the name is actually a personal name.

Moyarta (Clare), Magh Fhearta, 'plain of (the) grave'.

Moyasta (Clare), Maigh Sheasta, 'Seasta's plain'.

Moycullen (Galway), Maigh Cuilinn, 'plain of holly'.

Moydow (Longford), Maigh Dumha, 'plain of (the) burial mound'.

Moygashel (Tyrone), Maigh gCaisil, 'plain of (the) stone fort'.
This is the place that gave the name to the special kind of Irish linen.

Moyglass (Galway), Maigh Ghlas, 'green plain'.

Moygoish (Westmeath), Magh Uais, 'plain of (the descendants of) Colla'.
This was the Colla who was the father of Mughdhorn who gave his name to Cremorne.

Moygownagh (several), Magh Gamhnach, 'plain of (the) dairy cows'.
Irish *gamhnach* is the word for a 'stripper', or cow that yields milk in her second year after calving.

Moyle (several), Maol, 'bare hill'.

Moylett (Cavan), Magh Leacht, 'plain of (the) gravestones'.

Moylough (Galway), Maigh Locha, 'plain of (the) lake'.
The lake appears to be Summerville Lough, north-west of Moylough.

Moynalty (Meath), Maigh nEalta, 'plain of (the) flocks'.

Moyne (several), An Mhaighean, 'the precinct'.
The name usually refers to the enclosure round a fort or castle.

Moynoe (Clare), Magh Nó, 'plain of (the) yews'.
This is really the same name as Mayo, with an intrusive *n*.

Moyra (Donegal), Maighreach, 'place of salmon'.

This name may derive from Irish *maighre*, 'salmon' or else simply represent *Magh Rátha*, 'plain of (the) ring-fort'. It is on the river Ray, which supports the first theory, but is also known as Myrath, which seems to support the second.

Moyrus (Galway), Maigh Iorras, 'plain of (the) peninsula'.

Moytura (Mayo) Maigh Tuireadh, 'plain of (the) towers'.

The 'towers' or pillars are the stone circles that stand on the site of an ancient battle here between the Firbolg and the Dedanaans in the '303rd year of the world'.

Moyvalley (Kildare), Maigh Bhealaigh, 'plain of (the) road'.

Moyvore (Westmeath), Maigh Mhórdha, 'Moore's plain'.

Muckamore (Antrim), Maigh Chomair, 'plain of (the) confluence'.

The confluence is of the Six Mile Water and Lough Neagh.

Muckinagh (several), Muiceannach, 'place of pigs'.

The name denotes a place where pigs were kept or where they regularly fed or slept.

Mucknoe Plain (Monaghan), Machaire Mucshnámha, 'plain of (the) swimming place of pigs'.

The name denotes the narrowest part of the little lake here where pigs used to swim across.

Muckross (several), Mucros, 'pig peninsula'.

The name indicates a peninsula where pigs lived or were herded.

Muff (Donegal), Magh, 'plain'.

This is the same name as Maghera.

Muineagh (Donegal), Muineach, 'grove', 'shrubbery'.

Muine Bheag (Carlow), Muine Bheag, 'little grove'.

The former English name of Muine Bheag was Bagenalstown, from the Bagenal family who lived here from the 16th century, and in particular from Walter Bagenal who founded the town in the late 18th century. (He intended to build a grand architectural ensemble and to call it 'Versailles'.)

Muings (Mayo), Na Moingí, 'the ferns'.

As elsewhere, the Irish plural is shown by the 's' in the English name.

Muldonagh (Derry), Maol Domhnaigh, 'hill of (the) church'.

Mulhuddart (Dublin), Maol Eadrad, 'Eiderne's hilltop'.

Mullabohy (Louth), Mullach Boithe, 'hilltop of (the) hut'.

Mullacrew (Louth), Mullach Craoibhe, 'hilltop of (the) dense tree'.

Mullacurry (Louth), Mullach Curraigh, 'hilltop of the marsh'.

Mullagh (several), An Mullach, 'the hilltop'.

Mullaghanee (Monaghan), Mullach an Fhia, 'hilltop of the deer'.

Mullaghareirk (Limerick), Mullach an Radhairc, 'hilltop of the outlook'.

Mullaghareirk is the highest mountain (over 1,300 ft [390m]) of the Mullaghareirk range which extends over the border in south-west Limerick to north-west Cork.

Mullaghbrack (Armagh), Mullach Breac, 'speckled hilltop'.

Mullaghcarn (Tyrone), Mullach Carn, 'hilltop of (the) mound'.

The 'mound or cairn is the ancient fort of *Fiachra Éilgeach* or *Carn Amhalgaidh* ('burial mound of Amhalgaidh').

Mullaghglass (Armagh), 'green hilltop'.

Mullaghmast, Rath of (Kildare), Mullach Maistean, 'hilltop of Maiste'.

Mullaghmast was the place of assembly for the elders of the states of South Leinster. Maiste is said to be the name of an English adventurer who invited some 400 native chieftains here in 1577 for a New Year's banquet, then treacherously murdered them.

Mullaghmore (several), An Mullách Mor, 'the big hilltop'.

Mullaghroe (Sligo), An Mullach Rua, 'the red-coloured hilltop'.

This name was formerly interpreted, almost certainly wrongly, as 'hilltop of the druids' (*Mullach na nDruadh*).

Mullan (Fermanagh), Mullán, 'little hilltop'. Elsewhere, as in Monaghan, this name means 'the mill' (*An Muileann*).

Mullary (Louth), Má Lamhraí, 'Lamrach's plain'.

Mullaslin (Tyrone), Mullach Slinne, 'hilltop of flat stones'.

Mullinahone (Tipperary), Muileann na nUamhan, 'mill of the cave'.
This is not a 'hilltop' name like others above. The cave here is the one near the village through which the little river runs.

Mullinavat (Kilkenny), Muileann an Bhata, 'mill of the stick'.
Perhaps the stick (*bata*) here was a marker of some kind by the river Blackwater.

Mullingar (Westmeath) an Muileann gCearr, 'the wry mill'.
The name is said to derive from *muileann*, 'mill' and *cearr*, 'wrong', 'left-handed', meaning a mill whose wheel revolved anti-clockwise. But the second part of the name may actually be a personal name such as Carr.

Mullins Cross (Louth), Cros an Mhuilinn, 'crossroads of the mill'.

Mulnavannoge (Leitrim), Maol na bhFeannóg, 'hill of the hooded crow'.
These birds are still sometimes known in Ireland as 'scald crows'.

Mulrany (Mayo), An Mhala Raithní, 'the hilltop of (the) ferns'.

Mulroy (Donegal), An Mhaol Rua, 'the red-coloured hill'.
There is no obvious hill here by the shore of Mulroy Bay. Irish *maol* can mean anything that is bald or bare, as well as a hill, and so perhaps the reference is to the reddish-coloured sandbank in the middle of the lower part of the bay.

Multyfarnham (Westmeath), Muilte Farannáin, 'Farannán's mills'.

The '-ham' ending of the English name no doubt arose by association with the many English place-names ending thus.

Munster, An Mhuma, 'place of the Mumu (tribe)'.
Munster is one of the ancient kingdoms (a 'fifth', or *cúige*) of Ireland, and shares the same ending as Leinster and Ulster. This '-ster' is the Norse genitive *s* with Irish *tír*, 'land', 'territory' (as in Tyrone).

Murneen (Mayo), Muirnín, 'pleasant place'.

Murragh (Cork), Muighe Rátha, 'plain of (the) ring-fort'.
Murragh is a low-lying land by the river Bandon, 8 miles (12.8km) west of Bandon.

Murrisk (Mayo), Muraisc, 'sea marsh'.
Murrisk is a resort on Clew Bay.

Murroe (Limerick), Maigh Rua, 'red-coloured plain'.

Murvey (Galway), Muirbheach, 'sandy (place by the sea)'.

Muskerry (Cork), Múscraí, '(place of the) descendants of Cairbre Músc'.
Cairbre Músc (in older texts often called Carbery Musc) was the ancestor of the Muscraige (people of Muskerry) in early legend.

Mutton Island (Galway), Oileán Caorach, 'island of sheep'.
This island is in Galway Bay, as is another of the name off the west coast of Clare.

Mweelrea (Mayo), Maoil Réidh, 'smooth hilltop'.

Myshall (Carlow), Míseal, 'low plain'.

N

Naas (Kildare), An Nás, 'the assembly place'.

Naas was the residence of the kings of Leinster until the 10th century, and a meeting place for the great state assemblies. The central ring-fort is still here.

Nad (Cork), Nead, 'nest'.

Nafooey, Lough (Galway), Loch na Fuaithe, 'lake of the phantom'.

There must be a local legend to explain this name.

Nantinan (Limerick), Neanntanán, 'place of nettles'.

Narin (Donegal), An Fhearthainn, 'the rainy place'.

In its coastal location on this western peninsula of Donegal, the fishing village and resort of Narin is exposed to the frequent rainy weather that comes from the Atlantic.

Narrow Water (Down), Caoluisce, 'narrow water'.

Narrow Water Castle is at the head of Carlingford Lough, where the water narrows as the Newry Canal.

Naul (Dublin), An Aill, 'the cliff'.

Navan (Meath), An Uaimh, 'the cave'.

The 'cave' could have been a grotto somewhere on the Boyne or the Blackwater, which rivers meet here. In a poll taken earlier this century among local people, as to whether the town should be called officially Navan or An Uaimh, it was the former name that won the vote. The sense of Navan here is thus not the same as at Navan Fort (see **Emain Macha**).

Neagh, Lough (Antrim), Loch nEathach, 'Eochaid's lake'.

Eochaid (Eochaidh) was a legendary king of Munster who was said to have drowned in the lough when it suddenly flooded in the 1st century AD.

Neck of the Ballagh (Donegal), Cnoc an Bhealaigh, 'hill of the road'.

Both Irish nouns have been adopted untranslated in the English name.

Nenagh (Tipperary), An tAonach, 'the assembly place'.

Nenagh was one of the main assembly places of Munster in early times. Later, the assemblies took the forms of horse fairs, and these are continued today in the regular cattle markets.

Nendrum (Down), Naoindroim, 'nine ridges'.

This is a monastic site on Mahee Island, in Strangford Lough. The 'nine ridges' are the hillocks on the island here.

New Birmingham (Tipperary), Gleann an Ghuail, 'valley of the coal'.

When the site here was exploited for coal at the end of the 18th century, the resulting settlement was named after Birmingham, England, itself in the centre of a coalmining district. The Irish name reflects the nature of the location here below the Slieveardagh Hills.

New Bridge (several), An Droichead Nua, 'the new bridge'.

In historical terms, of course, the bridge today may not even be 'new' at all but several hundred years old. In some cases the Irish name is different in meaning, as at Newbridge in Galway, where it is *Gort an Iomaire*, 'field of the ridge'.

New Buildings (Derry), An Baile Nua, 'the new township'.

The Irish name has also been recorded as *Primite*, 'first fruits', 'primitiae'.

Newcastle (several), An Caisleán Nua, 'the new castle'.

As with the 'new bridges' of places called New Bridge or Newbridge, the 'new castle' will in modern terms often be an old one, and may now not even exist, or at any rate be in ruins. In Newcastle, Down, the 16th-century castle was pulled down in the 19th century to make way for a hotel. In Newcastle, Wicklow, the castle was an English royal one built at the beginning of the 13th century, and the land there was recorded at this time as *terra Mackineganorum*, 'land of the Mac Finnegans'. The Dublin Newcastle was built at the time of the Anglo-Norman invasion similarly, but now has only scant remains.

Newcastle West (Limerick), An Caisleán

Nua, 'the new castle'.

The castle here was built by the Knights Templar in the 12th century, but was burnt down in 1642. (Two 15th-century halls remain, however.) It is 'west' of one of the other many 'new castles', perhaps the Newcastle south-west of Clonmel in Tipperary.

New Chapel (Kerry), An Séipéal Nua, 'the new chapel'.

New Ferry (Antrim), An Caladh Nua, 'the new ferry'.

New Ferry is on the river Bann, and an alternative Irish name indicates an earlier way of crossing: *An Snámh Nuadh*, 'the new swimming place'.

New Geneva. See **Geneva**.

Newgrange (Meath), Sí an Bhrú, 'fairy mound of the palace'.

This is an important mound or cairn in the Brugh na Boinne complex, the burial ground of the kings of Tara. It has had several other Irish names in its time, including *Achadh Alla*, 'Alla's field', *Caiseal Aonghusa*, 'Aonghus's stone fort', and *Ros na Ríogh*, 'cemetery of the kings'. The English name is thus misleading for such an ancient monument.

Newmarket (Cork), Áth Trasna, 'oblique ford'.

An alternative Irish name for Newmarket is *Baile Nuadh Dhútha Ealla*, 'new town of (the) cattle estate'. The river here is the Dalva.

Newmarket-on-Fergus (Clare), Cora Chaitlín, 'Kathleen's weir'.

The English name is a borrowing of the horseracing centre in Suffolk, together with the name of the river on which it stands. There was a well known local racecourse here. The Irish name doubtless refers to a member of the family of the man who designed or constructed the weir.

New Mills (several), An Muileann Nua, 'the new mill'.

An alternative Irish name for Newmills in Tyrone is *Droichead Dubhrois*, 'bridge of (the) black wood'. The river here is the Swilly.

Newport (Mayo, Tipperary).

The Irish name of Newport, Mayo, on the Newport River, is *Baile Uí Fhiacháin*, 'O

Feehan's homestead'. Of Newport, Tipperary, on the Shannon, it is *An Tulach*, 'the hillock'. There are other places of the name elsewhere.

Newrath (Wicklow), An Iúrach, 'the yew land'.

This is not a 'new' name, therefore, and in origin is similar to Newry.

New Ross (Wexford), Rhos Mhic Thriúin, 'wood of the sons of Treon'.

The Irish name produced the anglicised version 'Rosmacrone' at one stage, resulting in an absurd legend about a woman here called Rose Macrone.

Newry (Down), An tIúr, 'the yew tree'.

Early records of the name show it as *Iobhar Chind Tráchta*, 'yew tree of (the) head of (the) strand', and according to tradition St Patrick is said to have founded the monastery here and to have planted the yew at the head of the strand of Carlingford Lough. Both monastery and yew, however, were burned down in the latter half of the 12th century.

Newtown (several), An Baile Nua, 'the new town'.

Newtownabbey (Belfast), Baile na Mainistreach, 'town of the (place that belongs to the) abbey'.

Newtownabbey is a new town development in the Belfast suburbs combining the originally separate places of Glengormley, Whitehall, Whiteabbey (giving the latter half of the name), Jordanstown, Cavehill, Carnmoney and Whitehouse.

Newtownards (Down), Baile Nua na hArda, 'new town of the promontory'.

The town was founded here in the early 17th century by Sir Hugh Montgomery, with the last past of the name (Ards) that of the district here at the head of Strangford Lough. (See **Ards**.) An alternative Irish name for Newtownards is *Baile Áird Uladh*, 'town of (the) heights of (the) Ulstermen'.

Newtownbreda (Down), Baile Nua na Bréadaí, 'new town of Breda'.

'Breda' means 'broken land' (Irish *bréad*, 'fragment', *bréadach*, 'breaking'.) Today Newtownbreda is a southern suburb of Belfast but still has much of the character of a small village.

Newtownbutler (Fermanagh), An Baile Nua, 'the new town'.
The English name, itself from a settler named Butler, gave the title of baron to the Butlers who were earls of Lanesborough.

Newtowncunningham (Donegal), An Baile Nua, 'the new town'.
Cunningham was the family name of Scottish settlers here.

Newtown Forbes (Longford), An Lios Breac, 'the speckled fort'.
The English name is that of the Scottish settler here in the early 17th century, Sir Arthur Forbes.

Newtown Hamilton (Armagh), Baile Úr, 'new town'.
The English name is that of the Scottish settler here in the late 17th century, Alexander Hamilton.

Newtownmountkennedy (Wicklow), Baile an Chinnéidigh, 'Kennedy's town'.
The English name is that of Sir Robert Kennedy, who was granted the manor here in the latter half of the 17th century.

Newtown Pery (Limerick).
This 18th-century settlement, now a district of the city of Limerick, is named after Viscount Pery, speaker of the Irish House of Commons.

Newtownstewart (Tyrone), An Baile Nua, 'the new town'.
The English name is that of William Stewart, who was given possession of lands here during the Plantations of the reign of James I.

Newtown-Trim (Meath), Baile Nua Átha Troim, 'new town of (the) ford of (the) elder'.
Newtown-Trim is on the river Boyne on the eastern outskirts of Trim.

Nine Mile House (Tipperary), Tigh na Naoi Míle, 'nine mile house'.
The village is approximately nine miles north of Carrick-on-Suir.

Noard (Tipperary), Nua-Ard, 'new height'.

Nobber (Meath), An Obair, 'the work'.
The 'work' is traditionally said to be the former Anglo-Norman castle here.

Nohoval (Cork, Kerry), Nuachabháil, 'new enclosure'.

Noughaval (Clare), Nuachongbháil, 'new establishment'.

Nurney (several), An Urnaí, 'the oratory'.

O

Offaly, Uíbh Fhailí, '(place of the) descendants of Failghe'.

Russ Failge was the son of Catháir Már (Cahirmore), and legendary ancestor of the Uí Failge, or Offaly people. The present county boundaries were established in 1556, when the territory was shired as King's County, named after Queen Mary's husband, King Philip II of Spain. The county reverted to the Irish name in 1920. (Compare **Laois,** which was formerly Queen's County.)

Offerlane (Laois), Uí Foirchealláin, '(place of the) descendants of Foircheallán'.

Oghermong (Kerry), Eochair Mong, 'edge of (the) swamp'.

Ogonnelloe (Clare), Tuath Ó gConáile, 'district of the O Connollys'.

Oldbridge (Meath), An Seandroichead, 'the old bridge'.

Oldbridge is on the river Boyne.

Oldcastle (Meath). An Seanchaisleán, 'the old castle'.

Old Court (Down), Seanchúirt, 'old court'.

Old Ross (Wexford), An Sean Ros, 'the old wood'.

Omagh (Tyrone), An Ómaigh, 'the plain'.

The first part of the Irish name, which was recorded in the 15th century as *Oghmaigh,* is of unknown meaning.

Omeath (Louth), Ó Méith, '(place of the) descendants of Méith'.

Oneilland (Armagh), Uí Nialláin, '(place of the) descendants of Niallán'.

Niallán is traditionally said to be descended from one of the three brothers Colla who was the father of the tribal chief who gave his name to Cremorne. The final *d* was apparently added by association with English 'land'.

Oola (Limerick, Waterford), Úlla, 'apple trees', 'orchard'.

Oran (Roscommon), Uarán, 'cold spring'.

Oranmore (Galway), Órán Mór, 'big cold spring'.

Oughter, Lough (Cavan), Loch Uachtair, 'upper lake'.

Lough Oughter is 'upper', i.e. further up the river Erne, with regard to Lough Erne.

Oughterard (Galway), Uachtar Árd, 'upper height'.

The village is on the approach to the Connemara Mountains.

Oughtmama (Clare), Ucht Mama, 'upper pass'.

Oughtmama is on the road through the hills of the Burren, north of Corofin.

Oulart (Wexford), An tAbhallort, 'the orchard'.

Ovens, The (Cork), Na hUamhanna, 'the caves'.

The English name is a misleading corruption of the Irish, which refers to the labyrinthine limestone caves in a quarry near the village. They extend for nearly 700 yards (630m).

Owenass (Laois), Abha an Easa, 'river of the waterfall'.

The river Owenass rises in the Slieve Bloom mountains and joins the Barrow near Mountnellick.

Owenbeg (several), An Abhainn Bheag, 'the little river'.

Owenboy (several), An Abhainn Bhuidhe, 'the yellow river'.

Owenduff (several), Abhainn Dubh, 'black river'.

Owenea Bridge (Donegal), Droichead Abha an Fhia, 'bridge of (the) river of the deer'.

Owenmore (several), Abhainn Mhór, 'big river'.

The name is often that of a river below the junction of two or more streams.

Owenreagh (several), Abhainn Riabhach, 'grey river'.

Oxmantown (Dublin).

Earlier names of Oxmantown (or Oxmanstown) were *Ostmantown, Ostmaneby* and *Austmannabyr,* showing it to be called after the 'eastmen' or Scandinavian settlers here.

Ox Mountains (Sligo), Sliabh Ghamh, 'mountain of storms'.

The English name is a mistranslation of the

99

Irish, taking the words as *sliabh dhamh*, 'mountain of oxen', instead of *sliabh ghamh*.

P

Pallas (Galway, Longford), Pailís, 'palisade'.

Pallas Green (Limerick), Pailís Ghréine, 'Grian's palisade'.
There is both New Pallas Green and Old Pallas Green, almost 2 miles (3.2km) apart. The name contains that of Grian, the sun goddess (Irish *grian*, 'sun') whose 'throne' was said to be in nearby Cnoc Greine.

Pallaskenry (Limerick), Pailís Chaonraí, 'Caonrach's palisade'.

Park (several), An Pháirc, 'the field', 'the pasture'.

Parkmore (Antrim), An Pháirc Mhór, 'the big field'.

Parknasilla (Kerry), Páirc na Saileach, 'field of the willows'.

Passage East (Waterford), An Pasáiste, 'the passage'.
Passage East is on the eastern side of the estuary of the Suir, above Waterford Harbour.

Passage West (Cork), An Pasáiste, 'the passage'.
Passage West is on the narrow western passage which joins the inner division of Cork Harbour with the chief outer section.

Phoenix Park (Dublin), Páirc an Fhionnuisce, 'park of the clear water'.
The English name is a corruption of the Irish, perpetuated in the erection of the so-called Phoenix Column in 1745, which is surmounted by a phoenix rising from the ashes. The original spring or 'clear water' is now underground.

Piltown (Kilkenny), Baile an Phoill, 'town of the hole'.
Irish *poll* means both 'hole', 'hollow' and 'pool', in the latter sense referring to a deep part of a river. Either of these could apply here. The English name is a corruption of the Irish.

Pluck (Donegal), Pluc, 'swelling', 'lump'.
The name presumably refers to some natural feature here.

Poisoned Glen (Donegal), An Cró Nimhe, 'the poisoned enclosure'.
The name is said to refer to the abundance of spurge here.

Pollagh (Offaly), Pollach, 'place of holes'.
See **Piltown** for an explanation of Irish *poll*.

Pollremon (Galway), Poll Réamainn, 'Réamonn's hole'.

Pollrone (Kilkenny), Poll Ruadhán, 'Ruadhán's hole'.

Pomeroy (Tyrone), Cabhán an Chaorthainn, 'hill of the rowan tree'.
The Irish name is often now the same as the English, which is itself a family name of Norman origin, here that of the owners of the 16th-century Pomeroy House.

Portacloy (Mayo), Port an Chlaí, 'harbour of the fence'.

Portadown (Armagh), Port an Dúnáin, 'landing-place of the little fort'.
Irish *port* means not only 'port', 'harbour', but also 'bank', 'passage', 'fort' or even just 'place'. Usually, however, it is a location by the sea or by a river. Here, the fort would have guarded a strategic crossing of the river Bann.

Portaferry (Down), Port an Pheire, 'harbour of the ferry'.
Portaferry is on the eastern side of the strait to the sea that forms the entrance to Strangford Lough.

Portarlington (Laois), Cúil an tSúdaire, 'secluded place of the tanner'.
The English name is that of Lord Arlington (Sir Henry Bennet), the owner of the lands here in the 17th century. Lord Arlington's title comes from Arlington in Devon.

Portavogie (Down), Port an Bhogaigh, 'harbour of the bog'.

Port Ballintrae (Antrim), Port Bhaile an Trá, 'harbour of (the) town of the strand'.
Port Ballintrae is near the mouth of the river Bush.

Portbraddon (Antrim), Port Bradán, 'harbour of salmon'.

Portglenone (Antrim), Port Chluain Eoghain, 'fort of (the) meadow of Eogan'.

Portlaoise (Laois), Port Laoise, 'fort of (the) descendants of) Lugaid'.

The personal name is the same as for Laois. From 1556 to 1920 Portlaoise was called Maryborough, after Queen Mary, just as Laois itself was Queen's County.

Portlaw (Waterford), Port Lách, 'landing place of (the) hill'.

Portlaw is on the Clodiagh and takes its name from the steep hill at the top of the village.

Portmagee (Kerry), An Caladh, 'the landing place'.

The origin of the name can be seen in the Irish alternative, *Port Mhig Aoidh*, 'harbour of Mac Gee' (or Magee, literally 'sons of Hugh').

Portmarnock (Dublin), Port Mearnóg, 'harbour of St Eirnín'·

The ruins of St Marnock's church and well can still be seen here. The saint's name is itself an affectionate diminutive of Eirnín (M'Earnóg, literally 'my little Eirnín'). The same saint's name occurs in Kilmarnock, Scotland.

Portmuck (Antrim), Port Muc, 'harbour of the pigs'.

Portnablagh (Donegal), Port na Bláiche, 'port of the milk'.

The name refers to the good pastureland here for cattle.

Portnoo (Donegal), Port Nua, 'new harbour'.

Portora (Fermanagh), Port Abhla Faoláin, 'landing place of (the) apple trees of Faolán'.

Portora is now best known as the name of Portora Royal School on the north-west edge of Enniskillen. In the grounds of the school, which is by Lough Erne, are the ruins of the early 17th-century Portora Castle.

Portrane (Dublin), Port Reachrann, 'port of Reachrann'.

Reachrann is the Irish name of Lambay Island, just off the coast here.

Portroe (Tipperary), An Port Rua, 'the red-coloured fort'.

Portrush (Antrim), Port Rois, 'harbour of (the) headland'.

The name refers to the basalt peninsula of Ramore Head here.

Portsalon (Donegal), Port an tSalainn, 'harbour of the salt'.

Presumably salt was landed at the harbour here at the mouth of Lough Swilly.

Portstewart (Derry), Port Stíobhaird, 'Stewart's harbour'.

The name is that of the Stewart family who held lands here in the mid-18th century.

Portumna (Galway), Port Omna, 'landing place of (the) oak'.

There must have been a prominent oak tree by the river Shannon here, possibly even a fallen one.

Poulaphouca (Wicklow), Poll an Phúca, 'pool of the sprite'.

The name refers to the waterfall under the road bridge here where the river Liffey plunges into the 'Pool of the Pooks' or 'Puck's Hole', so called from the water sprite thought to live in it (as in similar pools elsewhere).

Poulewhack (Clare), Poll an Bhaic, 'hole of the angular piece of land'.

Poulgorm (Kerry), Poll Gorm, 'blue hole'.

Powerscourt (Wicklow), Cúirt an Phaoraigh, 'Power's mansion'.

The name was probably given to the demesne here by the eighth earl of Kildare when he built the castle on this site at the end of the 15th century. The personal name was probably that of the landowners here some two hundred years earlier, the Le Poer family.

Poyntzpass (Armagh), Pas an Phointe, 'Poyntz's pass'.

The name refers to the engagement of 1598 in which English troops under Lieutenant Sir Toby Poyntz fought to prevent the Irish force, led by Hugh O Neill, from entering Down along this road. The route at that time here would have been through bogland and dense forest. (*See also* **Punchestown**).

Prosperous (Kildare), An Chorrchoill, 'the projecting wood'.

At the end of the 18th century there was a prosperous cotton industry here, promoted by Robert Brooke who had made a fortune in India. The industry was ruined by the rising of 1798 and by the government's refusal to finance Brooke's venture.

Pubblebrien (Limerick), Pobal Uí Bhriain,

'(land of the) descendants of O Brien'.
The name indicates that the land here was the patrimony of the O Briens.

Puckane (Tipperary), Pocán, 'little bag'.
The name probably indicates a small, secure place, a 'nest'.

Punchestown (Kildare), Baile Phúinse,

'Punch's homestead'.
The name is a family name of Norman origin (derived from the equivalent of Pontius) and is related to the name Poyntz, as in Poyntzpass. Punchestown has long been famous for its racecourse.

Q

Quilty (Clare), Coillte, 'woods'.

Quoile (Down), An Caol, 'the narrow (water)'.
This is the name of the river that flows past Quoile Quay and the ruined Quoile Castle into the south-west arm of Strangford Lough.

R

Raffeen (Cork), An Ráth Mhín, 'the level ring-fort'.

Rahan (Offaly), Raithean, 'place of ferns'.

Rahanisky (several), Ráthan Uisce, 'ring-fort of (the) water'.

The name applies to a ring-fort by a lake or a river.

Raharney (Westmeath), Ráth Fhearna, 'ring-fort of (the) elder tree'.

Raheen (several), An Ráithín, 'the little ring-fort'.

Raheens (Mayo), Na Ráithíní, 'the little ring-forts'.

The Irish plural is represented by the final English 's', as often happens in similar names.

Rahelty (Kilkenny, Tipperary), Ráth Eilte, 'ring-fort of (the) doe'.

Raheny (Dublin), Ráth Eanaigh, 'ring-fort of (the) marshes'.

This name could also be interpreted as 'Eanna's ring-fort'.

Rahine (Cork), An Ráithín, 'the little ring-fort'.

Raholp (Down), Ráth Cholpa, 'ring-fort of (the) bullock'.

Rahugh (Westmeath), Ráth hAodha, 'St Hugh's ring-fort'.

St Áed (whose name is usually anglicised as Hugh, although the two names are not connected) is said to have founded the church in the old ring-fort here in the 6th century. An earlier name of Rahugh was *Ráith Aedho mic Bricc*. This identifies the particular saint as Áed mac Bricc, of the royal race of the southern O Neills.

Ramelton (Donegal), Ráth Mealtain, 'Mealtan's ring-fort'.

Ramoan (Antrim), Ráth Madháin, 'Muadhán's ring-fort'.

Ramore (Antrim), Ráth Mhór, 'big ring-fort'.

Ramore Head is the basaltic peninsula on which Portrush stands.

Ramsgrange (Wexford), An Ghráinseach, 'the grange'.

An alternative Irish name for Ramsgrange is *Gráinseach Shéim*, 'St James's grange'.

English 'Ram-' appears to be a corruption of 'James', or more precisely, of its Irish equivalent.

Randalstown (Antrim), Baile Raghnaill, 'Randal's town'.

Randalstown derives its name from Randal Mac Donell, second viscount Dunluce and first marquis of Antrim, to whose wife, Rose O Neill, the manor of Edenduffcarrick was granted by Charles II in 1683. The settlement here was originally known as both 'Mainwater' (for its location on the river Main) and 'Ironworks' (for its forges and furnaces that smelted the iron ore here).

Randown (Roscommon), Rinn Dúin, 'headland of (the) fort'.

The headland of the name is the small peninsula, also called St John's, that projects south-east into Lough Ree. The original fort was probably where the castle ruins are today.

Raphoe (Donegal), Ráth Bhoth, 'ring-fort of (the) huts'.

The huts here were said to have surrounded the early monastery, which itself may have been founded by St Columb.

Rasharkin (Antrim), Ros Earcáin, 'Earcán's wood'.

Rashee (Antrim), Ráth Sidhe, 'ring-fort of (the) fairies'.

Ratallen (Roscommon), Ráth tSailainn, 'ring-fort of (the) salt'.

Perhaps salt was obtained from local springs here at one time.

Ratass (Kerry), Ráth Teas, 'southern ring-fort'.

Possibly the 'northern' ring-fort was on the other side of the hills that lie to the west of the Stacks Mountains here.

Rath (several), Ráth, 'ring-fort'.

Rathangan (Kildare), Ráth Iomgháin, 'Iomghán's ring-fort'.

The original ring-fort can be seen here in a field near the church, which is to the north of the town.

Rathanny (several), Ráth Eanaigh, 'ring-fort of (the) marsh'.

In the case of Rathanny, Carlow, the Irish name is *Ráth Sheanigh*, 'ring-fort of Seanach'.

Rathaspick (several), Ráth Easpuig, 'fort of (the) bishop'.

The name would have applied to a church built inside an old ring-fort, with the foundation belonging to a bishop.

Rathborney (Clare), Ráth Boirne, 'ring-fort of (the) Burren'.

The name indicates the location of the place in the district known as the Burren.

Rathclogh (Tipperary), Ráth Chloch, 'ring-fort of (the) stones'.

Rathconnell (Westmeath), Rubha Chonaill, 'Conall's salient'.

The first part of the Irish name has become assimilated to *ráth*, 'ring-fort'. Irish *rubha* means not only 'point of land', 'salient', but also in some cases 'brake', i.e. a thicket, especially one that could be used for trapping deer.

Rathconrath (Westmeath), Ráth Conarta, 'ring-fort of (the) covenant'.

This interpretation of the name assumes that the Irish represents *ráth connartha*, and relates to a pact of some kind made with the Norse builders of the ring-fort here.

Rathcoole (several), Ráth Cúil, 'ring-fort of (the) secluded place'.

In some cases, the second half of the Irish name may well represent the other sense of *cúil*, i.e. 'back', 'hill', since this would be a more likely site for a fort. For some places of the name, the Irish is given as *Ráth Chumhaill*, as if meaning 'ring-fort of Finn mac Cumaill (Finn Mac Coole)'. But he was not a historic person and can hardly have founded or owned a ring-fort.

Rathcormac (Cork, Sligo), Ráth Chormaic, 'Cormac's ring-fort'.

Rathcroghan (Roscommon), Ráth Cruachan, 'ring-fort of (the) mound'.

The name is usually interpreted as deriving from Irish *ráth cruacháin*, with the latter word meaning 'little hill'. There are many scattered earthworks here, and Rathcroghan is the most conspicuous of them. The complex is near Tulsk.

Rathdangan (Wicklow), Ráth Daingin, 'ring-fort of (the) stronghold'.

The 'stronghold' was probably the 'motte-and-bailey' fortress at Killamoat, just south of here.

Rathdowney (Laois), Ráth Domhnaigh, 'ring-fort of (the) church'.

It is possible that the Irish name is a corruption of *Ráth Tamhnaigh*, 'ring-fort of (the) green field', and that this pagan name was reinterpreted in its Christian sense, with a small spelling change, when a church was built on the site of the fort.

Rathdrinagh (Meath), Ráth Dhraighneach, 'ring-fort of (the) thorny place'.

Rathdrum (several), Ráth Droma, 'ring-fort of (the) ridge'.

Ring-forts were often built on low hills or ridges.

Rathfarnham (Dublin), Ráth Farnáin, 'Fearnan's ring-fort'.

For the final '-ham' of the English name, compare **Multyfarnham**.

Rathfeigh (Meath), Ráth Faiche, 'ring-fort of the sports field'.

Rathfran (Mayo), Ráth Bhranduibh, 'Brandubh's ring-fort'.

Rathfriland (Down), Ráth Fraoileann, 'Fraoile's ring-fort'.

The English name has acquired a final 'd' by association with 'land'. The original large ring-fort can be seen to the east of the village.

Rathgar (Dublin), Ráth Garbh, 'rough ring-fort'.

Rathgormack (Waterford), Ráth Ó gCormaic, 'ring-fort of (the) descendants of Cormac'.

Rathkeale (Limerick), Ráth Caola, 'Caola's ring-fort'.

Rathkeeran (Kilkenny), Ráth Ciarán, 'St Ciarán's ring-fort'.

It is believed that St Ciarán (Kieran) who founded the church near the pagan ring-fort here was probably St Ciarán the Elder of Seir.

Rathkeevin (Tipperary), Ráth Chaoimhín, 'Caoimhín's ring-fort'.

The name of Caoimhín is traditionally anglicised as Kevin.

Rathkenny (Antrim, Meath), Ráth Cheinnigh, 'Ceannach's ring-fort'.

Rathlacken (Mayo), Ráth Leacan, 'ring-fort of (the) flat stones'.

Rathlee (Mayo, Sligo), Ráth Lao, 'ring-fort

of (the) calves'.

Rathlin (Antrim), Reachlainn.
The exact meaning of this very old name is still a mystery. It was recorded by Ptolemy in the 2nd century AD as *Rikini* and in Old Irish as *Rechru*. It can hardly be based on the Irish word for 'tree' (modern *crann*) and is certainly not *Ráth Éireann*, 'fort of Ireland', as has been suggested. The most that can be proposed is that some Celtic word or root lies hidden in the name, and that perhaps this might be the one seen in modern Welsh *rhygnu*, 'to rub', 'to scrape', referring to an island that has been 'rubbed' or eroded over the centuries. The same name lies behind Lambay Island, Dublin (with *l* changed to *r* to give *Reachrainn*), and the Irish name of Rathlin O Birne Island, Donegal, is *Reachlainn Uí Bhirn*.

Ráth Luirc (Cork), An Ráth, 'the ring-fort'.
The first name here means 'Lorc's ring-fort'. From the mid-17th century until the 1920s the name of the town was Charleville, after Charles II.

Rathmacknee (Wexford), Ráth Mac Naoi, 'ring-fort of the sons of Naoi'.

Rathmichael (Dublin), Ráth Mhichíl, 'Michael's ring-fort'.

Rathmines (Dublin), Ráth Maonais, 'ring-fort of de Moenes'.
The original name of the ring-fort here was just *Ráth*. In the first half of the 14th century ownership passed to the de Moenes family, and this gave the name its present form.

Rathmolyon (Meath), Ráth Moliain, 'Moladhan's ring-fort'.

Rathmore (several), An Ráth Mhór, 'the big ring-fort'.

Rathmoyle (Kilkenny), An Ráth Mhaol, 'the bald ring-fort'.
The name implies a fort that is dilapidated or broken.

Rathmullan (Donegal, Down), Ráth Maoláin, 'Maolán's ring-fort'.

Rathnew (Wicklow), Ráth Naoi, 'Naoi's ring-fort'.
It is possible that the personal name here is a corruption of *nua*, 'new', and that it was introduced, consciously or unconsciously, to explain a local legend.

Rathnure (Wexford), Ráth an Iúir, 'fort of

the yew tree'.
The *n* of the English name comes from Irish *an*, 'the', as it does in the name of Newry.

Rathowen (Westmeath), Ráth Eoghain, 'Eógan's ring-fort'.

Rathreagh (Longford, Mayo), Ráth Riabhach, 'grey ring-fort'.

Rathroan (Meath), Ráth Ruáin, 'Ruán's ring-fort'.

Rathroe (Wexford), An Ráth Ruadh, 'the red-coloured fort'.

Rathronan (Limerick, Tipperary), Ráth Rónáin, 'Rónán's ring-fort'.

Rathvilly (Carlow), Ráth Bhile, 'ring-fort of (the) ancient tree'.

Rattoo (Kerry), Ráth Tuaidh, 'northern ring-fort'.
This is the so called Round Tower of Rattoo, south of Ballyduff (near Ballybunion), but it is not clear where the 'southern' fort or place-reference is.

Ravensdale (Louth), Gleann na bhFiach, 'valley of the ravens'.
Ravensdale is a glen through which the river Flurry flows.

Ray (Donegal), An Ráith, 'the ring-fort'.
There was at one time a monastery here called Moyra, 'plain of (the) fort', with its site where the ruined 16th-century church now stands.

Ray Bridge (Donegal), Droichead na Ráithe, 'bridge of the ring-fort'.

Rear Cross (Tipperary), Crois na Rae, 'crossroads of the plain'.
Irish *rae* has a primary meaning 'duelling ground', 'battlefield', but there is no evidence that the name should be interpreted in this way here. The English name is a corruption of the Irish.

Reban (Kildare), Fásach Réaban, 'wilderness of (the) white mountain-flat'.
The English name represents the second half of the Irish name, itself a contraction of *réidh bán*. In Kildare, the name in these forms is recorded for Reban Castle, northwest of Athy, and it would be more realistic to interpret *réidh* here as 'level area between mountains'.

Recess (Galway), Sraith Salach, 'fenland of willows'.
Recess is on Glendalough Lough, so that

sraith (or *srath*) here applies to the low-lying land by the lake. The English name suggests that an earlier or alternative Irish name might have been based on *cúil*, 'corner', 'angle', 'recess', usually appearing in the English spelling as 'Coole'.

Red Bay (Antrim), Cuan an Deirg, 'bay of the red colour'.
Perhaps the 'red colour' is a personal nickname (as 'the Red'). It can hardly be for the sunsets here on the east coast.

Red Island (Dublin), An tOileán Rua, 'the red island'.

Ree, Lough (Longford/Westmeath/Roscommon), Loch Ríbh, 'grey lake'.

Reenard (Kerry), Rinn Árd, 'high headland'.

Reens (Limerick), Roighne, 'best place'.
The English plural 's' suggests that the Irish name is a corruption of some other word. From the location of Reens, it is not likely to be *reanna*, 'headlands', 'edges'. Perhaps it is *riana*, 'tracks', 'paths'.

Rehins (Mayo), Raithíní, 'little forts'.
The English name, as often, has taken a plural 's' to represent the Irish plural.

Richhill (Armagh), Log an Choire, 'hollow of the whirlpool'.
If the English name does not derive from a personal name it may refer to the rich fruit-growing land here.

Rineanna (Clare), Rinn Eanaigh, 'headland of (the) marsh'.
This is the name of the peninsula west of Shannon Airport that juts into the wide river Shannon here.

Ring (several), An Rinn, 'the headland', 'the point of land'.

Ringaskiddy (Cork), Rinn an Scidígh, 'headland of the Skiddy family'.
The Irish family name Skiddy (Scideadh) derives from the Scottish island of Skye.

Ringrone (Cork), Rinn Róin, 'headland of seals'.

Ringsend (Derry), Droichead na Carraige, 'bridge of the rock'.
The river here is the Aghadowney. The English name is a compound of Irish *rinn*, 'point of land', and English 'end'. Ringsend is just north of Farm Hill and east of the higher Boyds Mountain. Compare the next entry.

Ringsend (Dublin), An Rinn, 'the headland'.
English 'end' has been added to the Irish word. Ringsend was once a port of Dublin, now it is an eastern district of the city.

Ringville (Waterford), Rinn Ó gCuanach, 'headland of (the) O Cooneys'.
The English name represents the same Irish origin as for Rinville, so means 'headland of the ancient tree'.

Rinkippeen (Galway), Rinn na gCipín, 'point of land of the little sticks'.
This name, if correctly interpreted, may refer to some local natural or constructed feature.

Rinneen (several), Rinnín, 'little headland', 'little point of land'.

Riverstick (Cork), Áth an Mhaide, 'ford of the stick'.
The stick or staff must have acted as a marker for the ford. Riverstick is actually on the river Stick.

Riverstown (several).
The Irish names of places called Riverstown vary considerably. Riverstown in Cork is *Baile Roisín*, 'town of the little wood'. The village is on the Glashaboy River close to its confluence with two smaller rivers. In Tipperary, Riverstown is *Baile Uí Lachnáin*, 'O Lachnain's town'. In Sligo the place of this name is Irish *Baile idir Dhá Abhainn*, 'town between two rivers', and in Louth it is *Baile Nua*, 'new town'.

Riversville (Galway), Baile na hAbhann, 'town of the river'.

Roachtown (Meath), Baile an Róistigh, 'Roche's town'.
Roche is a Norman name that soon became widely established as a virtually native Irish family name.

Roadford (Clare), Áth an Bhealaigh, 'ford of the road'.
The ford took the road here over the river Aille.

Robertstown (Kildare), Baile Riobaird, 'Robert's homestead'.

Rochestown (Cork), Baile an Róistigh, 'Roche's town'.
This is the same family name as for Roachtown.

Rochfort Bridge (Westmeath), An

Droichead, 'the bridge'.

The English name is that of Robert Rochford, member of parliament for Westmeath, who owned lands here in the latter half of the 17th century. The full Irish name is *Droichead Chaisleán Loiste*, 'bridge of (the) burnt castle'. This refers to Castlelost, one mile (1.6km) north-west of here, whose scant stone fragments remain.

Rockabill (Dublin) Cloch Dhábhiolla, 'Dábhiolla's rock'.

The English name is a part translation, part transliteration of the Irish name of this twin-peaked island. A local legend tells how Dábhiolla, the pet dog of Bóinn, the goddess of the river Boyne, was drowned with its mistress here and its body washed up on this little island.

Rockcorry (Monaghan), Buíochar, 'yellow land'.

The second half of the English name represents the latter half of the Irish.

Rockmills (Cork), Carraigan Mhuilinn, 'rock of (the) mill'.

Roe (Derry), An Rua, 'the red (place)'.

Roosky (several), Rúscaigh, 'marshy place'.

Rosbeg (Donegal), Ros Beag, 'small headland'.

Roscommon (Roscommon), Ros Comáin, 'St Comán's wood'.

The Dominican friary here is believed to stand on the site of the original foundation of St Comán in the 8th century.

Rosconnell (Laois), Ros Chonaill, 'Conall's wood'.

Roscor (Fermanagh), Ros Corr, 'round promontory'.

Roscrea (Tipperary), Ros Cré, 'Cré's wood'.

Rosegreen (Tipperary), Faiche Ró, 'Roe's green'.

The Irish name appears to be a translation of the original English, which itself then became distorted so that the family name was obscured.

Rosenallis (Laois), Ros Fhionnghlaise, 'wood of (the) clear stream'.

Roskeen (several), Ros Caoin, 'beautiful wood'.

Roslea (Fermanagh), Ros Liath, 'grey wood'.

Rosmuck (Galway), Ros Muc, 'headland of pigs'.

Rosmult (Tipperary), Ros Moilt, 'wood of (the) wether'.

Rosnaree (Meath), Ros na Rí, 'wood of the kings'.

Ross (Meath), An Ros, 'the wood'.

Rossard (Wexford), Ros Árd, 'high wood'.

Rossbeigh (Kerry), Ros Beithe, 'headland of birches'.

This is a peninsula on Dingle bay.

Ross Carbery (Cork), Ros Ó gCairbre, 'wood of (the) O Cairbre (family)'.

Rosserk (Mayo), Mainistir Ros Eirc, 'monastery of (the) headland of St Earc'.

Ross Errilly (Galway), Ros Oirbhealagh, 'wood of the eastern road'.

The road past Ross Errilly Friary here runs to the east of Lough Corrib.

Rosses, The (Donegal), Na Rosa, 'the headlands'.

The English name does everything but translate the main Irish word. The Rosses is a coastal area with many headlands.

Rossglass (Down), Ros Glas, 'green headland'.

Rossglass is on the west coast of Ringmore Point.

Rossin (Louth), Roisín, 'little wood'.

Rossinver (Leitrim), Ros Inbhir, 'headland of (the) estuary'.

Rossinver is properly the name of Ross Point, which projects into the southern part of Lough Melvin just north of the village, where a small river runs into it.

Rosslare (Wexford), Ros Láir, 'middle headland'.

The headland here is between The Raven Point to the north (the other side of Wexford Harbour) and Greenore Point to the south.

Rossmore (several), An Ros Mór, 'the big wood'.

This frequent name also mean 'the big headland'.

Rossnowlagh (Donegal), Ros Neamhlach, 'wood of the apple trees'.

The Irish name is a corruption of *ros an abhla*.

Rossroe (Clare, Galway), Ros Ruadh, 'red-coloured wood'.

Rostellan (Cork), Ros Tialláin, 'Tillán's peninsula'.

Rostrevor (Down), Ros Treabhair, 'Trevor's wood'.

The old oaks here have been preserved as a forest nature reserve.

Rosturk (Mayo), Ros Toirc, 'headland of boars'.

Roughty (Kerry), An Ruachtach, '(glen of) the O Ruachtan (family)'.

The river Roughty took its name from the valley here.

Roundstone (Galway), Cloch na Rón, 'rock of the seals'.

The English name is a part translation, part corruption of the Irish.

Roundwood (Wicklow), An Tóchar, 'the causeway'.

An earlier Irish name here was 'Leitrim' (or some similar spelling), 'grey ridge'.

Rousky (Tyrone), Rúscaigh, 'marshy place'.

This is the same name as Roosky.

Rower, The (Kilkenny), An Robhar, 'the red-coloured land'.

Royal Oak (Carlow), Cloch Rúsc, 'stone (building of the) marsh',

The English name is that of an old inn here.

Ruan (Clare), An Ruán, 'the red-coloured land'.

Rush (Dublin), An Ros, 'the headland'.

Rutland Island (Donegal), Inis Mhic an Doirn, 'Mac an Doirn's island'.

The English name derivers from the fourth duke of Rutland, Charles Manners, who attempted to establish a port here in the late 18th century.

Rylane (Cork), Réileán, 'level land of the meadow'.

The Irish name represents *réidh léana*.

S

Saggart (Dublin), Teach Sagard, 'house of St Sacra'.

St Sacra (Mo-Shacra) is said to have founded a monastery here in the 7th century. A few fragments of the original remain in the old graveyard.

Saintfield (Down), Tamhnaigh Naomh, 'field of (the) saints'.

St John's Point (Down), Tigh Eoin, 'John's house'.

St John's Point is the headland to the east of Dundrum Bay, south of Killough. The English name was recorded in an early spelling as *Styoun*, derived from the Irish with 'St-' instead of the single Irish 'T-'. The 'St' ('Saint') was thus not in the original, although *Tigh* did probably mean 'church' rather than just 'house'. The same conversion of *T-* to *St-* is seen in the name of Stillorgan.

St Johnstown (Donegal), Baile Suingean, 'St John's town'.

The village arose as an English settlement in the late 17th century.

St Macdara's Island (Galway), Oileán Mhic Dara, 'Mac Dara's island'.

The church here was said to have been founded by St Mac Dara in the 6th century. The unusual name means 'son of the oak'.

St Mullin's (Carlow), Tigh Moling, 'St Moling's house'.

The monastery here was founded in the 7th century by St Moling, who became bishop of Ferns and Glendalough.

St Patrick's Island (Dublin), Inis Phádraig, 'St Parrick's island'.

This island off Skerries is said to have been where St Patrick landed on his journey from Ulster to Wicklow, and where he stayed for three weeks, crossing daily to Red Island.

St Patrick's Purgatory (Donegal), Purgadóir Phádraig, 'St Patrick's purgatory'.

This is a deep cave on Station Island, in Lough Derg. St Patrick is said to have fasted here to drive evil spirits away from the island. The cave is also said to be the gateway to Hell. It was once a great place of pilgrimage, although now the cave is sealed.

Sallins (Kildare), Na Solláin, 'the willow groves'.

Sallybrook (Cork), Srugh na Saileach, 'stream of the willows'.

Sally Gap (Wicklow), Bearnas na Diallaite, 'gap of the saddle'.

The Irish name, of which the English is a corruption, means 'saddle' in the geographical sense of 'mountain pass', and Sally Gap is in fact a high crossroads in the Wicklow Mountains.

Salruck (Galway), Oileáin an tSáile, 'islands of the sea'.

Salruck is not itself an island but is on the coast at the head of Little Killary Bay, so that the 'islands of the sea' are all further offshore.

Salt (Kildare), Salt, 'leap'.

There may have been a place where animals leaped through a gap here, or a river where fish leaped as at Leixlip.

Saltee Islands (Wexford), Na Sailtí, 'the salt islands'.

These are two uninhabited islands off the south coast of Wexford.

Salthill (Dublin), Cnoc an tSalainn, 'hill of the salt'.

The name inplies a location by the sea, as is shown more clearly in the Irish name of Salthill, Galway, which is *Bóthar na Trá*, 'road of the strand'.

Sandycove (Dublin), Cuan an Ghainimh, 'cove of the sand'.

According to one source, the name actually derives from a Scot here called (or nicknamed) Sandy. Support for this is said to lie in the name of the bay here, Scotsman's Bay. But certainly Sandycove is a good descriptive name for this bathing beach in Dún Laoghaire.

Santry (Dublin), Seantrabh, 'old tribe'.

This name may be a corruption of some other sense.

Saul (Down), Sabhall, 'barn'.

According to legend, the name refers to a barn here that was presented to St Patrick for use as a church by one of his first converts.

Scalp (several), An Scailp, 'the cleft', 'the chasm'.

Scaralwalsh (Wexford), Scairbh Solais, 'shallow of light'.

If the name does not mean 'place of clear, shallow water', the second half may be a personal name, as suggested by the English 'Walsh'.

Scardaune (Mayo), Scardán, 'cataract'.

Scarriff (Clare), An Scairbh, 'the shallow'.

The name properly applies to Scarriff Bay here.

Scart (several), Scairt, 'thicket', 'shrubbery'.

Scartaglen (Kerry), Scairteach an Ghlinne, 'grove of the valley'.

Scarteen (several), Scairtín, 'little shrubbery'.

Scarva (Down), Scarbhach, 'rough place'.

The name refers to the ford over the stream here.

Scattery Island (Clare), Inis Cathaigh, 'Cathach's island'.

The English name is a corruption of the Irish, beginning with the final *s* of *inis*.

Schull (Cork), An Scoil, 'the splinters'.

This is a controversial name. It may derive from *scolb*, 'splinter', 'thin stick', and perhaps refer to a place where sticks or timber could be got for building, thatching or the like. On the other hand, the origin may lie in *scoil*, 'school', and relate to an early school founded by monks here. The English version of the name is sometimes found as Skull.

Scrabo Hill (Down), Screabach, 'crusted (place)'.

The name implies rough land.

Screeb (Galway), Scríob, 'track', 'furrow'.

Screggan (Offaly), An Screagán, 'the rough ground'.

Scullogue Gap (Wexford), Bearna Scológ, 'gap of (the) farm servants'.

Scurlogstown (Meath), Baile Scorlóg, 'Scurlóg's town'.

Seaforde (Down), Baile Forda, 'Forde's town'.

The English name, with its Irish translation, derives from that of Colonel M.

Forde, who promoted development here in the early 19th century.

Seagoe (Armagh), Teach Daghobha, 'Daghobha's house'.

The English name has altered the initial Irish 'T-' to 'S-'.

Seefin (Limerick), Suidhe Finn, 'seat of Finn'.

The name refers to the pseudo-historical hero, Finn mac Cumaill (Finn Mac Coole).

Seirkieran (Westmeath), Saighir Chiaráin, 'fountain of St Ciarán'.

Saighir was said to be the name of the fountain here where St Ciarán founded a monastery in the 6th century.

Seskanore (Tyrone), Seisceann Odhar, 'pale-coloured marsh'.

Seskilgreen (Tyrone), Seisíoch Chill Ghrianna, 'the *seisíoch* of (the) church of Grianna'.

A *seisíoch* is an old measure of land, equal to 60 acres (24 hectares).

Shanachashel (Kerry) Seanachaiseal, 'old stone fort'.

Shanagarry (Cork), An Seangharraí, 'the old garden'.

Shanagolden (Limerick), Seanghualainn, 'old hill shoulder'.

Shanakill (Cork), Seanachoill, 'old wood'.

The English form of the name suggests that the original Irish could have meant 'old church' (i.e. from *cill*, not *coill*).

Shanboth (Kilkenny), Seanbhoth, 'old hut'.

Shandon (Cork), Seandún, 'old fort'.

The fort was probably on the hill here, in the northern district of the city of Cork.

Shane's Castle (Antrim).

This is the better known name of the castle of Edenduffcarrick (see **Randalstown**). It derives from Shane O Neill, who built it in the 16th century. He was the grandfather of Rose O Neill, who named Randalstown. The name of Edenduffcarrick (*Eadan Dubhcharraige*) means 'hilltop of (the) black rock'.

Shangarry (several), Seangharraidhe, 'old garden'

Shankill (several), Seanchill, 'old church'.

In Belfast, the 'old church' was sited on the old graveyard on the Shankill Road.

Shanmullagh (Monaghan), Seanmhullach,

'old summit'.

Shannon (Limerick/Clare), An tSionna, 'the old one'.
The name of Ireland's longest river almost certainly means something like 'old one' (almost 'old man river'), implying an ancient river god personified by the flowing water. The name was recorded by Ptolemy in the 2nd century AD as *Senos*.

Shannon Bridge (Offaly), Droichead na Sionainne, 'bridge of the Shannon'.

Shannon Pot (Cavan), Lag na Sionna, 'hollow of the Shannon'.
This is the name of the small pool on the mountain of Tiltinbane that is said to be the source of the Shannon.

Shantallow (Derry), Seantalamh, 'old land'.

Shantonagh (Monaghan), Seantonnach, 'old rampart'.
This is presumably a reference to an old fort here.

Sharavogue (Offaly), Searbhóg, 'bitter (place)'.
The name suggests barren or difficult land, unless it refers to some incident here.

Sheean (Mayo), An Sidheán, 'the fairy hill'.

Sheelin, Lough (Cavan/Meath/Westmeath), Loch Sithleann, 'lake of (the) fairies'.

Sheep Haven (Donegal), Cuan na gCaorach, 'harbour of the sheep'.
It is possible that the original English name was 'Ship Haven', which would have produced an Irish version *Cuan na Long*. The present Irish name is a translation of the English as it stands. An alternative Irish name for Sheephaven Bay here is *Báighe na nDúnaibh*, 'Downings Bay', from the village of Downings on the coast.

Sheeroe (Longford), Sidh Ruadh, 'red-coloured fairy hill'.

Shehy Mountain (Cork), Cnoc Seithe 'hill of (the) fairies'.

Shelburne (Kerry, Wexford), Síol mBrain, '(place of) descendants of Bran'.
Bran was a popular name of early warriors and rulers of Ireland.

Shelmaliere (Wexford), Síol Maoluidhir, '(place of) descendants of Maolughra'.

Shelton (Wicklow), Teach na gCanónach, 'house of the canons'.
This is the name of Shelton Abbey. The English name is not a corruption of the Irish, but is apparently the name of the house here in the mid-17th century of Robert Hassells, with the house named by his wife. Shelton is a fairly common English place-name.

Sheskin (Mayo, Monaghan), Na Seiscinn, 'the marsh'.

Shillelagh (Wicklow), Síol Éalaigh, '(place of the) descendants of Éláthach'.
Éláthach was a 9th-century hero. The cudgel called the 'shillelagh' is said to have been originally made from the wood of oaks here.

Shimna (Down), '(river) of bulrushes'.

Shinrone (Offaly), Suí an Róin, 'seat of the seal'.
This name can hardly apply literally, since Shinrone is well inland. Perhaps the other sense of Irish *rón* apart from 'seal' should be considered. This is 'hair', and could perhaps be understood as a nickname, so that the whole name means 'seat of the hairy man'.

Shrule (Mayo), Sruthair, 'stream'.
The final *r* of the Irish name has become the English *l*. Shrule is on the Black River.

Silvermines (Tipperary), Béal Átha Gabhann, 'ford-mouth of (the) smith'.
The village has been a mining centre since at least the 14th century, and there are still silver-bearing ores here. The 'ford-mouth' is unusual, however, since Silvermines is nowhere near the mouth of a river.

Sion Mills (Tyrone), Muileann an tSiáin, 'mill of the fairy hill'.
The English name, which almost suggests a biblical origin, is actually a rendering of the Irish.

Sixmilebridge (Clare), Droichead Abhann Ó gCearnaigh, 'bridge of (the) river of the descendants of Cearnach'.
The Irish name refers to the river Owengarney, with O Cearnaigh giving the modern family name O Kearney. (Irish *ceárnach* means 'victorious'.) The English name appears to refer to Newmarket-on-Fergus, which is six miles away.

Skagh (Dublin), Sceach, 'thorn bush', 'whitethorn'.

Skahanagh (several), Sceachanach, 'place of

whitethorns'.

Skeagh (several), Sceach, 'thorn bush', 'whitethorn'.

Skegoneill (Belfast), Sceithiog an Iarla, 'whitethorn of the earl'.

There must be some legend or tradition to account for this name, although none has been recorded. Perhaps the 'earl' was one of the earls of Ulster. The name was printed in 1604 as *Balliskeighog-Inerla*, showing an initial 'Bally-' ('town'). Very likely the last part of the name came to be '-neill' by association with nearby Legoneil.

Skelligs (Kerry), Na Scealaga, 'the splinters'.

The name refers to the rocky 'splinters' of the three little islands that form the Skelligs.

Skenakilla (Cork), Sceach na Cille, 'thorn bush of (the) church'.

Skerries (Dublin), Na Sceirí, 'the skerries', 'the reefs'.

The name relates to the rocky islands off the coast here: Red Island (now joined to the mainland), Colt Island, and St Patrick's Island.

Skibbereen (Cork), An Sciobairín, 'the place of the little boats'.

The Irish name is based on *scib*, 'skiff', 'small boat'. Skibbereen has long been a fishing port.

Skreen (Sligo), an Scrín, 'the shrine'.

An early monastery here founded by St Columba was called *Scrín Adhamhnáin*, as a collection of the relics of St Adhamhnán, biographer of Columba, had been deposited here. At Skreen in Meath, called in Irish *Scrín Choilm Chille* ('shrine of St Columba'), Columba's own relics were preserved, having been transferred in 878 from Iona, Scotland, to protect them from the Viking invaders.

Slea Head (Kerry), Ceann Sléibhe, 'head of (the) mountain'.

Sleaty (Laois), Graigue Shléibhte, 'village of (the) mountain'.

Sleaty, also known as Sleatygraigue, is to the east of a mountain group.

Slemish (Antrim), Sliagh Mis, 'Mis's mountain'.

Mis is a woman's name.

Slieveardagh (Kilkenny/Tipperary), Sliabh Árdachad, 'mountain of (the) high field'.

Slieve Bernagh (Down), Sliabh Bearnach, 'gapped mountain'.

The word 'gapped' *(bearnach)* is often applied to forts, as for Lisdoonvarna.

Slieve Bloom (Offaly), Sliabh Bládhma, 'Bladhma's mountain'.

Slieve Donard (Down), Sliabh Dónairt, 'Donart's mountain'.

Slieve Donard is the highest of the Mourne Mountains, and Donart, or Domhanghart, is traditionally said to have been a disciple of St Patrick who built his church on the summit.

Slieve Gullion (Armagh), Sliabh gCuillin, 'mountain of (the) steep slope'.

This is the highest mountain in Armagh.

Slieve League (Donegal), Sliabh Liag, 'mountain of (the) flat stones'.

Slieve na Calliagh (Meath), Sliabh na Caillí, 'mountain of the hag'.

Slievenamon (Tipperary), Sliabh na mBan, 'mountain of the women'.

According to legend, the mountain is named after the women who ran a race from the bottom to the top to win the hand of the famous hero Finn mac Cumaill (Finn Mac Coole).

Slieve Reagh (several), An Sliabh Riabhach, 'the grey mountain'.

Slieverue (Kilkenny), Sliabh Rua, 'red-coloured mountain'.

Sligo (Sligo), Sligeach, 'shelly place'.

The name refers to the river Garavogue here. The town gave its name to the county.

Sluggary (Cork), An Slogaire, 'the quagmire'.

Slyne Head (Galway), Ceinn Léime, 'headland of (the) leap'.

Perhaps animals leapt here, or a local legend exists. The English name is a corruption of the second half of the Irish name, with *s* added.

Smithborough (Monaghan), Na Mullaí, 'the hilltops'.

The English name, recorded as *Smithsborough* in 1778, was that of a landowner called Smith who lived here at some time in the 18th century.

Snave (Cork), An Snámh, 'the swimming place'.

Snave, or Snave Bridge, is where the Coomhola River runs into Bantry Bay. The name implies that the river was too deep to be forded here.

Sneem (Kerry), An tSnaidhm, 'the knot'.

Irish *snaidhm* means 'knot', 'joining', 'junction', and here at the head of an inlet on the long estuary of the Kenmare River the name must apply to the many roads and rivers that meet at Sneem, among the latter the Sneem, Small and Ardsheelhane.

Solloghod (Tipperary), Sulchóid, 'willow wood'.

Sonnagh (Longford, Mayo), Sonnach, 'palisade', 'rampart'.

Spancel Hill (Clare), Cnoc an Urchaill, 'hill of the spancel'.

A spancel is a hobble or tether for a cow. There seems no reason to doubt this origin, and the land here is mostly grazing ground.

Spanish Point (Clare), Rinn na Spáinneach, 'point of the Spaniard'.

The name refers to the ships from the Spanish Armada that were wrecked here in 1588. The survivors were killed by order of Sir Richard Bingham, the English governor of Connacht.

Speenoge (Donegal), Spíonóg, '(place of) gooseberries'.

Spelga Pass (Down), Bearna na Speilge, 'pass of the pointed rock'.

The pass is in the Mourne Mountains, now the B27 road from Hilltown to Kilkeel.

Sperrin Mountains (Derry/Tyrone), Cnoc Speirín, 'pointed hills'.

Spiddal (Galway), An Spidéal, 'the hospital'.

The name refers to a former hospice here, some traces of which still remain.

Spink (Laois), An Spinc, 'the pointed rock'.

Srah (Mayo), An tSraith, 'the riverside meadow'.

Sraheen (Mayo), Sraithín, 'little riverside meadow'.

Srahlea (Mayo), An Srath Liath, 'the grey riverside meadow'.

Srahmore (Mayo), An Srath Mór, 'the big riverside meadow'.

Srahnamanragh (Mayo), Srath na mBan-

rach, 'riverside meadow of the enclosures'.

Stabannon (Louth), Tigh Banán, 'Bannán's house'.

The initial *T-* of the Irish name has been prefixed by *S-* in the English, as in the name of Stillorgan.

Stackallen (Meath), Stigh Colláin, 'Collán's house'.

The added *S-* of the English name (as in Stabannon, above) has here also transferred to Irish *teach*, 'house'.

Staffordstown (Antrim), Baile Stafard, 'Stafford's town'.

Staholmog (Meath), Teach Cholmóg, 'Colmog's house'.

The English name has added *S-* to the Irish, as frequently happens with *teach*.

Staigue (Kerry), Stéig, 'strip', 'rocky ledge'.

Staigue Fort is one of the best known stone forts in Ireland, some 500 ft (150m) up near the coast between two streams.

Stamullen (Meath), Steach Maoilín, 'Meallán's fort'.

The spelling of the Irish name reflects the initial *S-* of the English, added to *teach*, 'house'. An earlier version of the Irish name was *Teach Mealláin*.

Stewartstown (Tyrone), An Chraobh, 'the mansion'.

The Irish name is the figurative sense of *craobh*, which is literally 'branch', 'tree'. Stuart Hall here, the residence of Lord Castlestewart, was built by John Stewart in about 1760. Roughan Castle nearby was built by Sir Andrew Stewart in 1618. These men belonged to the family that gives the English name.

Stillorgan (Dublin), Stigh Lorgan, 'Lorcán's house'.

An earlier version of the Irish name was *Tigh Lorcáin*, showing that as with many names above, English initial *S-* has been added to Irish *teach*, 'house'. In most names of this kind, the 'house' means a church, and here it was the one founded by Lorcán Ó Tuathail (Laurence O Toole), archbishop of Dublin, in the 12th century.

Stone Bridge (Monaghan), An Droichead, 'the bridge'.

Stonybatter (Dublin), An Botar Clochach, 'the stony road'.

The English name is half English, half Irish. Compare **Batterstown** and **Booterstown**.

Stonyford (Kilkenny), Áth na Staing, 'ford of the pole'.

The English name is a part corruption, part translation of the Irish. Stonyford is just south of the Kings River.

Strabane (Tyrone), An Srath Bán, 'the white riverside land'.

Strabane is on the Mourne River.

Stradbally (several), An Sráidbhaile, 'the village'.

The Irish name literally means 'street town', denoting a village running along a single main street. At Stradbally in Laois, the village extends for almost a mile along the road (the T16 Port Laoise to Carlow). Originally, a 'street town' was understood to be one that was undefended, with no fort or castle.

Strade (Mayo), An tSráid, 'the street'.

Stradone (Cavan), Sraith an Domhain, 'riverside land of the deep (place)'.

Stragolan (Fermanagh), Srath Gabhláin, 'riverside land of (the) fork'.

Straid (several), An tSráid, 'the street'.

Straidarran (Derry), Sráidbhaile Uí Árain, 'O Aran's village'.

See **Stradbally** regarding Irish *sráid-bhaile*.

Strancally (Waterford), Srón na Caillighe, 'nose of the hag'.

Strancally Castle, now ruined, was built on a rock overhanging the river Blackwater, and this rock is the 'hag's nose'. Irish *srón* has acquired a *t* in the English name.

Strandhill (Sligo), An Leathros, 'the half-headland'.

Strandhill is a small resort on a peninsula projecting into Sligo Bay, at the foot of the hill Knocknarea.

Strangford (Down), Baile Loch Cuan, 'town of Loch Cuan'.

Loch Cuan ('haven lake') is the Irish name of Strangford Lough, which itself has an Old Norse name meaning 'violent inlet' (almost 'strong fjord'), referring to the strong current in the Narrows between the lough and the open sea. The village takes its name from the lough.

Stranmillis (Belfast), Sruthán Milis, 'pleasant stream'.

Stranooden (Monaghan), Sraith Nuadáin, 'Nuadán's riverside land'.

Stranorlar (Donegal), Srath an Urláir, 'riverside land of the level place.'

The village is in the valley of the river Finn.

Stratford-on-Slaney (Wicklow), Áth na Sráide, 'ford of the street'.

The Irish name translates the first part of the English, which derives from Edward Stratford, second earl of Aldborough, who founded the village as an industrial enterprise here on the river Slaney in the late 18th century. The name may have been modelled on the English Stratford-on-Avon. An earlier Irish name was *Baile an Taibhirne*, 'town of the inn'.

Streamstown (Galway), Baile an tSrutháin, 'town of the stream'.

Streamstown is at the head of Streamstown Bay where a stream flows into it.

Street (Westmeath), An tSráid, 'the street'.

Strokestown (Roscommon), Béal na mBuillí, 'ford-mouth of the strokes'.

The name appears to refer to a battle here, since Irish *buille* means 'stroke', 'blow', unless the 'stroke' is that of some agricultural implement such as a scythe. Perhaps the Irish *béal* in the name does not represent *béal átha*, 'ford-mouth', but *baile*, 'town', thus corresponding with the English. Strokestown is anyway not at the mouth of a ford.

Struel (Down), Srúill, 'stream'.

The name is that of the Holy Wells of Struel near Downpatrick.

Suil, Lough na (Sligo), Loch na Súile, 'lake of the eye'.

The 'eye' is the opening in the lake called Balor's Eye, through which, according to tradition, all the lake water completely disappears every hundred years. This last happened in 1933.

Summerhill (several).

The Irish name varies from one place to another. Summerhill in Meath is *Cnoc an Línsigh*, 'Lynch's hill', in Waterford *Cnoc na gCaorach*, 'hill of the sheep', and in Laois *Achadh na hÁirne*, 'field of the sloes'.

Sutton Cross (Dublin), Suí Fhiontáin, 'St Fiontan's seat'.

The English name is a corruption of the Irish.

Swilly, Lough (Donegal), Loch Súilí, 'lake of (the) eyes'.

The name of the lough comes from the river that flows into it, and the Swilly River has a name that probably means 'full of bubbles', 'full of whirlpools', with *súil* literally meaning 'eye'.

Swinford (Mayo), Béal Átha na Muice, 'ford-mouth of the pigs'.

Doubtless the name refers to the stream near here where pigs regularly crossed, or were driven across. However, Swinford is not at the mouth of a river.

Swords (Dublin), Sord, 'well'.

The name does not appear to derive from *sord*, 'sward', and is certainly not from English 'sword'. Traditionally, the name is said to refer to the well here blessed by St Columba. No early relics remain of the monastic site, however.

T

Tacumshane (Wexford), Teach Coimsín, 'Coimsín's house'.

Taghadoe (Kildare), Teach Tua, 'St Tua's house'.

The original church no longer exists, although part of the tower remains in the churchyard.

Taghboy (several), Teach Buidhe, 'yellow house'.

In a general name like this, without a personal name, Irish *teach* need not always mean 'church' but may mean what it says, simply 'house'.

Taghmon (Wexford, Westmeath), Teach Munna, 'St Munna's house'.

Taghmon in Wexford is on the site of an Augustinian monastery founded by St Munna in the early 7th century. Munna was buried here, and the head and base of his cross are in the graveyard.

Tagoat (Wexford), Teach Gót, 'St Cód's house'.

Tallaght (Dublin), Tamhlacht, 'plague burial-ground'.

The name is said to refer to a large number of plague victims buried here in prehistoric times. An earlier Irish name for the place was *Tamhlacht Maolruain*, after Maolruain who founded the site in the 8th century, See also **Tamlaght**.

Tallanstown (Louth), Baile an Tallúnaigh, 'Tallan's homestead'.

Tallow (Waterford), Tulach an Iarainn, 'little hill of the iron'.

The latter half of the name refers to the former iron ore workings here.

Tallowbridge (Waterford), Droichead Tulach an Iarainn, 'bridge of Tallow'.

Tallowbridge is just north of Tallow on the river Bride.

Tamlaght (several), 'plague burial-ground'.

This is the same name as Tallaght. Tamlacht in Derry, in the parish of Magilligan, was earlier called *Tamhlacht Arda*, 'burial-ground of (the) promontory'.

Tamnamore (Tyrone), An Tamhnach Mhór, 'the big green field'.

The name indicates a plot of arable ground in a less fertile district.

Tamney (Donegal), An Tamhnaigh, 'the green field'.

See **Tamnamore** for the basic sense of *tamhnach*.

Tandragee (Armagh), Tóin re Gaoith, 'backside to the wind'.

The name represents Irish *tón-le-gaoith*, literally 'bottom by wind', i.e. having the wind in one's rear, denoting a bleak place.

Tang (Westmeath), An Teanga, 'the tongue'.

The name indicates a tongue of land.

Tara (Meath), Teamhair, 'elevated place', 'assembly hill'.

This is the traditional interpretation of the name of this famous ancient royal site, as well as of other places called Tara, such as Tara Hill in Wexford. But recent place-name scholarship suggests that the true meaning is probably based on the personal name of the earth goddess Temair, whose own name may mean 'dark one'.

Tarbert (Kerry), Tairbeart, 'isthmus'.

This name, whether here or elsewhere, indicates a fairly narrow neck of land where boats and their contents can be carried across. In Kerry, Tarbert is on a steep slope overlooking the river Shannon, and to the south of Tarbert Island which is connected by a causeway to the main headland. The name also occurs in Scotland, with the same meaning.

Tarmon (several), Tearmon, 'refuge', 'church land'.

The name denotes a place of sanctuary on church ground.

Tattygare (several), Taite Gearr, 'short *tate*'.

A *tate* is an old Irish land measure equal to 60 Irish acres (i.e. a quarter of a *ceath-ramha*, or quarter, and one sixteenth of a *baile*, or townland).

Tattymoyle (Tyrone), Taite Maol, 'bare *tate*'.

Tattymoyle is a hill. See last name for its meaning.

Tattyreagh (Tyrone), An Táite Riabhach, 'the grey *tate*'.
See **Tattygare**.

Taughmaconnell (Roscommon), Teach Mhic Conaill, 'house of the sons of Conall'.

Tawlaght (several), Tamhlacht, 'plague burial-ground'.
See **Tallaght** and **Tamnaght**.

Tawnagh (Sligo), Tamhnach, 'green field'.
See **Tamnamore** for an explanation of *tamhnach*.

Tawnaghlahan (Donegal), Tamhnach Leathan, 'broad green field'.
See **Tamnamore** for an explanation of *tamhnach*.

Teebane (several), Taobh Bán, 'white house'.
In many cases, Irish *teach* has been assimilated to *taobh*, 'side, 'region', as here.

Teltown (Meath), Tailtean, 'Taillte's place'.
Teltown arose as the location of the most famous of the ancient August assemblies, and is named after Taillte (Tailltiu), the legendary queen or goddess who in some stories is said to be the daughter of the king of Spain and wife of Eochaid. Her name may mean 'beautiful one'. The '-town' of the English name is thus a corruption of the original.

Templeboy (Sligo), Teampall Baoith, 'St Baoth's church'.

Templebredon (Tipperary), Teampall Uí Bhrídeáin, 'church of the descendants of Bradan'.

Templebreedy (Cork), Teampall Bríde, 'St Brigid's church'.
An earlier name here was *Cill Cúile*, 'church of (the) corner', 'secluded church'.

Templecarn (several), Teampall Carna, 'church of (the) monument'.
The name denotes a church built by a pagan burial place, marked by a cairn.

Templederry (Tipperary), Teampall Doire, 'church of (the) oak wood'.

Temple Douglas (Donegal), Teampall Dúghlaise, 'church of (the) dark stream'.
St Columba is said to have been baptized in the old ruined church here that stands on the Glashagh River.

Templeetney (Tipperary), Teampall Eithne, 'St Eithne's church'.

Eithne is a woman's name.

Templeglantine (Limerick), Teampall an Ghleanntáin, 'church of the little glen'.

Templemichael (Cork), Teampall Michíl, 'St Michael's church'.

Templemartin (Cork), Teampall Mártan, 'St Martin's church'.

Templemolaga (Cork), Teampall Molaga, 'St Molaga's church'.

Temple Monachan (Kerry), Teampall Manacháin, 'St Manchán's church'.

Templemore (several), An Teampall Mór, 'the big church'.
In Templemore, Tipperary, the remains of the 'big church' can be seen in the Town Park, where the Knights Templar had their castle and monastery.

Templemoyle (several), Teampall Maol, 'bald church'.
The name indicates a disintegrating or dilapidated church.

Templenacarriga (Cork), Teampall na Carraige, 'church of the rock'.

Templenoe (several), Teampall Nua, 'new church'.

Templeogue (Dublin), Teach Mealóg, 'St Maológ's house'.
The original Irish name here has become assimilated to *teampall*, 'church', even though *teach* does mean 'church' in this context.

Templepatrick (several), Teampall Phádraig, 'St Patrick's church'.

Templeport (Cavan), Teampall an Phuirt, 'church of the bank'.
The name is also that of a lough here, south of Slieve Rushen.

Templeshanbo (Wexford), Teampall Seanbhoth, 'church of the old hut'.

Templetogher (Galway), Teampall an Tóchair, 'church of the causeway'.

Templetuohy (Tipperary), Teampall Tuaithe, 'church of (the) territory'.
The church here was the main one for the district.

Tempo (Fermanagh), An tIompú Deiseal, 'the right-hand turn'.
The name may refer to a ritual in pagan sun worship, in which a clockwise turning towards the sun was made.

Terenure (Dublin), Tír an Iúir, 'land of the

yew tree'.

The former English name of the district here was Roundtown, for the circular group of cottages on the Harolds Cross-Rathfarnham road.

Termon (several), An Tearmann, 'the refuge', 'the church land'.

This is the same name as Tarmon.

Termonbarry (Roscommon), Tearmann Bearaigh, 'church land of St Bearach'.

Termonfeckin (Louth), Tearmann Feichín, 'church land of St Feichín'.

Terryglass (Clare, Tipperary), Tír Dhá Ghlas, 'land of (the) two streams'.

In Tipperary, Terryglass is on a stream near the upper reaches of Lough Derg.

Tevrin (Westmeath), Teamhairín, 'little hill'.

Thomastown (Kilkenny, Tipperary), Baile Thomáis, 'Thomas's homestead'.

In Kilkenny, the Irish name of Thomastown is *Baile Mhic Andáin*, 'Fitzanthony's homestead', referring to Thomas Fitzanthony, the Anglo-Norman seneschal of Leinster who had a castle here in the 13th century.

Thompson's Bridge (Fermanagh), Droichead Mhic Thomáis, 'Thompson's bridge'.

The Irish name translates the English family name literally ('son of Thomas').

Three Castles (Kilkenny), Bábhún Ó nDuach, 'enclosure of the descendants of Duach'.

The Irish name relates to a 'bawn', a fortification or enclosure. Only two castle ruins can be traced here now.

Thurles (Tipperary), Durlas, 'strong fort'.

Thurles was strategically important in the Middle Ages, when it was surrounded by several castles.

Tiaquin (Galway), Teach Dáchonna, 'St Dáchonna's house'.

Tibberaghny (Kilkenny), Tigh Braichne 'St Braichne's house'.

Another origin of this name is seen in Irish *Tiobra Fhachtna*, 'St Fachtna's well'.

Tibohine (Roscommon), Tigh Baoithín, 'St Baoithín's house'.

Tieve (several), Taobh, 'side', 'hillside', 'district'.

Tievemore (Donegal), Taobh Mór, 'big hillside'.

Timahoe (Laois), Tigh Mochua, 'St Mo-Chua's house'.

Timogue (Laois), Tigh Maodhóg, 'St Maodhóg's house'.

Timoleague (Cork), Tigh Molaige, 'St Molaga's house.'

The monastery here was founded in the 6th century by St Molaga of Templemolaga.

Timolin (Kildare), Tigh Moling, 'St Moling's house'.

The monastery here was established in the 7th century by St Moling, bishop of Ferns.

Tinahely (Wicklow), Tigh na hEille, 'house of the thong'.

This interpretation assumes that the last part of the name derives from Irish *éillín*, 'thong', 'small strap', although it is difficult to see what this could mean. The name has also been derived from that of a river called *Ely*, but the river here is the Derry and there is no record of it ever having been called by another name.

Tinamuck (Offaly), Tigh na Muc, 'house of the pigs'.

Tinnahinch (several), Tigh na hInse, 'house of the riverside land'.

Tintern (Wexford), Mainistir Chinn Eich, 'monastery of (the) head of (the) horse'.

The English name is not a corruption of the Irish but a borrowing of the name of Tintern Abbey in Wales (now in Gwent). The Wexford foundation was a daughter house of the Welsh Cistercian abbey, and was established in the early 13th century by William le Mareschal, Earl of Pembroke, in fulfilment of a vow he had made when he was in danger of losing his life at sea in a shipwreck. For a similar borrowing of a Welsh monastic name, see **Bangor**.

Tipperary (Tipperary), Tiobraid Árann, 'well of (the river) Ara'.

The river took its own name from that of the district here, meaning 'ridged (place)'. The original well was in Main Street, but is now covered.

Tipperkevin (Kildare), Tiobraid Caomhghein, 'St Caoimhín's well.

This saint's name is usually anglicised as Kevin.

Tiranascragh (Galway), Tír Chinn Eascrach 'land of (the) head of (the) esker'.

Irish *eiscir*, anglicised as 'esker', means a ridge of mounds or sandhills.

Tirawly (Mayo), Tír Amhalghaidh, 'land of Amhalgaidh'.

Amhalgaidh was an early king of Connacht.

Tirconnell, Tír Conaill, 'land of Conall'.

Tirconnell is the old name of Donegal, from Conall Gulban, ancestor of the O Donnells and other Donegal families.

Tireragh (Sligo), Tír Fhiachrach, 'district of Fiachra'.

Tirerrill (Sligo), Tír Ailealla, 'district of Olioll'.

Tirkeeran (Derry), Tír Mic Cairthinn, 'district of the sons of Ciarán'.

The Irish name Ciarán is usually anglicised as Kieran.

Tisaran (Offaly), Tigh Sárán, 'St Sárán's house'.

Tiscoffin (Kilkenny), Tigh Scoithín, 'St Scoithín's house'.

The *-th-* of the Irish name has produced the *-ff-* in the English.

Tober (several), An Tobar, 'the well'.

Tobercurry (Sligo), Tobar an Choire, 'well of the cauldron'.

The name may refer to the shape of the well. The English version of the name is also spelt Tubbercurry.

Toberdoney (Antrim, Derry), Tobar an Domhnaigh, 'well of the church'.

Tobermoney (Down), Tobar Muine, 'well of (the) thicket'.

Tobermore (Derry), An Tobar Mór, 'the big well'.

Tobereendoney (several), Tobar Righ an Domhnaigh, 'well of the king of Sunday'.

The 'king of Sunday' is God. Such wells were visited on Sundays.

Toberroe (Galway), Tobar Ruadh, 'red-coloured well'.

Togher (several), An Tóchar, 'the causeway'.

Tollymore (Down), Tulaigh Mhór, 'the big hillock'.

Tomfinlough (Clare), Tuaim Fionnlocha, 'burial mound of (the) bright lake'.

The name refers to the old church by Lough Fin, 4 miles (6.4km) north-west of Sixmilebridge.

Tomgraney (Clare), Tuaim Gréine, 'burial mound of Gráinne'.

In ancient legend Gráinne was the daughter of Cormac mac Airt who, after a number of amatory adventures, was drowned in Lough Graney and subsequently, when her body had been found in the River Graney, was buried at Tomgraney. Her name means 'sun' (Irish *grian*).

Tomhaggard (Wexford), Teach Moshagard, 'Moshagra's house'.

Tonragee (Mayo), Tóin re Gaoith, 'backside to the wind'.

This name has the same origin as Tandragee.

Toom (several), Tuaim, 'burial mound'.

Toombeola (Galway), Tuaim Beola, 'Beola's burial mound'.

Toome (Antrim), Tuaim, 'burial mound'.

Toomebridge, (Antrim), Droichead Thuama, 'bridge of (the) burial mound'.

Toomebridge is on the river Bann.

Toomore (Mayo), Tuaim Mhór, 'large burial mound'.

Toomyvara (Tipperary), Tuaim Uí Mheára, 'burial mound of the O Mearas'.

The original name of Toomyvara was *Tuaim Donnáin*, for the monastery founded by St Donnán in the 7th century. The present name relates to the O Mearas, who held the priory and burial place here in the 15th and 16th centuries.

Tooreen (Mayo), An Tuairín, 'the little bleaching-green'.

Toormore (Cork), An Tuar Mór, 'the big bleaching-green'.

Torc (Kerry), An Torc, 'the (mountain of) boars'.

Torr Head (Antrim), Torbhuirg, 'pointed head'.

Tory Island (Donegal), Toraigh, 'place of towers'.

The 'towers' are the high cliffs and isolated tors in many parts of the island.

Tourmakeady (Mayo), Tuar Mhic Éadaigh, 'bleaching-green of the sons of Éadach'.

Tralee (Kerry), Trá Lí, 'strand of Lí'.

The name refers to the river Lee, which runs into the sea here just south of Tralee. The 'strand' is probably the sea shore here.

Tramore (Waterford), Trá Mhór, 'big strand'.

Tramore is noted for its 3 mile (4.8km) strand along Tramore Bay here.

Trasna Island (Fermanagh), Inis Trasna, 'island across'.

The name implies an island that has to be reached by crossing a narrow stretch of water. Today there is a bridge here in Upper Lough Erne taking the B127 road onto and off the little Trasna Island.

Treanboy (Derry), Trian Buidhe , 'yellow third'.

The 'third' is a land measure.

Treanlaur (Galway, Mayo), Trian Láir, 'middle third'.

The name denotes the central portion of a tripartite division of territory.

Trevet (Meath), Trefoit, 'three sods'.

This is the traditional interpretation of the name, the legend being that when Art, son of Conn Cétchathach ('of the Hundred Battles'), was buried here, three sods (Irish *fód*, 'sod', 'piece of turf') were dug over his grave to represent the Trinity.

Trillick (several), Treileac, 'three flagstones'.

Trim (Meath), Baile Átha Troim, 'town of (the) ford of (the) elder tree'.

The trees would have marked the ford over the river Boyne here, and the site of the original fort can still be seen above the town bridge.

Trough (several), Triúcha, 'cantred'.

A cantred is a 'hundred', a division of land.

Tuam (Galway), Tuaim, 'burial mound'.

The full name of Tuam is *Tuaim an Dá Ghualainn*, 'burial mound of the two shoulders', referring to its original shape.

Tuamgraney see **Tomgraney**.

Tubber (Galway), An Tobar, 'the well'.

Tubbercurry see **Tobercurry**.

Tubbrid (several), Tiobraid, 'well', 'spring'.

Tulla (Clare), An Tulach, 'the hillock'.

Tulla is a small town on a hill.

Tullaghan (Leitrim), An Tulachán, 'the little hill'.

Tullaghgarley (Antrim), Tulach Garlach, 'hillock of (the) babies'.

The origin of this name is not clear. Perhaps there is some reference to illegi-

timate children.

Tullaghmelan (Tipperary), Tulach Maolán, 'Maolán's hillock'.

Tullaherin (Kilkenny), Tulach Iarainn, 'hillock of iron'.

The name appears to refer to iron ore deposits here.

Tullamore (Offaly), Tulach Mhór, 'big hill'.

The 'big hill' is the one on which St Catherine's church stands, on the east side of the town.

Tullaroan (Kilkenny), Tulach Ruáin, 'little red-coloured hill'.

Tullig (several), Tulaig, 'hillock'.

Tulloha (Kerry), Tulach Átha, 'hillock of (the) ford'.

Tulloha is in the valley of the Sheen River, on the T65 road from Kenmare to Glengarriff.

Tullow (several), An Tulach, 'the hillock'.

Tullyallen (Laois, Louth), Tulach Áluinn, 'beautiful hillock'.

Tully Bay (Fermanagh), Bá na Tulaí, 'bay of the hillock'.

Tullybeg (Donegal), Tulaigh Bheag, 'little hill'.

Tullycorbet (Monaghan), Tulaigh Carbaid, 'little hill of (the) chariot'.

This name, if correctly interpreted, must have some local legend or incident behind it.

Tullydonnell (Armagh), Tulach Dhónaill, 'Donal's hillock'.

Tullyhogue (Tyrone), Tulaigh Óg, 'hillock of (the) youths'.

The name refers to the games and sports held here. Tullyhogue (or Tullaghoge) is better known, however, for being the place where the kings of Ulster were inaugurated as 'The O Neill'.

Tullyhommon (Fermanagh), Tulaigh Uí Thiomáin, 'hillock of the O Tiomains'.

The family name of O Tiomain is commonly anglicised as Timmons.

Tullylease (Cork), Tulach Léis, 'hillock of (the) huts'.

Tullymongan (Cavan), Tulaigh Mongáin, 'Mongán's hillock'.

Tullymore (Donegal), Tulaigh Mhór, 'big hill'.

Tullymurry (Down), Tullach Mhuire, 'St

Mary's hill'.

Tullynagrow (Monaghan), Tulach na gCró, 'hillock of the cattle pens'.

Tullyrap (Donegal), Tulach Rap, 'hillock of (the) fragments'.
Irish *rap* is 'piece', 'fragment', but the exact sense here is uncertain.

Tullyrusk (Antrim), Tulach Roisc, 'hillock of (the) marsh'.
The name implies that the hill where the old church is here was formerly surrounded by marshland.

Tulrohaun (Mayo), Tulach Shrutháin, 'hillock of (the) stream'.

Tumna (Roscommon), Tumna, 'burial mound of (the) woman'.
This name seems to represent *tulach mna*, the second word being the genitive of *bean*, 'woman'.

Ture (Donegal), An tIúr, 'the yew tree'.
This is a similar name to Newry, with the first letter of the English name from the Irish definite article.

Turlough (Mayo), Turlach, 'dry lake'.
A 'dry lake' is one that dries up in summer.

Turloughmore (Galway), An Turlach Mór, 'the big dry lake'.
See **Turlough**.

Twelve Bens, The (Galway), Na Beanna Beola, 'the peaks of Beola'.
This is the name of the mountain range in Connemara which has Benbaun as the highest peak. Beola is said to have been an old Firbolg chief. The English name is sometimes given as The Twelve Pins.

Twomileborris (Tipperary), Buiríos Léith, 'borough of Liath'.
Twomileborris is 2 miles (3.2km) from Leigh or Leighmore (or Leamakevoge), whose Irish name is *Liath Mór Mo-*

Chaomhóg, 'big grey place of Mo-Chaomhog'. This saint's name could be rendered in English as 'my little Kevin'.

Tybraughney (Tipperary), Tigh Braichne, 'Braichne's house'.

Tydavnet (Monaghan), Tigh Damhnaita, 'Damhnait's house'.
Damhnait (whose name has been anglicised as Dymphna) was the wife of Áed Bennán, king of Munster in the early 7th century.

Tyholland (Monaghan), Teach Thaláin, 'Talan's house'.

Tymon (Dublin), Teach Motháin, 'Mothán's house'.

Tynan (Armagh), Tuíneán, 'water course'.
This is the conjectured origin of the name, from Irish *tuidhidhean*, 'mill-leat'. It was recorded in the late 8th century as *Tiughnetha* and in the late 11th century as *Tuidhnigha*, being first found as *Tynan* in 1603.

Tyone (Tipperary), Tigh Eoghain, 'Eoghan's house'.

Tyrella (Down), Teach Riala, 'St Riail's house'.

Tyrone, Tír Eoghain, 'Eoghan's land'.
According to historical legend, the territory here (much larger than the present county) was possessed by the descendants of Eoghan (Owen), son of Niall of the Nine Hostages.

Tyrrellspass (Westmeath), Bealach an Tirialaigh, 'Tyrrell's road'.
The name refers to the road through bogland here where in 1597 Captain Richard Tyrrell and Piers Lacy ambushed and defeated an English force led by Christopher Barnwell, son of Lord Trimleston. The village of Tyrrellspass first arose in the late 18th century.

U

Ullard (several), Ulard, 'high place'.

Ulster, Ulaidh, '(place of the) Ulaidh (tribe)'.

The name, like those of Leinster and Munster, consists of the tribal name followed by the Old Norse genitive *s* and Irish *tír*, 'district'. The Norse record of the name appears as *Uladztír*. Ulster was one of the ancient provinces of Ireland. Today the name is commonly used synonymously with Northern Ireland.

Ummerafree (Monaghan), Iomaire Fhraoigh, 'ridge of (the) heath'.

Unshinagh (several), Uinnseannach, 'place of ash trees'.

The name derives from *uinneas*, genitive *uinnse*, an early form of modern *fuinnseog*, 'ash tree'.

Upperchurch (Tipperary), An Teampall Uachtarach, 'the upper church'.

The village of Upperchurch lies in the Slievefelin Hills.

Upperland (Derry), Áth an Phortáin, 'ford of the little bank'.

Upperland lies on the eastern edge of a hilly district north-east of Maghera.

Urbal (several), Urbal, 'tail'.

The name refers to a tail of land, or to a location at the 'tail' end of some natural feature. The Irish name also appears as *Eirball* or *Earball*.

Urbalshinny (Donegal), Eirbal Sionnaigh, 'fox's tail'.

This name may denote the shape of the land here, thought to resemble a fox's tail, or refer to actual foxes.

Uregare (Limerick), Iubhar Gearr, 'short yew tree'.

Yew trees are not normally tall, and this name apparently refers to an unusually short yew tree, or group of yew trees.

Urlanmore (Clare) Urlann Mhór, 'big forecourt'.

The name is that of Urlanmore Castle here, south-west of Newmarket-on-Fergus. The castle is now in ruins.

Urlaur (Mayo), Urlár, 'floor', 'level place'.

Urlingford (Kilkenny), Áth na nUrlainn, 'ford of the forecourts'.

If this is the correct interpretation of the name, the reference may be to the courts or gardens of the many (now ruined) castles of the district.

Urney (several), An Urnaí, 'the oratory', 'the prayer house'.

Ushnagh (Westmeath), Uisneagh, 'place of fawns'.

The Hill of Ushnagh (or Usnagh) is the reputed central point of Ireland, where one of the great assemblies of Gaelic Ireland was held annually on May Day.

V

Valentia (Kerry), Dairbhre, 'place of oaks'.

The English name, whose spelling may have been influenced by the Spanish province Valencia, represents Irish *Béal Inse*, 'estuary of the island'. This properly applies to the 5 mile (8km) sound here that separates the island from the mainland.

Vartry (Wicklow), Abha bhFear Tire, 'river of (the) men of (the) district'.

The name of the river Vartry seems to indicate that it was regarded as a kind of local communal possession, 'our river'.

Ventry (Kerry), Ceann Trá, 'head of (the) strand'.

The English name derives from the sandy beach here, whose Irish name is *Fionn Traigh*, 'white strand'. This is thus the same name as that of Fintragh Bay, Donegal. The current Irish name of the village refers to its location at the head of Ventry Harbour.

Vilanstown (Westmeath), Baile na Bhileanach, 'town of the villeins'.

The name refers to the original farmworkers on the homestead here.

Villierstown (Waterford), An Baile Nua, 'the new town'.

The English name is that of the Villiers-Stuart family, who held lands here and who lived at the demesne of Dromana.

Vinegar Hill (Wexford), Cnoc Fiodh na gCaor, 'hill of (the) wood of the berries'.

The English name is an unexpected corruption of the Irish.

Virginia (Cavan), Achadh an Iúir, 'field of the yew tree'.

The little market town was founded by James I during the English colonisation of Ulster and was named after his predecessor, Queen Elizabeth I, the 'Virgin Queen'.

W

Waddingtown (Wexford), Baile Uaidín, 'Wadding's town'.

Walshestown (Down), Baile an Bhreatnaigh, 'Walshe's homestead'.
The name is that of Walshestown Castle, a 16th-century stronghold on Strangford Lough.

Waringstown (Down), Baile an Bhairínigh, 'Waring's homestead'.
The name derives from William Waring, who built Waringstown House here in 1667. Another member of this family, Samuel Waring, introduced the manufacture of linen damask here in 1691.

Warrenpoint (Down), An Pointe, 'the point'.
The English name is said to derive from the rabbit warren once here to the north of Carlingford Lough, with the Irish name borrowed from the English. The earlier Irish name for the location was *Rinn Mhic Ghiolla Ruaidh*, 'headland of (the) Mac Gilroys'.

Waterford (Waterford), Port Láirge, 'bank of (the) haunch'.
The English name looks obvious, but is actually of Norse origin and means 'wether inlet' (Norse *Vadrefjord*), referring to the point on the estuary of the river Suir where wethers (castrated rams) were loaded onto boats for transportation to other ports. The Vikings established Waterford in the late 9th century. The Irish name refers to the contour of the river bank here. An earlier Irish name for the location was said to be *Cuan na Greine*, 'harbour of the sun'.

Watergrasshill (Cork), Cnocán na Biolraí, 'little hill of the water cresses'.

Waterville (Kerry), An Coireán, 'the little whirlpool'.
The name derives from that of Waterville House here, which became the residence of James Butler in 1844. The house name itself refers to the little Finglas River, which here flows into the larger Currane, with '-ville' a standard ending (suggesting 'villa') of house names. The whirlpool of

the Irish name can still be seen in front of Waterville House where the Finglas joins the Currane.

Wellington Bridge (Wexford), Droichead Eoin, 'John's bridge'.
The English name commemorates the Duke of Wellington, who was born in Dublin. The river here is the Corock.

Wells (Wexford), Tobar Scoilbín, 'Scoilbean's well'.

West Cove (Kerry), Bun Inbhir, 'end of (the) estuary'.
Both West Cove and Castle Cove are on the north shore of the wide estuary of the Kenmare River.

Westmeath, An Iarmhí, 'western Meath'.
The name is based on that of Meath ('middle province'), with the county of Westmeath created by statute in 1542.

Westport (Mayo), Cathair na Mart, 'stone fort of the beef cattle'.
Irish *mart* is the word for a cow or ox fattened for the butcher. The English name describes the location of the town on the west coast.

Wexford (Wexford), Loch Garman, 'lake of (the river) Garma'.
The Irish name refers to the pool here at the mouth of the river Slaney, whose earlier name here was the Garma (Irish *garma*, 'headland', perhaps alluding to the point of land to the north of the narrow approach to Wexford Harbour). The English name is an Old Norse one, given by the Vikings when they established a base here in the 9th century. It means 'esker fjord', that is, 'inlet by the sandbank'. The county name came from that of the town.

Whiteabbey (Antrim), An Mhainistir Fhionn, 'the white monastery'.
Whiteabbey is now part of the new district of Newtownabbey.

Whitegate (several), An Geata Bán, 'the white gate'.

Whitehead (Antrim), An Cionn Bán, 'the white headland'.
The name refers to the chalk cliffs of the

headland here, contrasting with those of Black Head to the north.

Whitehouse (Antrim), An Teach Geal, 'the white house'.

The name refers to a distinctive white-coloured house or church here at some time.

White's Cross (Cork), Crois an Fhaoitigh, 'White's crossroad'.

The English name refers to someone named White who must have lived by the crossroad here at some time. Earlier Irish names of the location have been *Baile Rua Chorcaí*, 'red-coloured townland of Cork' and *Baile Nuadh Corcaigh*, 'new townland of Cork'. White's Cross is only 3 miles (4.8km) north of Cork.

Wicklow (Wicklow), Cill Mhantáin, 'St Mantán's church'.

The English name is actually an Old Norse one, meaning 'vikings' meadow', from Old Norse *vikingr*, 'viking' and *ló*, 'meadow'. An early record of the name appears as *Wykynoelo*. St Mantán of the Irish name is said to have been a disciple of St Patrick.

Wilkinstown (Meath), Baile Uilcín, 'Wilkin's homestead'.

Williamstown (several), Baile Liam, 'William's homestead'.

Windgap (Kilkenny), Bearna na Gaoithe, 'gap of the wind'.

Windgap is on a pass (now the L26a road) through the hills east of Slievenaman. Compare the next name.

Windy Gap (Laois), Bearna na Gaoithe, 'gap of the wind'.

Windy Gap is a high pass through the hills south of Stradbally, on what is now the T16 road.

Woodenbridge (Wicklow), Garrán an Ghabhláin, 'grove of the (river) fork'.

Woodenbridge is at the second Meeting of the Waters, where the valleys of the rivers Aughrim and Avoca combine. The English name is first recorded in 1799. Perhaps the original wooden bridge led across the Avoca to Ballyarthur House.

Wood of O (Offaly), Coill Eo, 'yew tree wood'.

This name is a kind of inversion of the name of Youghal. The English name thus translates Irish *coill*, 'wood', but not *eo*, 'yew tree'.

Woodsgift (Kilkenny), Baile na Lochán, 'town of the small lake'.

The English name appears to be based on a family name.

Woodtown (Meath), Baile na Coille, 'town of the wood'.

Y

Yellowbatter Park (Louth), Páirc an Bhóthair Bhuí, 'park of the yellow road'. Yellowbatter Park is near Drogheda.

Yellow Ford, The (Armagh), Béal an Átha Bhuí, 'mouth of the yellow ford'. The Yellow Ford is 2 miles (3.2km) north of Armagh, on the river Callan.

Youghal (Cork), Eochaill, 'yew wood'. Yew trees still exist in various parts of the town. Compare the name of Youghal with that of the **Wood of O**.

Elements Commonly Found as the First Part of an Irish Place-name

Abbey- translates Irish *mainistir*, 'monastery', 'abbey', usually to refer to an establishment of the 12th century or later, i.e. one founded by the Anglo-Normans; *see also* **Monaster-**.

Agha-, Augh- Irish *achadh*, 'field', 'land'.

Anna- Irish *eanach*, 'marsh', 'watery place', or *áth na*, 'ford of the. . .'.

Ard- Irish *ard*, 'height', 'hill', 'high ground'.

Ath- Irish *áth*, 'ford'; often follows *béal* (*see* **Bella-** below).

Ballagh- Irish *bealach*, 'road', 'way', or *béal átha*, 'ford-mouth'.

Ballin(a)- Irish *baile na*, 'town of the. . .', or *béal átha na*, 'ford-mouth of the. . .'.

Bally- Irish *baile*, 'farmstead', 'homestead', 'townland', 'town'; Ireland is divided administratively into some 60,000 townlands, each of which has a name and which in area can vary from about an acre to as much as 7,000 acres (2,800 hectares); English 'Bally-' can also occasionally represent Irish *béal átha* or *bealach* (*see* **Ballagh-**).

Bel(la)- (1) represents Irish *béal*, literally 'mouth', i.e. 'river-mouth', 'estuary'; very often followed by *átha*, 'of (the) ford', meaning thus 'ford-mouth', 'approach to a ford'; (2) represents *baile* (*see* **Bally-** above); (3) represents *bealach* (*see* **Ballagh-** above).

Boher- Irish *bóthar*, 'road', 'way'.

Bool- Irish *buaile*, sometimes rendered in English as 'booley', i.e. a place where cattle are kept for milking, especially in the summer; such a place can be open or enclosed, and is often a pasture on a hill.

Bun- Irish *bun*, 'bottom', 'base', 'origin', 'end'; as applied to a river usually means 'mouth'.

Caher- Irish *cathair* (from Latin *castrum*), 'fort', meaning first 'circular stone fort', then 'monastic establishment'; can also translate as 'city', 'court'.

Carn- Irish *carn*, 'cairn', 'burial mound'; in practice a mound of stones over a prehistoric grave, often a chambered tomb (as at Carnfree).

Carrick- Irish *carraig*, 'rock', 'large stone', 'crag'.

Carrow- Irish *ceathrú* (earlier *ceathramha*), 'quarter', i.e. a land measure, usually a fourth part of a townland (*baile*, *see* **Bally-** above).

Cashel- Irish *caiseal*, 'ring-fort', usually meaning an ancient stone enclosure surrounding a defended settlement; sometimes rendered in English as 'cashel'.

Castle- (1) usually translates Irish *caisleán*, 'castle', denoting an Anglo-Norman one, with a personal name added; (2) corresponds to Irish *baile* (*see* **Bally-**) but in the late 16th- or 17th-century sense of 'mansion', denoting an English or Scottish settler's family residence (e.g. **Castlecaulfield**.

Clogh- Irish *cloch*, 'stone', meaning a stony place or denoting a stone structure such as a fort or castle; the related *clochán* frequently indicates the ruins of an old fort, a heap of stones, a burial ground, or stepping stones over a marsh or stream; for a famous example of *clochán see* **Giant's Causeway**.

Clon- Irish *cluain*, 'meadow', 'pastureland'.

Cool- Irish *cúil*, 'corner', i.e. a nook or secluded place.

Cor- (1) Irish *corr*, 'hill', usually a round one; (2) *cora*, 'weir'.

Cross- Irish *cros*, 'cross', 'crossroads'.

Cul- usually the same as **Cool-**.

Derry- Irish *doire*, 'oak grove', 'oak wood'; there are many 'Derries' in Ulster.

Desert- Irish *díseart* (from Latin *desertum*), 'hermitage' (i.e. a 'desert'); the name usually implies a secluded monastery, especially one with a strict rule.

Donagh- Irish *domhnach* (from Latin *dominicum*), 'church', especially one associated with St Patrick or one of his missionaries; the name thus implies an early, pre-7th-century church; its later equivalent was generally *cill* (*see* **Kill-**).

Doon- Irish *dún*, 'fort', usually a grand or important one of a king or chieftain; many such forts are on the coast, a hill, or some other prominent site, and several became the locations for early churches or monasteries.

Drom-, Drum- Irish *droim*, literally 'back', so meaning 'ridge', 'long low hill'.

Dun- *see* **Doon-** (although Dun- is the more common English rendering).

Ennis- *see* **Inch-**.

Glan-, Glen- Irish *gleann*, 'glen', 'valley', 'hollow'.

Gort- Irish *gort*, 'field', especially a cornfield and often a field of oats.

Green- Irish *grianán* 'sunny place' (from *grian*, 'sun'); the name often implies an elevated or important place (*see* **Greenane**).

Inch-, Inis- Irish *inis*, 'island', meaning either a literal island in the sea or on a lake, land by a river, or raised land standing as an 'island' in a marsh.

Kil(l)- (1) Irish *cill* (from Latin *cella*), 'cell', 'church', usually implying a pre-12th-century monastery or a post-12th-century church or graveyard (compare *domhnach*, see **Donagh-**); (2) Irish *coill*, 'wood', 'grove'; it is often difficult to distinguish these two elements, especially as they are so common.

Kin- Irish *ceann*, 'head', 'headland', 'promontory', 'hill summit'.

Knock- Irish *cnoc*, 'hill', 'height', 'mountain', a fairly general term; related *cnocán* means 'small hill', 'hillock'.

Lack- (1) Irish *leac*, 'flagstone', 'slab of rock'; (2) *leaca*, literally 'cheek', so denoting a flat slope or a hillside.

Letter- Irish *leitir*, 'hillside', especially one wet with running streams.

Lis- Irish *lios*, 'ring-fort', properly, the enclosed area inside a *ráth* (*see* **Rath-**), but in place-names usually denoting the fort as a whole; the element is not so frequent in place-names as *dún* or *ráth*, but in the north of Ireland denotes the type of fort that is called *ráth* in the mid-east and south-east of the country; a *lios* was not often an ecclesiastical site.

Lough Irish *loch*, 'lake', 'lough'; the lake is not necessarily land-locked, but can be open to the sea as Lough Swilly, Lough Foyle and Belfast Lough.

Maghera- Irish *machaire*, 'plain', i.e. flat, low-lying land, technically known as 'champaign'.

Monaster- Irish *mainistir* (from Latin *monasterium*), 'monastery'; almost all places beginning with this element had post-12th-century monastic houses, but the single notable exception is Monasterboice; *see also* **Abbey-**.

Money- (1) Irish *muine*, 'grove', 'thicket', 'shrubbery'; (2) *moin*, 'moor', 'bog' (i.e. peat bog).

Moy- Irish *má* (earlier *magh*), 'plain', 'level district'.

Mulla(gh)- Irish *mullach*, 'summit', 'hilltop'.

Mullin- Irish *muileann*, 'mill'.

Newtown- corresponds to Irish *An Baile Nua*, 'the new settlement', and usually indicates an English or Scottish Plantation dwelling or settlement of the 16th or 17th century.

Owen- Irish *abhainn*, 'river' (compare the common English river-name Avon).

Port- Irish *port*, 'bank', 'shore', 'port', 'harbour', 'passage', 'fort', 'house', 'monastery'; a much more wide-ranging term than English 'port'.

Rath- Irish *ráth*, 'ring-fort'; this term virtually corresponds to *dún* (*see* **Doon-**), and like it was often an early ecclesiastical site, so that the word can denote: 1) a former complete church or monastic unit, 2) a church named after the *ráth* near which it was built, or 3) a church or monastery built actually inside a *ráth*; in the mid-east and southeast of the country the term corresponds to *lios* (*see* **Lis-**).

Rin(g)- Irish *rinn*, 'point', 'headland', 'promontory', 'edge'.

Ros- Irish *ros*, 'wood', 'point', 'headland'; the name often indicates the site of an old cemetery or burial ground.

Shan- Irish *sean*, 'old'.

Slieve(-) Irish *sliabh*, 'mountain', 'range of mountains', 'upland'.

Temple- Irish *teampall* (from Latin *templum*), 'church'; the term usually indicates a post-12th-century church, often with a well-known saint's name.

Tober-, Tubber- Irish *tobar*, 'well', 'spring', especially a holy one.

Tulla(gh)-, Tully- Irish *tulach*, 'little hill', often one that was an assembly point.

Elements Commonly Found as the Final Part of an Irish Place-name*

-aglish Irish *eaglais* (from Latin *ecclesia*), 'church'; the term is similar to *teampall* (*see* **Temple-** in Appendix I), and so denotes a post-12th-century church.

-anna 'marsh' (*see* **Anna-** in Appendix I).

-bane Irish *bán*, 'white'.

-beg Irish *beag*, 'little', 'small'.

-boley 'milking place' (*see* **Bool-** in Appendix I).

-boy Irish *buidhe*, 'yellow'.

-dangan Irish *daingean*, 'stronghold'.

-derg Irish *dearg* 'red' (bright red, crimson; compare **-roe** below).

-drohid Irish *droichead*, 'bridge'.

-keel, -kill Irish *caol*, 'narrow'.

-lack 'flagstone' (*see* **Lack-** in Appendix I).

-more Irish *mór*, 'big', 'large' (also in sense 'important').

-roe Irish *rua* (earlier *ruadh*), 'red' (russet, copper-coloured; compare **-derg** above).

-tullagh, -tully 'little hill' (*see* **Tulla(gh)** in Appendix I).

-vally 'town' (*see* **Bally-** in Appendix I).

-villa, -villy Irish *bile*, 'ancient tree', 'sacred tree', meaning one where assemblies were held, chiefs inaugurated, games held, and the like.

-voley, -vooly 'milking place' (*see* **Bool-** in Appendix I).

-vullen 'mill' (*see* **Mullin-** in Appendix I).

* Examples of the elements listed here are: Glennahaglish, Rinneanna, Strabane, Drombeg, Knocknaboley, Mullaghboy, Ballindangan, Barnderg, Carrigadrohid, Carrowkeel, Ballinalack, Baltimore, Coolroe, Kiltullagh, Lavally, Knockavilla, Ballyvooly, Killavullen.

Select Bibliography

Appletree Press, *Irish Touring Guide*, Appletree Press, Belfast, 1985

Automobile Association, *Road Book of Ireland*, Automobile Association, Dublin, 1969

Beach, Russell P. O. (ed.), *Touring Guide to Ireland*, Automobile Association, Basingstoke, 1976

Bulletin of the Ulster Place-Name Society, Series 2, vols 1-4, Belfast, 1978-82

Cassell's Gazetteer of Great Britain and Ireland (6 vols), Cassell, London, 1893-8

Coghlan, Ronan, *Pocket Dictionary of Irish Myth and Legend*, Appletree Press, Belfast, 1985

Dinneen, Patrick S., *Foclóir Gaidhilge agus Béarla/ An Irish-English Dictionary*, Educational Company of Ireland, Dublin, 1979

Field, John, *Place-Names of Great Britain and Ireland*, David & Charles, Newton Abbot, 1980

Foclóir Tíreolaíochta agus Pleanála mar aon le Téarmaí Seandálaíochta/ Dictionary of Geography and Planning incorporating Archaeological Terms, Oifig an tSoláthair, Baile Átha Cliath, 1981

Joyce, P. W., *Irish Local Names Explained*, Fred Hanna, Dublin, 1968 [1970]. (Reissued in a new edition in 1984 as *Pocket Guide to Irish Place Names* by Appletree Press, Belfast.)

Joyce, P. W., *The Origin and History of Irish Names of Places*, EP Publishing, East Ardsley, 1972 [Dublin, 1875]

Killanin, Lord and Duignan, Michael V., *The Shell Guide to Ireland*, Ebury Press, London, 1969

Lewis, Samuel, *A Topographical Dictionary of Ireland* (2 vols), Genealogical Publishing Co., Baltimore, Md., 1984 [London,1837]

MacLysaght, Edward, *The Surnames of Ireland*, Irish University Press, Dublin, 1973.

O'Connell, James, *The Meaning of Irish Place Names*, Blackstaff Press, Belfast, 1979

Ó Corráin, Donnchadh and Maguire, Fidelma, *Gaelic Personal Names*, The Academy Press, Dublin, 1981

Ó Foghludha, Risteárd, *Log-ainmneacha/Dictionary of Irish Placenames*, n.p., n.d. (c. 1960)

Price, Liam, *The Place-Names of Co. Wicklow* (7 vols), Dublin Institute for Advanced Studies, Dublin, 1945-67
Room, Adrian, *A Concise Dictionary of Modern Place-Names in Great Britain and Ireland*, Oxford University Press, Oxford, 1983
Room, Adrian, *Guide to British Place Names*, Longman, Harlow, 1985
tSuirbheireacht Ordanáis, An [The Ordnance Survey], *Ainmneacha Gaeilge na mBailte Poist* [Irish Names of Postal Towns], Oifig an tSoláthair, Baile Átha Cliath, 1969

Maps

Éire, 1:575000, An tSuirbheireacht Ordanáis, Baile Átha Cliath, 1970
Ireland, Travel Map, 1:253440 (Quarter-inch to the mile) (5 sheets), John Bartholomew & Son, Edinburgh, 1977, 1981
Map of Ulster, 1:253440 (Quarter-inch to the mile), John Bartholomew & Son, Edinburgh, 1981